KICKER

KICKER

R Grey Hoover

To order additional copies of this book, contact:
Xlibris Corporation
1-888-795-4274
www.Xlibris.com
Orders@Xlibris.com

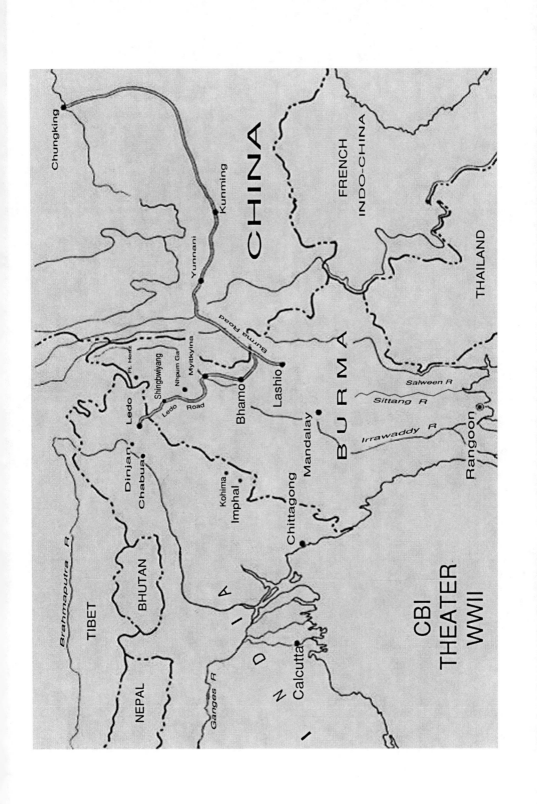

PREFACE

As CHILDREN GROWING up, my brothers and I would occasionally ask our father about his experiences during World War II. Dad was an aircrew member in the U.S. Army Air Corps and served in the CBI (China-Burma-India) Theater. Like most veterans of that war, he would not speak much about his experiences, and when he did, it was usually only to relate some funny story or memory of a good time. Throughout his life, we continued to ask about his war experiences, but he never fully talked about them. Dad died in 1978 at the age of fifty-six, and with him went all firsthand knowledge of his time at war. I decided then to document his wartime experiences for my brothers and myself. Over the years, I have researched military records, attended meetings of CBI veterans groups, and talked with many CBI veterans about their experiences. What I learned about the CBI Theater and the heroic efforts of the men and women who fought there has touched me deeply.

The CBI Theater has been called the forgotten front. It was fourteen thousand miles from the United States and had the lowest priority for supplies of all the WWII theaters receiving only what supplies were left after the European and Pacific theaters were supplied. When Dad would talk of the war, it was often in terms of the meager rations they had. He would tell of subsisting on powdered eggs and what little rice or fruit they could barter from the natives.

CBI was the largest theater in land area of all the WWII theaters. It stretched northeast to southwest some four thousand miles from Manchuria to the southern tip of India and east to west some 3,500 miles from eastern China to western India. It was an area that encompassed the highest mountains on earth and some of the world's thickest jungles and driest deserts. Temperatures ranged from well below zero to over 110 degrees Fahrenheit, and in some areas, the storms of the monsoon season brought hundreds of inches of rain and some of the worst flying conditions in the world. Aircrews often encountered severe icing, winds up to 250 miles per hour, and vertical air currents that hurled their aircrafts up or down at over three thousand feet per minute. The combination of monsoon weather, the Himalayan Mountains, and enemy action resulted in the loss of one in five aircrafts that flew in the CBI Theater. The scattered wreckage of lost aircraft over the stretch of the Himalayan Mountains between India and China became known as the aluminum trail. The aerial supply lines for troops fighting in Burma and China were the longest of the war, crossing sections of the Himalayas that rose over twenty thousand feet and traversing the dangerous swamps and jungles of Burma. The flight route over the Himalayas between India and China became known as the Hump.

Although it was the "forgotten front," the CBI Theater was noteworthy in that it saw the first glider invasion in the history of warfare and the building of the Ledo Road through jungle mountains and valleys flooded by monsoon rains. In addition, it saw the monumental effort to keep China in the war by flying hundreds of thousands of tons of supplies over the dangerous and foreboding Himalayan Mountains. The success of this effort kept thousands of Japanese troops tied down in China, where they were unable to aid their comrades in the war in the Pacific. Perhaps the most significant accomplishments of the CBI Theater were the greatest sustained combat air-supply missions the world has ever seen. These missions over the jungles of Burma kept more than seven hundred thousand Allied troops completely supplied from the air as they successfully defeated some of Japan's best jungle fighters.

My father was part of this air-supply effort. His official military title was flight traffic clerk, but he and others like him were better known as kickers. They were aircrew members whose job was to properly load bundles of supplies onto their aircraft and then unload those supplies by dropping them from the planes to soldiers on the ground below. Sometimes the supplies were specially bundled with parachutes, and at other times, they were not. The job was neither easy nor safe and usually required unloading six thousand to seven thousand pounds of supplies while their plane flew over frontline positions at very low altitudes and speeds. It would typically take seven to fifteen passes over their target to completely unload the supplies. During these passes, they were often subjected to deadly fire from enemy aircraft and ground forces. The term "kicker" came from one of the methods the crew often used to unload the supplies. As they approached their target area, bundles of supplies would be stacked in the open doorway of the plane's cargo bay. One of crewmen would then lie on his back behind the stacked bundles, with his knees flexed and his feet firmly planted in the center of the supplies. At a signal from the pilot, the kicker would literally kick the supplies out of the door to the waiting troops on the ground below.

This book is a historical novel depicting the efforts of my father and other veterans as they fought the war in China, Burma, and India and is based in part on their actual experiences. My hope is to provide some enlightenment of the war that was fought in the little-known CBI Theater. I began with the intention of honoring my father by writing his story, but after meeting so many veterans of that war, I have written this book in honor of them all. Tom Brokaw has so aptly labeled the men and women who fought in World War II as the Greatest Generation, and yet when you talk to them, they simply say they did what they had to do. I am humbled to be a son of parents of that generation and to have befriended many of those veterans. This is part of the story they were so very reluctant to tell.

1

JULY 4, 1939
MOSHANNON VALLEY, PENNSYLVANIA

As a youth, Sam Huber had no idea he would be involved in the largest world war in the history of mankind. Neither did he know he would participate in events that would lead to his generation being called the Greatest Generation. He was born and raised in the Moshannon Valley of central Pennsylvania. The valley is thickly wooded and nestles snuggly against the western slopes of the Allegheny Mountains. It was a good place for a boy to grow up and had plenty of fishing, hunting, and outdoor activities close at hand. He enjoyed them all until his idyllic childhood was interrupted by the Great Depression. Sam's family, like many others of that era, fell upon hard times. Sam quit school after the eighth grade and, in an effort to help his family, went to work in the local brick yard. When he reached the age of eighteen, he joined the CCC (Civilian Conservation Corps). There he trained as an automotive mechanic and continued to earn extra money for his struggling family. Little did he know that his life was about to be profoundly and permanently changed.

On this July 4, life in the Moshannon Valley was difficult, but everyone was looking forward to the annual Independence Day celebration in Osceola Mills. During the week of the Fourth of July, the local volunteer fire company always sponsored a carnival with rides, games, food booths, high-wire acts, and nightly bingo. It was always a time when family and friends returned to their roots to enjoy the festivities, renew friendships, and celebrate the national holiday. Of course, the high point of the week was the Fourth of July parade.

In previous years, Sam could be found among the spectators watching the parade, but this year, he was participating in the parade as a member of the CCC. He had donned his CCC uniform early and went to the high school complex where units for the parade were gathered. After the traditional 11:00 a.m. start, the parade followed the usual twisted route through town with the final leg progressing down Curtin Street past the carnival and the judge's stand. Sam's unit had almost completed the parade route and was marching past the judge's stand when he saw her. She was standing on the sidewalk, holding the hand of a smaller girl, and both were waving small American flags. She wore a white cotton dress that accentuated her trim figure and shapely legs. Her long black hair fell to her shoulders, framing a stunning face accented by high cheekbones and pale blue eyes. For a moment, Sam thought his heart had stopped beating. He knew he was supposed to keep his eyes front while they marched, but as he passed by, he turned his head in her direction and beamed his best smile. Their eyes met and held for several seconds. Sam nearly stumbled and fell out of step with the rest of the unit.

Eleanor was stunned and almost dropped her flag. One moment she was watching the parade with her sister, and the next she was gazing into a pair of amazing dark brown eyes. Those eyes were accompanied by the most handsome face she had ever seen, with flashing white teeth and a smile meant only for her. Her sister, Mim, who was almost three years younger than Eleanor, realized what was happening and couldn't suppress a little giggle. Oblivious to her sister,

Eleanor watched Sam until his unit passed out of sight. Mim looked up at her sister with knowing eyes and continued to giggle.

Sam regained his composure and continued marching down the street. There were only three blocks remaining in the parade route, and he could hardly wait for it to end. He knew he had to go back and find her. After what seemed like an eternity, his unit finally reached the end of the route. Sam broke ranks and hurried back up Curtin Street. His unit had been near the front of the parade, so he hoped she would still be in the same spot watching the remainder of the procession. His eyes scanned the crowd for that unforgettable figure. The final unit of the parade was just passing by when Sam saw her standing in the same spot. He didn't know she had stayed there, hoping he would return. She wasn't disappointed, and neither was he. Casting aside any semblance of reserve, Sam approached.

"Hi, I'm Sam Huber. I saw you from the parade. Would you and your friend like to go to the carnival with me?" Sam held his breath, waiting for an answer.

"Well, this isn't my friend. She's my sister, and I usually don't date someone I've just met, but I think my sister would enjoy the carnival. My name is Eleanor Hale, and this is Mim."

Mim giggled as she cast shy glances at the handsome young man.

It turned out to be a glorious afternoon filled with fun and laughter. They rode the carnival rides, ate cotton candy, and Sam won Kewpie dolls for both girls at a ringtoss booth. Eleanor reveled at the envious glances she received from other girls, and Sam chaffed at constantly being distracted to introduce her to yet another of his CCC buddies. Although they just met, Sam and Eleanor quickly developed a rapport that would have been the envy of lifelong friends. Eleanor was enthralled with Sam's stories about life in the CCC camps, and Sam was surprised to learn that Eleanor would be attending Penn State University as a freshman in the fall. Evening came much too quickly for either of them, and Sam escorted the girls to their home.

He really didn't want the day to end but finally asked if he could see her again the following weekend. Trying not to seem too eager, Eleanor accepted and waved as he departed. Mim waved too and giggled.

They continued to see each other throughout the summer of 1939, and their romance blossomed. However, it was a sad parting in September when Sam left for CCC Camp Roosevelt near Edinburg, Virginia, and Eleanor went off to study at Penn State. They saw little of each other that winter but faithfully wrote many letters. In the spring, Sam returned from Virginia and was assigned to a camp near Penfield, Pennsylvania. Eleanor finished her freshman year at Penn State, and they continued their romance during the summer of 1940. Whenever the couple got together, Mim was always close at hand. Her impish presence became second nature to Sam, but Eleanor often became exasperated with her little sister. Eleanor's discomfort only delighted Mim even more.

The summer passed quickly, and Eleanor began her second year at the university. However, she had to withdraw at the end of the fall semester due to a lack of funds. As 1940 came to an end, Sam and Eleanor knew they wanted to spend the rest of their lives together. Since neither family had enough money to give them a traditional wedding, they eloped along with Eleanor's brother and his fiancée and were married by a justice of the peace in Winchester, Virginia, on February 28, 1941. The couples spent their honeymoon driving through the Blue Ridge Mountains and the Shenandoah Valley of Virginia. During the day, Sam took them to all the places he remembered from his CCC days in the area. Each night, the couples looked forward to going to their own rooms and the opportunity to be alone. They enjoyed their time together, and on occasion, Sam and Eleanor even missed the presence of Mim.

The remainder of 1941 was quite eventful for the young couple. Two months after their marriage, Eleanor proudly announced they were going to have their first child. In August, they moved into a two-bedroom bungalow in Osceola Mills, and in November, Sam landed a much-coveted job as a brakeman with the Pennsylvania Railroad. Life was looking good, and they were very happy. Their first child was due around the seventh of December. Even with war raging in Europe, it seemed that nothing could spoil the ideal life they were living.

2

DECEMBER 7, 1941
MOSHANNON VALLEY, PENNSYLVANIA

IT WAS CUSTOMARY for Sam and Eleanor to have Sunday dinner with one of Sam's older half sisters, May and Lynette. Lynette was eighteen years older, and May was nine years older than Sam. Their common mother was sickly during most of her second marriage to Sam's father, so the sisters were like surrogate mothers to Sam and his younger brother, Francis. This particular Sunday, Sam and Eleanor arrived at May's home eager to share the news that Eleanor had begun her labor pains. Eleanor was nine months pregnant and overdue with their first child. Her pains began at five o'clock that morning, and by the time they reached May's house at eleven, her contractions had strengthened and were fifteen minutes apart. May, who could not have children of her own, was very close to the young couple and was like a mother hen around them. As they entered the house, Sam could smell the wonderful aroma of dinner cooking in the kitchen. May was preparing one of Sam's favorite meals, roast beef with mashed potatoes, gravy, and creamed corn. She had a special way of preparing a roast by first browning the meat in an iron skillet and then transferring it to a covered roasting pan where she finished cooking it slowly, adding small amounts of water until it was done. She then used the water and juices from the beef to prepare rich brown gravy. This day, May was also preparing another favorite for Sam: homemade bread which would be served hot with butter and an elderberry jelly she preserved the previous summer.

May's husband, Paul, met Sam and Eleanor at the door. Paul was short in stature and always had a twinkle in his eyes. He was a master machinist by trade and had lost his index finger and part of the middle finger on his right hand in an industrial accident several years previously. The missing fingers hadn't inhibited his ability to play the banjo and violin at local square dances. In his younger days, Paul even had his own local radio show and was known as Decker Hollow Dan. Paul wasn't the only musician in the family. May was also musically talented. Her mother taught her to play the piano at an early age, and throughout the 1920s, she played at the local silent movie theater. It was always a pleasure for Sam and Eleanor to sit and listen as May and Paul accompanied one another on their respective instruments.

As Sam and Eleanor entered the house, Paul could tell immediately something special was happening.

"I'm sure May's cooking isn't the only reason for the smiles on your faces. What's going on here?" Paul asked.

"Well, I hope Eleanor can hold off until after dinner. But I think we may have a new addition to the family before the day is over," Sam responded.

May entered the room just in time to hear Sam's statement. She immediately ushered Eleanor to the sofa where she made her sit down and then covered her with a hand-crocheted afghan.

"Can I get you anything, Eleanor?" May asked. "How far apart are your contractions? Maybe you should go to the hospital. Do you have enough gas in your car, Sam?"

"I'm okay, May. I think we have a while to go before we rush off to the hospital," Eleanor explained. "Besides, I agree with Sam. I hope the baby can wait until after dinner. It smells so good, and I'm famished."

May smiled and held Eleanor's hand. Her eyes revealed a mixture of joy for Eleanor and sadness for herself. At the age of twelve, May's appendix ruptured, spilling bacteria-laden intestinal contents into her abdomen, causing peritonitis. She barely survived the ordeal, but her ovaries had been infected, and she was left infertile. May knew she could never have the true experience of motherhood.

"You know I am going to spoil this baby, don't you?" May said.

"I know you will, May, and you'll have my blessings in doing just that," Eleanor replied.

Eleanor loved May as much as she loved her own sisters and could only imagine the emptiness she must feel inside. Joy returned to May's eyes.

"Well, you two got here early today, and dinner won't be ready for another fifteen minutes. So just relax, Paul and I will set the table, and, Sam, you take care of Eleanor." With that, she returned to the kitchen.

Sam observed the exchange between his wife and sister and felt honored that they were part of his life. He looked at Eleanor and marveled at the glow on her face and felt the same tug at his heart that he felt the first time he saw her. He put his arm around Eleanor's shoulder and thought about what it was going to be like to be a father. He was stirred from his reverie when May entered the living room.

"Dinner is ready," she said. "Come and get it while it's hot."

Sam loved May's cooking and heartily ate the sumptuous meal. Eleanor, who also enjoyed May's meals, continued to have contractions and hardly touched her food. At the end of the meal, she returned to the sofa. Her contractions continued to strengthen and, within half an hour, were eight minutes apart.

"I think I better get the car started and warm it up," Sam said, with a note of nervousness in his voice.

"I believe that's a good idea," Eleanor responded. "May, would you help me with my coat?" she asked.

Sam put on a jacket and hurried to the door but stopped short when he realized the jacket didn't fit, and his car keys were not in the pocket. He stood there with a confused look on his face. Paul, who was quite a bit shorter than Sam, removed another jacket from the coat tree and handed it to Sam.

"Here, this is your jacket. You put mine on by mistake." He chuckled.

Sam's face reddened with embarrassment, and he quickly changed jackets, retrieved his car keys, and opened the living room door. Before he could step outside, he was almost bowled over by Nan Herring, May's widowed next-door neighbor. Nan was a plump little lady in her seventies who rarely got excited, but she was positively flustered as she entered the house. Her face was flushed, and it was obvious she was short of breath from hurrying between the two houses.

"They've done a terrible thing, a terrible thing," she finally gasped. There were notes of obvious terror and concern in her voice. Sam gently placed his hands on her shoulders to steady her.

"What terrible thing, Nan? Who are you talking about?" he asked.

Nan seemed unable to respond. Tears streamed down her face as Sam led her to a chair where she sat down and was immediately surrounded by her concerned friends. None of them could imagine what would so greatly disturb this gentle woman. Nan continued to sob for a moment and then composed herself enough to continue.

"I just heard it on the radio. The Japanese have bombed Pearl Harbor, it was a sneak attack. Turn on your radio," she pleaded.

No one moved. They just stood there shocked by the news, looking at each other with expressions of disbelief on their faces. Finally, Paul went to the radio and turned it on. They listened while the announcer recounted details of the tragic events that had so recently occurred.

The little group continued to listen, each one wondering in their own mind how they were going to be affected, yet knowing deep down their lives would never be the same. They had all followed the events of the war that was raging in Europe, and everyone hoped and prayed the United States would not be drawn into that war. But now they sullenly listened to the dreadful details of death and destruction that had occurred in Hawaii. No one spoke as reports continued to flow from the radio. They were consumed by the enormity of what was happening.

It wasn't until several hours passed that Eleanor realized her labor stopped the moment they heard the news from Nan. Uncontrollable dread seemed to fill her. At first, she feared something was wrong with the baby, but when it finally kicked, she was relieved and at the same time shuddered at the thought of bringing a new life into the uncertainty of a world at war. However, it would be several more days before that life was ready to face the troubled world.

3

DECEMBER 11, 1941
MOSHANNON VALLEY, PENNSYLVANIA

IT WAS A typical work day for Sam and his fellow trainmen on the Pennsylvania Railroad. They began the day in the crisp coolness of the winter morning by forming a train of more than 150 hopper cars loaded with coal from various mines around the Moshannon Valley. The cool weather kept them moving, and by early afternoon, they were transporting their load over the Sandy Ridge summit to the freight yard at Tyrone. Sam enjoyed the slow ride over the summit as the train wound its way around sharp curves and down the steep inclines of the Appalachian front. It gave him the opportunity to watch for wildlife as they rumbled along the track, and it was not unusual to see a deer, a wild turkey, and the occasional black bear. He was especially watchful when they passed McCann's Crossing. It was at that site on May 31, 1893, that the Walter L. Main circus train derailed, spilling fourteen cars and their load of circus animals into the surrounding forest. The toll from the accident was high. Five circus employees were killed, and nineteen were injured. Fifty show horses were either killed outright or had to be destroyed, and a tiger was shot by a local farmer as it attacked one of his cows. Most of the surviving animals were recaptured and tied to trees to keep them from escaping. However, a lion and a black panther were never recaptured. Forty-seven years later, there were still rumors of panther sightings in the neighboring woodlands. But on this day, the only black thing Sam saw was their load of coal, which was destined for the coke ovens of western Pennsylvania and eventually the steel mills of Pittsburgh. At the end of the day, the crew deposited the loaded hoppers at Tyrone and brought back 250 empty cars to the Moshannon Valley.

Sam loved his job with the railroad and realized he was making a significant contribution to the fledgling war effort. However, as he drove home from work this Thursday evening, he thought back over the unbelievable events of the previous four days.

On Sunday, December 7, two waves of Japanese naval planes struck the Pacific fleet at Pearl Harbor, destroying or badly damaging sixteen navy vessels and most U.S. planes on the ground. More than twenty-four hundred military and civilian personnel were killed. That same day, the Japanese attacked Clark Field on the Philippine island of Luzon and destroyed most of the heavy bombers stationed there. On Monday, December 8, Sam listened to President Roosevelt as he delivered his Date of Infamy speech and announced the declaration of war against Japan. Later that day, he heard of the Japanese attacks against the United States held islands of Midway, Wake, and Guam. Tuesday, December 9, brought news of the Japanese invasion of the Philippines, and Wednesday, the tenth, there was news of the fall of the island of Guam to the seemingly unstoppable Japanese military.

All those events tore at Sam's soul, and he desperately wanted to strike back and avenge the loss of so many of his fellow Americans. Throughout the day, members of his train crew expressed the same sentiment and his friend Shorty Renford announced he was going to enlist in the army. Sam was seriously considering enlisting himself, but he was torn between his patriotic feelings and his responsibility to Eleanor and their unborn child.

As he drove alone through the waning light of the December evening, Sam's mind was tormented with indecision. He turned on the car radio, hoping the sound of music or another voice would help quiet the turmoil raging in his head. But it was not to be so easy for Sam, because he tuned in the radio just in time to hear the news that on this day, December 11, 1941, Germany and Italy had declared war on the United States, and we in turn declared war on them. After more than two years of walking the tightrope of neutrality, America, in just four frenzied days, was embroiled on two fronts in a world war.

As he listened to the latest bad news, the turmoil he felt inside seemed to grow until it was almost unbearable. There seemed to be no relief. Just yesterday, he tried to discuss his feelings with Eleanor, but it had not gone well. She sensed what Sam wanted to do, and her fear of losing the love of her life and the prospect of raising a child without a father was more than she could stand. Their conversation ended when she ran from the room crying and refused to listen as Sam tried to further explain the anguish he felt. How could he blame her, and yet, how could he ignore what he considered to be a sacred duty to his country? Needing time to think, he pulled his car to the side of the road and stopped the engine. He sat there as the last rays of light dimmed in the western sky, remembering the stories his father had told him about their family's long history of service to America.

Sam's father had served as a member of the Fifth Field Artillery in France during World War I. Sam remembered his tales of life in the trenches of Europe. He recalled stories about his great-grandfather, Philip Huber, who was a sergeant in the Twenty-second Pennsylvania Calvary during the Civil War and fought in many battles around Winchester, Virginia, and the Shenandoah Valley. Although Philip survived, two of his brothers lost their lives during the Civil War. He also remembered his father's account of a distant grandfather, a farmer near Allentown, Pennsylvania, during the Revolutionary War. Although that ancestor was too old to fight in the revolution, he provided General Washington's army with gunpowder and food during their winter encampment at Valley Forge. As a member of the Zion Reformed Church, he also helped hide the Liberty Bell in the basement of the church after the British captured Philadelphia. Patriotism ran long and deep in Sam's veins, and tears came to his eyes as he pulled back onto the highway. He made his decision and knew he had to tell Eleanor of his intention to enlist.

As Sam approached his home, he steeled himself for the task he knew was not going to be easy. When he pulled into his driveway, he was immediately met by his sister May.

"Don't get out of the car, Sam. We have to go to the hospital right away," May exclaimed as she jumped into the passenger's seat.

"Eleanor began her labor about an hour ago. Paul took her to the hospital, and I waited here for you. Where have you been?" she asked. "You should have been home forty-five minutes ago."

Sam thought of the time he just spent sitting along the road and realized he missed being with Eleanor when she needed him most. Without saying a word to his sister, he put the car in gear and hurriedly pulled onto the street and headed for the hospital. Sam was silent during the five-mile drive to the hospital, and May attributed his silence to concern for his wife. They arrived at the hospital in record time and rushed to the maternity ward where they met Paul in the waiting room.

"Dr. Flynn was just here and said everything is progressing nicely. He expects it won't be much longer," Paul reassured them.

Sam was relieved to hear that Dr. Flynn was there. Not only was he one of the best doctors in the area, he was also Sam and May's uncle. He had delivered all of the children in their family, and his skill had saved May's life when she suffered from peritonitis as a young girl. Now in his midseventies, the doctor had long ago given up his pediatric practice, but he couldn't resist the opportunity to deliver one more family member. Sam knew childbirth was painful, and he knew any number of things could go wrong, so he sat quietly and nervously waited as the minutes dragged on. May and Paul were seated nearby, holding hands and thinking of their own unfulfilled dreams of a family.

Finally, at 7:50 p.m., Dr. Flynn entered the waiting room and approached the anxious family.

"Well, Sam," he said, "you have a brand-new baby boy born at exactly seven thirty-five. Eleanor did a great job, and she is doing fine."

Sam felt as though a great weight was lifted from his shoulders, and he was immensely relieved and elated at the news, but then he caught a somber glance between May and their uncle and realized something was wrong. The kindly doctor looked deep into Sam's eyes.

"I understand you are naming the baby William after your father, and you're going to call him Billy."

Sam nodded, but the tightness in his stomach kept him from responding.

"Billy is having some problems breathing, and we currently have him under an oxygen tent," the doctor said. "I don't think it is anything really serious. He is breathing on his own, which is a good thing. Once we have the little guy stabilized, I'll be able to examine him more closely. In the meantime, why don't all of you visit Eleanor?"

With that, the old doctor left them and returned to his little patient. As Sam, May, and Paul walked silently to the recovery room, the turmoil he had gone through earlier in the day was replaced by new and more immediate concerns. Sam began to realize that service to his country would have to wait. What he didn't realize was how long that wait would be.

4

MAY 24, 1943
MOSHANNON VALLEY, PENNSYLVANIA

ELEANOR STOOD TREMBLING with the newly delivered letter in her hands. The return address on the envelope read:

AVIATION CADET EXAMINING BOARD
Tenth St. & Howard Avenue
Altoona, Pennsylvania

Tears welled in her eyes, and she started to sob uncontrollably. The moment she had been dreading had finally arrived. Sam would soon be leaving her and Billy, perhaps forever. She felt as if her world was coming to an end. Still sobbing, she placed the unopened letter on the kitchen table for Sam to see when he got home from work. She sat down, staring at the unopened letter. Memories flooded her mind of the past year and a half since Billy's birth, just a few days after the Japanese attack on Pearl Harbor. Billy's breathing problems at birth had put Sam's plans to enlist on hold. Those problems persisted throughout his first six months of life and nearly cost him his life due to pneumonia at the age of four months. Billy eventually overcame his health problems, and now he was a normal little boy. The experience of seeing their baby near death had brought Sam and Eleanor closer together, but it hadn't lessened Sam's longing to serve his country.

All through 1942, Sam worked for the Pennsylvania Railroad and had become comfortable with his job as a brakeman. However, he never lost sight of what was happening in the war zones around the world and was greatly disheartened as the Japanese steadily advanced throughout the Pacific, capturing Luzon, Hong Kong, and the islands of Guam and Wake all in the month of December 1941. He was even more dismayed in 1942, when Japanese forces overran Borneo, Sumatra, Bali, Java, and other islands of the East Indies and then captured Singapore and occupied all of Burma. MacArthur's evacuation of the Philippines in March of 1942 was the lowest point thus far of the war for Sam, but those events only served to deepen his desire to fulfill his patriotic duty.

Throughout the early war years, Eleanor tried to understand why Sam had such strong patriotic feelings, and when the opportunity arose, she would draw him into conversation on the subject. She remembered the stories of his many ancestors from the Revolutionary War through World War I and how they had faithfully served their country. One particular incident that happened to his father deeply affected Sam.

Three years before Sam was born, his father was a soldier in the trenches of France during World War I. On one fateful day, while he was standing in an underground bunker, a German artillery shell crashed through the ceiling and lodged into the floor just inches from his feet. Fortunately the shell was a dud and did not explode. Had it served the purpose for which it was intended, his father would have been killed and would not have returned home to eventually marry Sam's mother. Sam felt fate had intervened in his father's life to ensure that Sam would be born and brought to a place and time where he too could serve his country. Maybe some future action on his part was destined to alter the life of someone else, perhaps his own children.

Eleanor had eventually come to see how important military service was to Sam, and she reluctantly agreed when he asked her support in his enlistment and application for aviation cadet training in the spring of 1943. However, as she sat looking at the letter on the table before her, she felt the terrible loneliness that was to come when she wouldn't have the comfort of her husband at night and wouldn't know from one moment to the next where he was, what he was facing, or even if he was alive.

Eleanor tried to go about her daily tasks around the house, but every time she saw the letter on the table, her emotions welled within her, until finally, she felt she could stand no more. She had to talk to someone. Sam's sister May lived just across the street, so she put a jacket on Billy, grabbed the letter from the kitchen table, and hurried over to May's house.

May was dusting in her living room when she heard her front door open. She looked up and saw Eleanor and Billy as they entered. May was very fond of Eleanor and had come to love Billy like the child she could never have. Normally, she would have rushed to greet them, but the look on Eleanor's face told her something was very wrong.

"What's wrong, Eleanor?" May dropped her dust cloth and hurried to the door. Billy held out his arms for May to take him, and she gladly accommodated his wishes. Eleanor sank into an overstuffed chair next to the sofa, and tears once again streamed from her eyes.

"This came in today's mail," Eleanor said, holding the letter out for May to see. "It looks like Sam is finally going to get his wish. I had hoped he would be exempt from serving because of his job with the railroad," she sobbed.

Billy spotted one of his favorite toys and squirmed in May's arms. She put him down, and he scurried off to play with a metal replica of a P51 fighter plane. May walked over and placed a comforting hand on Eleanor's shoulder. Noticing the toy Billy had chosen, May remarked, "He's just like his daddy. Sam had loved airplanes since he was a little boy too. He had always wanted to fly. It didn't surprise me when he applied for aviation cadet training."

"What am I going to do, May? What if he doesn't come back? I shouldn't have agreed to let him enlist."

May's heart was aching for Eleanor and, although she didn't show it, for herself also. She was nine years older than Sam, and because their mother was sickly after Sam's birth, she had played a major role in raising him. Over the years, they had become very close.

"Sam will come back, Eleanor. I know in my heart that he will, and while he's gone, we will take care of you and Billy," May stroked Eleanor's long dark hair and watched Billy play contentedly with his toy airplane. "If you hadn't agreed to let him go, he would have been miserable. You know our family's military tradition. Sam has to be part of that. He feels very strongly about doing his share."

"I know you're right, May. Sam has been miserable since the war started. I just don't know what I'm going to do without him. We've never been apart since we were married. I love him so much."

"We all love him, Eleanor, but we have to make this easy for him. We have to let him know that we support what he is doing and that we will always be here for him." May sensed the tension beginning to ease from Eleanor's body. "Do you love him enough to do that for him, Eleanor?"

Eleanor knew May was right. She knew Sam was going to be facing some very difficult times, and she had to suppress her own feelings and let him know she would always be here for him.

"I understand what you are saying, May, and I agree with you. I shouldn't be so selfish. I know it will be difficult and lonely when he is gone, but I also know you and Paul and the entire family will be here for Billy and me."

"We will, Eleanor, you can count on it. Now Sam will be home from work in a few hours. Why don't you leave Billy here for the night and go home and fix Sam a nice supper? Pretty yourself up and let him know how much you love him."

Eleanor considered May's advice as she watched Billy playing contentedly with his airplane. She had always been afraid of airplanes, and the thought of her husband flying in one terrified her. She knew it was too late to change Sam's mind and that she had to put up a brave front in order to support him. After a moment, she decided to accept May's offer to keep Billy for the night as she had often done when she and Sam needed a babysitter.

"Thank you, May. I'll bring Billy's night clothes right over and then start supper for Sam, and thank you for your support and advice. As usual, you have been very helpful and a comfort to me."

"You're welcome, dear, and thank you for letting Paul and me care for Billy. You know how much we both love him."

As Eleanor departed, May watched Billy playing for a moment and then picked him up and gave him a warm hug and a kiss, which always elicited a happy giggle from the little guy. She watched Eleanor cross the street and enter her own home. The thought of Sam going to war made her heart heavy, and she knew how difficult it was going to be for Eleanor in the coming months. She held Billy even tighter as she went into the kitchen to prepare supper.

Sam arrived home from work right on time, and Eleanor had supper waiting on the table as he walked in the door. Before he could even put his lunch pail down, Eleanor hurried to him and gave him an ardent hug and passionate kiss. She clung to him a little longer than normal, and Sam sensed something had happened that day. He peered inquisitively into her eyes.

"That was quite a greeting. What brought all this about?" he asked.

Trying to keep a smile on her face, Eleanor reached into her apron pocket, removed the unopened letter, and handed it to him. "This came for you today. I think it's the letter you've been wanting."

Sam peered at the return address on the envelope and then eagerly tore it open and began reading the letter inside. Eleanor watched the excitement grow on his face as he read.

"Well, what does it say, Sam?"

"It says they have received my application for aviation cadet training. Here, you read it." He handed the letter to Eleanor, and she halfheartedly began to read,

AVIATION CADET EXAMINING BOARD
10th St. & Howard Avenue
Altoona, Penna.

Date <u>May 21, 1943</u>

<u>Mr. Samuel D. Huber</u>
<u>Osceola Mills,</u>
<u>Penna.</u>

Dear Sir:

This office acknowledges receipt of your application and allied papers for training as an Aviation Cadet. You will report to this office on <u>Friday, May 28, 1943</u> at 8:00 A.M., <u>SHARP</u> for your mental examination.

Upon successful completion of the mental test, you will be given a preliminary physical examination and also appear before a Board of Officers for a moral examination. It will then be necessary for you to proceed to either Pittsburgh, Pa., or Middletown Air Depot for your physical examination, and this is entirely at your own expense. Upon successful completion of that examination you will return to the Aviation Cadet Examining Board, 10th St. & Howard Avenue, Altoona, Pa., for your enlistment.

For the President of the Board:

J. C. Diesel,
2nd Lieut., A.U.S.
Recorder.

Eleanor hadn't expected events would happen so quickly. She fought back the desperation she felt building within her. She handed the letter back to Sam and forced a smile upon her face.

"This is what you have been wanting for a long time, Sam. Can we be ready in four days?"

Sam knew how Eleanor was feeling inside. He too was saddened by the thought of leaving his family, but he also knew this was something he had to do. He couldn't explain his feelings; he just knew he could never look at himself in a mirror again if he didn't do his share to defend his country. His brother, Francis, and so many of his friends had already answered the call, and a few were never coming back.

"I'll take this letter to my boss tomorrow. He will do whatever is necessary for the railroad. My job will be here when I get back."

He walked over and took Eleanor into his arms.

"Are you going to be okay with this?"

She buried her face in his chest so he couldn't see the tears forming in her eyes and took a few moments to compose herself as they clung to each other. Finally, she stepped back and looked directly into his eyes.

"You do what you know you have to do. Billy and I will be here waiting for you when it's all over. You know I will always love you, Sam."

The lump in Sam's throat kept him from answering right away. After a moment, he was finally able to speak. "I love you too, Eleanor, and I will come back to you."

They embraced each other once again with an intensity that arises only when two people are truly in love. They stood there holding each other for long moments until Sam noticed that Billy wasn't there to greet him as he usually did.

"Where's Billy?" Sam asked.

"May is keeping him for the night. Let's eat supper before it gets cold and then we have the rest of the night to do whatever we want," she responded.

Sam knew exactly what he wanted to do, and so did Eleanor.

5

JUNE 1, 1943
MIDDLETOWN AIR DEPOT, PENNSYLVANIA

S AM HAD CHOSEN to go to Middletown Air Depot for his enlistment physical. The depot was located about 120 miles away, just south of Harrisburg, Pennsylvania. He departed from Osceola Mills at 3:00 a.m. in order to arrive at Middletown before eight. He was accompanied by Kerburt "Kerby" Kline, a longtime friend, who was also enlisting in the army. Sam and Kerby now found themselves waiting for their physical examinations with a group of other young men from various parts of the state. As they stood in loose formation, their attention was riveted upon what had to be the largest person Sam had ever seen.

At six feet five inches tall and 280 pounds, Sergeant Ricks towered over everyone in the room. He wore a permanent scowl on his face and was to be in charge of the group of fifty men throughout the day. Like a lion on the prowl, he paced back and forth before them. He stopped in front of Kerby who was standing next to Sam. Kerby was all of five feet three inches tall and couldn't weigh more than 105 pounds. In addition to his diminutive stature, Kerby was a nervous person and also rather naïve. He was constantly worrying about one thing or another. With the gigantic sergeant looming over him, Kerby literally seemed to wilt. He was noticeably pale, and his knees were shaking. Sergeant Ricks looked as if he were about to eat Kerby alive when Sam came to his friend's rescue by addressing the sergeant.

"Excuse me, Sergeant. What do you want us to do first?" Sam asked.

The sergeant's glare was averted to Sam who looked directly into the noncom's eyes and evidenced no sign of fear. Through his CCC experience, Sam knew Sergeant Ricks was just doing his job and returned his stare with no indication of disrespect. After a moment, the sergeant gave a nod of approval to Sam and then turned and spoke to the group.

"You maggots will strip down to your socks and undershorts. Place your belongings in the metal baskets behind you and then line up in front of the door on your left."

The men hurriedly obeyed the sergeant and began stripping off their clothing. Sam was nearly undressed when he noticed that Kerby was just standing there and had not removed a single item of clothing.

"Kerby! Do you want that sergeant back on your case? Get undressed before he notices you," Sam said.

"I can't, Sam," Kerby replied.

"What do you mean you can't? Surely you know how to undress yourself," Sam said.

"I can't undress. I'm not wearing any underwear," Kerby said meekly.

Sam stared at Kerby in disbelief, but it was too late. Sergeant Ricks noticed Kerby standing there fully dressed and pounced upon the hapless little fellow.

"What's your problem, Shorty? Didn't you hear my order, or are you afraid to undress in front of real men?" the sergeant said.

Kerby was speechless and couldn't respond. His face was turning paler by the second, and he made no effort to move.

"If you're not undressed in twenty seconds maggot, I will personally peel your clothes off like a banana and your skin along with them," roared the sergeant.

Kerby needed no further prompting and hurriedly began undressing. In record time, he stood before the sergeant and the assembled men in nothing but his socks. Beads of sweat had formed on his forehead. There was a long pause of silence in the room. Sam turned his back, so Kerby could not see the amusement on his face as a scattering of laughter erupted from the other men. Sergeant Ricks stared in disbelief and then erupted.

"I don't have a thimble to give you to cover that thing, so you will have to use your hand," he snarled at Kerby. Then turning to the other men, he shouted, "Now all of you line up in front of the door on the left and prepare to give urine samples, and will someone get this clown a band aid or something to cover himself?"

A towel was found for Kerby, and he quickly covered his nakedness. However, the towel was very small, and he couldn't tie it around his waist, so he had to hold it in place with one hand. As they entered the next room, each man was given a small labeled jar with a lid and told to write their names on the label and then go into the adjoining men's room and fill it with urine. Kerby was immediately faced with a dilemma, since it would take two hands to write his name on the label. He didn't want to expose himself by letting go of the towel, so he finally asked Sam to write his name for him. Sam obliged his friend, and they proceeded into the men's room. Sam quickly filled his jar but noticed Kerby was having trouble with his. He was trying to fill his jar with one hand while holding the towel in place with the other. He was succeeding only in peeing all over the outside of the jar and his hand. Finally, he dropped the towel and managed to partially fill his jar. Upon completion of their tasks, they exited the men's room and deposited the jars in metal trays along the wall. The label on Kerby's jar had a distinctive yellow color. Sam could only imagine what lay in store for them the rest of the day. Sergeant Ricks continued to glower at Kerby as he directed them into another room where he formed them into four lines and told them they would be giving blood samples. Kerby received some odd stares from the female nurses when he entered the room. His complexion turned a bright red as he fumbled to keep his towel in place.

"How do they take blood samples, Sam? Does it hurt?" Kerby inquired.

"It won't hurt if you stay relaxed, Kerby. They just stick a needle into a vein in your arm and extract a little blood," Sam said.

"I hate needles, Sam. I know it's going to hurt," Kerby complained.

"You'll be okay. Just close your eyes until it's all over," Sam said.

Kerby was in front of Sam as they approached one of four chairs where the men sat while a nurse took the blood sample. The man in front of Kerby sat down and extended his right arm to the nurse. Kerby watched intently as the nurse took a syringe and inserted it into the man's arm. The man flinched noticeably as the needle entered his arm. Kerby stepped back, bumping into Sam. Not finding a vein, the nurse removed the needle and inserted it again, this time eliciting a small groan from the man. Kerby groaned as well. Still not finding a vein, the nurse again removed the needle and began inserting it in another location. This time, the hapless fellow groaned louder, and his head rolled from side to side as the nurse turned the needle this way and that, seeking a vein. It was all too much for Kerby, and he released his grip on his towel and passed out on the spot. Sam caught him as he fell and gently guided him to the floor.

Addressing the nurse, Sam said, "I think it would be a good idea to get a blood sample from him before he wakes up."

The nurse agreed and proceeded to get a blood sample with no problems. However, Kerby regained consciousness just as the nurse was removing the needle from his arm, and he promptly passed out again when he saw the blood-filled syringe. When he came to the second time, Sergeant Ricks was there to greet him.

"Well, hero, you've proven how brave you are in the face of a little nurse with a needle. I think I'll recommend you be sent directly to the frontlines. The enemy will be so busy laughing, they won't be able to fight, and the war will be over in no time. Now get back in line, maggot," the sergeant roared.

Kerby hurriedly got in line next to Sam as the sergeant directed the men into an adjoining room and formed them into two rows. Kerby stood to the right of Sam and tried to become as invisible as possible. Sergeant Ricks addressed them again.

"Now, gentlemen, you are going to be examined for hemorrhoids. I want you to turn around and face the wall behind you. Drop your shorts, then bend over and with both hands reach back and spread your butt cheeks. Remain in that position until I tell you differently," ordered the sergeant.

As they turned around, Kerby whispered to Sam, "What are hemorrhoids, Sam? This doesn't involve a needle, does it?"

"There are no needles, Kerby. They just look at your behind for signs of hemorrhoids," Sam explained.

"What are hemorrhoids, Sam?" Kerby asked.

"They are like swollen veins that can bleed and itch," Sam said.

"Well, how do you get rid of them?" Kerby was getting noticeably nervous again.

"In some cases, they have to cut them out," Sam explained.

"Geez, Sam, you don't think they'll find any of them hemorrhoids on me, do you?" Kerby asked.

"Don't worry about it, Kerby, if you had them, believe me you would know it. Now be quiet and do what the sergeant says, or he will give us all a good case of hemorrhoids," Sam said.

After what seemed like an eternity, the hemorrhoid examination was soon over in spite of a great deal of grumbling on the part of Kerby as to why they had to stand in that awkward position so long and why someone had to look at his butt anyway. Sergeant Ricks then ordered them to stand up and turn around. Kerby quickly wrapped his towel around himself and turned around to find the sergeant towering over him once again. "I didn't tell you to cover yourself, Shorty," he bellowed. "Drop that towel and stand at attention."

Kerby's towel immediately fell to the floor, eliciting scattered snickers from the men around him. The sergeant turned his attention back to the entire group, "You will now be examined for hernias. Everyone stand at attention, and when the doc gets to you, turn your head to the right and cough when he tells you."

Sam and Kerby were standing in the middle of the front row as the doctor approached from their left. Kerby was still grumbling under his breath about the hemorrhoid examination.

"Oh geez, Sam," Kerby whispered.

"Kerby, shut up. You'll get us in trouble," Sam said.

"But, Sam," Kerby insisted.

"What's wrong now, Kerby?" Sam glanced over to see Kerby covering himself with one hand and pointing to the right with the other hand. Sam moved his eyes in the direction Kerby was indicating and was brought up short by what he saw. Standing in the doorway on the right side of the room were two middle-aged cleaning ladies leaning on their mops and taking in the sight of fifty young American men clad in nothing but their socks. Sam's first reaction was to cover himself with his hand too, but at that moment, the doctor stepped in front of him and told him to turn his head and cough. Reluctantly, he turned his head in the direction of the doorway, and his eyes were met by those of the cleaning ladies who smiled and nodded their approval to him. Sam could feel the heat of embarrassment as their eyes traveled up and down his naked body. He was shaken from his predicament by the growl of Sergeant Ricks's voice in his ear.

"Well, pretty boy, are you going to cough for the doctor, or do you want to go and introduce yourself to the lovely ladies?" Ricks said.

Sam half-choked a cough, and mercifully, the doctor moved on to Kerby. Thankful that attention was no longer centered on him, Sam began to recover but then noticed that all activity had stopped and the doctor was just standing in front of Kerby with a shocked expression on his face. Sergeant Ricks's voice cut through the silence as he bent over nose to nose with Kerby and growled, "I have to give you credit, little man. It isn't much, but it stands at attention better than you do."

Sam looked down at Kerby and was amazed to see that his friend had managed quite an erection. The room erupted into laughter, and the cleaning ladies added a round of applause. The remainder of the physical was anticlimactic and was soon over. The cleaning ladies stayed at their station in the doorway, dispensing approving nods and lascivious leers until the room cleared.

On their drive back to the Moshannon Valley that night, Sam and Kerby chuckled and teased each other over the events of the day. Both had passed their physical examinations, but Sam couldn't help feel that his friend was going to have a difficult time meeting the challenges of military life. He also wondered what the future held for himself. He had previously passed the mental and moral tests for aviation cadet training but still faced a series of written exams after his enlistment. He worried that his eighth grade education would not be enough to get him into the program.

6

JUNE 28, 1943
FT. INDIANTOWN GAP, PENNSYLVANIA

Sam's fears about his limited education had not been groundless. After his enlistment in Altoona, he was sent to the New Cumberland Army Depot for further testing for the aviation cadet program. His scores were one point short of qualifying for the program. However, due to his experience in the CCC, he would be trained as an automotive mechanic in the army. His farewell to his family at the train station in Altoona had been emotional, but he assured Eleanor and his sisters that he would get back to see them before he was sent overseas. He currently found himself in basic training at Ft. Indiantown Gap, Pennsylvania, with none other than his old friend Kerby Kline.

His platoon was eight miles into a simulated ten-mile night patrol. They had been told the enemy might be nearby and to maintain silence at all costs. Things were going fine for Sam, but it was a different story for Kerby, who was hanging on to the back of Sam's belt and groaning with every step. Because of his short stature, Kerby had to take two steps for every one Sam took.

"Slow down, Sam. I can't keep up," Kerby moaned. He was literally being dragged along as he clung to Sam's belt.

"I can't go any slower, Kerby, or we'll lose the rest of the platoon." They were already the last men at the end of the patrol, and Sam was carrying Kerby's rifle as well as his own. "And keep quiet. We're supposed to be on patrol behind enemy lines."

"The enemy can have me, Sam. I just want to sit down for a while."

"Hang in there, Kerby. This march is almost over, and then you can rest. Remember what the sergeant told us—if a flare goes up, hit the dirt and take cover along the road."

"Oh, that would be great. I hope one does go up, and then I can rest," Kerby groaned. At that moment, as if in answer to his prayers, a flare shot high into the night sky, illuminating the narrow road they were on and the surrounding countryside. The rest of the platoon disappeared into the bushes along the road. Sam tried to take cover but was unable to with Kerby hanging on to him. The two of them were left standing alone in the bright light of the flare. Bewildered and exhausted, Kerby stood there, blinking at the descending flare, until the voice of their sergeant boomed out of the darkness.

"Get your sorry asses undercover, or you'll be on KP for the rest of the war."

Galvanized into action by the sergeant's command, Sam dove into a ditch on the left, and Kerby leapt far into the bushes to the right. As soon as he hit the ground, Kerby realized he had made the mistake of jumping into the middle of a briar patch. "Oh… oh… ow, Sam, get me out of here," Kerby wailed as he was pierced from every angle by the briars. Every movement he made to extricate himself only resulted in more pain and louder moans.

"Quit thrashing around in there, Kerby. We'll try to get you out," Sam responded.

Any semblance of stealth by the patrol had long been destroyed.

As Sam and several other soldiers removed Kerby from the briar patch, their irate sergeant was there to meet them.

"If this would have been a real patrol in enemy territory, you two would now be dead along with half the platoon," roared the sergeant, "But you'll wish you were dead when I'm through with you. Both of you report for KP duty as soon as you get back to the barracks." With that, the sergeant turned and stormed off into the darkness.

Kerby looked at Sam and said, "Does this mean we won't get any sleep tonight, Sam?"

Sam just shook his head and followed the rest of the platoon into the darkness.

July 8, 1943
Ft. Indiantown Gap, Pennsylvania

For the past two weeks, when they were not in training sessions, Sam and Kerby were on KP duty. Thankfully, it would soon be over for Sam because he was shipping out in a few days for advanced automotive mechanics training at Ft. McPherson, Georgia. As usual, he and Kerby were on KP duty along with four other trainees. They were assigned to sweep out the mess hall before the evening meal, and Sam felt confident Kerby would not get into any trouble. Everything seemed to be going well until Kerby appeared at Sam's side and shoved a piece of apple pie into his hands.

"Where the hell did you get the pie?" Sam inquired as he tried to give the pie back to Kerby.

"No, you have to keep it, Sam. The cooks just put two dozen pies on the serving counter. The other guys and I are taking turns sweeping behind the counter and heisting a slice as we go by. If we all take a slice, one pan will be empty, and we can hide it in the trash. No one will miss it."

Before Sam could say another word, Kerby was heading for the serving counter with his broom. Sam looked quickly around. The KP sergeant was nowhere in sight, and he noticed the other men were seated around a table. Each man had one hand under the table and would periodically lower his head and sneak a bite of pie. Sam couldn't just stand there holding his pie, so he decided he might as well join them. Everything seemed to be going okay as they sat eating the pie and joking about their great pie caper.

"Did you get rid of the empty pie pan, Kerby?" Sam asked.

"Yeah, I hid it deep in the trash can," Kerby responded through a mouthful of pie. Everyone chuckled until they noticed Kerby turn pale as he stared at the far end of the room. They turned in the direction Kerby was looking and were dismayed to see the KP sergeant entering the mess hall. Each man still had a couple of bites of pie remaining. Their only recourse was to cram the remaining pie in their mouths as the sergeant quickly approached their table. Sam's back was toward the sergeant so he began to chew furiously in an attempt to empty his mouth. The other men, being in plain view of the NCO, could only sit there with their mouths full of pie, unable to speak or chew. Sam had not quite accomplished his goal when the sergeant reached their table.

"Have you lowlifes finished sweeping up in here?" the sergeant asked. Not a single man was able to open his mouth to respond. Kerby nodded his head yes, which immediately infuriated the noncom.

"Don't you know how to properly respond to a superior soldier?" screamed the sergeant.

Kerby's eyes grew twice their normal size, and he looked like he was about to pass out. You could see he was having difficulty keeping the pie from erupting from this mouth. With the noncom's attention riveted upon Kerby, Sam was finally able to swallow the last of his pie.

"Yes, sir, the mess hall has been completely swept, sir," Sam responded.

There were a few tense moments as the sergeant looked around the room. While the sergeant's attention was elsewhere, Kerby took the opportunity to spit his half-eaten pie into his hand and then shove it into his pocket. Finally, the sergeant turned back to the group, apparently satisfied with what he saw.

"Okay, gentlemen. Get off your butts and get back to your barracks." With that, he spun around and headed for the door.

Relieved that they had escaped a close call, the men stowed their brooms and proceeded to leave the mess hall. As they reached the door, they were brought up short by a voice from the kitchen.

"Hope y'all enjoyed the pie. Y'all be sure and come back now." Laughter from the cooks in the kitchen followed them as they jostled through the door.

JULY 11, 1943
FT. INDIANTOWN GAP, PENNSYLVANIA

Sam was stretched out on his bunk on the first floor of the barracks. It was Sunday evening, and he was happy to have the opportunity to relax after a grueling week of basic training. He was doubly pleased he had managed to keep Kerby out of any serious trouble during the week. It suddenly occurred to Sam that he hadn't seen Kerby for a while, and he began to feel uneasy.

"Has anyone seen Kerby lately?" he inquired from the other soldiers nearby.

"Yeah, he went upstairs to join a poker game about an hour ago," replied a soldier a few bunks away.

Sam immediately became concerned. He knew from firsthand experience that Kerby was not a very good poker player, and he also knew Kerby liked to cheat at cards. His first inclination was to go upstairs and check on his friend, but then he remembered Lieutenant Vance, the officer of the day (OD), had just checked the barracks and found everything shipshape. Besides, it was only one hour until lights out, and the poker game would have to break up at that time. Satisfied there was no need to worry, Sam relaxed and began thinking about his upcoming transfer to Fort McPherson.

He was almost to the point of dozing off when he was startled by the sound of running feet and angry voices from the floor above. He rose quickly from his bed and turned in the direction of the stairway leading to the second floor. He could hear the pounding of feet as they descended the stairs, but due to the design of the barracks, he was unable to see who was coming until they reached the bottom of the steps. As the footsteps drew nearer, Sam hoped beyond hope that he would not see who he suspected was hurrying down the steps. His hopes were dashed instantly when Kerby slid into view from around the corner of the stairway. Behind him came six angry soldiers from the second floor.

Sam knew immediately that Kerby had been caught cheating. As the mob approached, he looked about for some way to help his friend without causing a full-scale riot in the barracks. As Kerby sped by, Sam grabbed a pillow from his bunk and swung it at the nearest pursuer, knocking him over a footlocker. Aroused by the noise but not knowing what was really going on, other soldiers grabbed their pillows to join in the hijinks. In a matter of moments, the entire first floor was engulfed in a gigantic pillow fight. More soldiers from the second floor arrived, and in the ensuing melee, bunks were overturned and feathers from torn pillows were spewed everywhere.

After five minutes of an all-out pillow fight, the men from the second floor retreated up the stairway and immediately blocked the top of the stairs with footlockers and mattresses. Some of the first-floor soldiers, eager to carry the battle to the enemy's turf, charged up the stairs, only to be stopped at the barricade and repulsed by defenders wielding push brooms. Repeated attempts to ascend the stairway met with no success. Finally, Kerby, who had been hiding under his bunk the entire time, came up with a plan. He pointed out the fact that anyone coming down from the second floor had to go past the latrine to enter the first floor. He convinced his coconspirators to taunt and cajole the upstairs mob to come down and resume the fracas on the turf already trashed. In the meantime, Kerby would hide in the latrine with several buckets of cold water. His plan was to douse the villains as they passed by the latrine doorway.

Sam tried to reason with them to let well enough alone, but the fever for revenge was too high, and Kerby's plan was immediately put into action. Kerby went into the latrine, and the others withdrew into the first floor where they began a loud outpouring of catcalls and jeering directed at those above. Sam stood by helplessly, as Kerby positioned himself just inside the latrine doorway with bucket in hand.

Lieutenant Vance, who was known throughout the company for his attention to detail and his spotless appearance, heard the commotion in the barracks and came to investigate. The noise from the hecklers was so loud that Kerby did not hear the door to the barracks open. A body appeared in the latrine doorway, and Kerby struck. He didn't realize until it was too late that the person he was dousing was not a nemesis from the second floor, but the OD, Lieutenant Vance. A great hush fell over the entire first floor as the dripping lieutenant took in the wasteland before him. The rage building inside him was only intensified when the troops on the second floor, not knowing what had transpired below, directed a barrage of coat hangers and catcalls down the stairway.

Everyone was amazed at the agility the water-logged lieutenant displayed as he bounded up the stairs and kicked the barricade out of the way. It was a subdued bunch of soldiers who were formed up in front of the barracks, many of them in their underwear, and were ordered to march to the headquarters building. There they were told they would toil until 5:00 a.m., cleaning and polishing every inch of the building. Only then could they return to their barracks and have it ready for inspection by the company commander at 6:00 a.m.

Sam's only thoughts for the remainder of the night were of ways to get his hands around Kerby's throat.

JULY 13, 1943
SOUTHERN VIRGINIA

As Sam rode south aboard a train for Atlanta and Ft. McPherson, he thought of Kerby back at Ft. Indiantown Gap and wondered if his friend would survive in the army. Because of the difficulties he experienced in boot camp, Kerby was going to be trained as a cook. At least, Sam knew, the little soldier wouldn't go hungry. Sam's thoughts then turned to Eleanor and Billy, and he hoped the next three months of training would pass quickly so he could go home to see them.

7

NOVEMBER 14, 1943
MOSHANNON VALLEY, PENNSYLVANIA

IT WAS THE last night of Sam's leave, and he was asleep at his home in Osceola Mills. He hadn't gotten much sleep in the six months since he enlisted in the army, and this night was to be no exception. He awoke disoriented and sweating in the darkness. His fitful slumber was disturbed once again. He had been having a nightmare almost every night since receiving orders to be shipped to the China-Burma-India war zone. The nightmare was the same each time and always left him breathless and trembling.

In his nightmare, he dreamed he was being pursued through a dense jungle by Japanese soldiers. As he ran, the thorns of the jungle plants and creepers clawed and tore at his clothing and exposed flesh. It was as though the plants were participating in some morbid plot with the Japanese to slow him down. He could hear his enemy as they closed the gap behind him; his heart pounded violently in his chest. As he approached the point of total exhaustion, his strength began to wane. He looked back and caught a glimpse of his pursuers and saw the menacing long sword carried by their leader. Desperation gripped him, and he tried to run faster, but his legs wouldn't respond. He tripped over a hidden jungle vine, and suddenly, everything seemed to slow down. As he fell, panic overcame him, and he realized there was to be no escape. The enemy soldiers were upon him. He curled up in a fetal position, covering his face and head with his hands and arms, as the soldiers viciously kicked his body and struck him with the butts of their rifles.

The soldiers screamed at him in Japanese, and he struggled to understand what they wanted. Their words were guttural and harsh to his ear. He tried to respond, to tell them he couldn't understand, but no matter how hard he tried, words would not escape his lips. A command from their leader momentarily stopped his torment. He looked up into the face of the officer standing above him and hoped desperately to see some sign of understanding or compassion. He saw only hatred in the eyes glaring back at him. Slowly, he looked at the soldiers surrounding him. Their uniforms were mildewed and rotting, and their emaciated bodies were dirty and covered with jungle sores. Without exception, their eyes revealed the malevolence and hatred they felt toward him. A cold chill ran down his spine, and panic gripped his soul as he realized what was in store for him.

The officer barked another command, and two soldiers stepped forward. He could feel their rough hands as they lifted him into a kneeling position and forced his head down. The soldiers stepped back, and the officer's eyes gleamed in anticipation of the elimination of one more enemy of the Japanese empire. Clasping his sword with both hands, he raised it far above his head. The tropical sun filtering through the jungle foliage glistened off the blade as it was poised to strike. Shouts of triumph erupted from the throats of the soldiers. They were about to witness the culmination of a grizzly ritual from their ancient past. He could hear the hiss of the blade as it arched down toward his exposed neck. He never felt the touch of that blade, as he always awoke before it struck.

Sam was startled by a movement beside him and then remembered he was home in bed with his wife, Eleanor. He looked at his wristwatch in the dim light of the street lamp filtering through the bedroom window and saw that it was four o'clock in the morning. A deep sadness filled him when he realized that in just two short hours, he would have to rise and prepare to leave his home and loved ones. From the day he enlisted, Sam knew this day would come, and yet he wasn't ready for it to happen. His bags were packed and were waiting by the living room door. He would travel to the nearby town of Tyrone, where he would catch a troop train bound for San Francisco. Eventually, he was to board a ship destined for India. He would be at war halfway around the world, not knowing how long he would be gone or if he would ever return. The thought weighed heavily upon him that those he loved so dearly might someday have to face the news of his death. He knew this was Eleanor's greatest fear, and he could do little to comfort her. Evidence of the war's horrible toll was all around them. Several families in town had already received the terrible news of the loss of loved ones. One family lost a son in North Africa and another son in the South Pacific.

Eleanor stirred again and rolled tightly against his side. A contented murmur escaped her lips as she placed her head upon his chest and draped her arm over his abdomen. Sam cradled her gently, stroking her long dark hair. He knew he would not be able to go back to sleep and lay there thinking over the events that had transpired in his first six months in the army…

He had arrived at Fort McPherson in mid-July and immediately began advanced automotive mechanic training. He had only been there a week when he received word from Eleanor that she was coming to Atlanta to be near him. He objected at first but soon realized he could not dissuade her from her decision. She left Billy in the capable hands of his sister May and departed for Atlanta on July 20. Almost immediately, she found work in a textile factory, making cloth for the war effort. She settled into a small apartment on Peachtree Street that was within walking distance of her new job.

Sam was able to get liberty passes on the weekends, and they relished every moment together exploring the Atlanta area. In the evenings, they took long walks through the neighborhoods of Atlanta, and most of the time, Eleanor prepared their meals in the apartment. On rare occasions, they would dine in some quaint little neighborhood restaurant that they discovered in their explorations. During these times together, their discussions always revolved around plans for the future. In a superstitious way, those plans were assurances to them of their future together. The possibility it would not happen was never discussed. All in all, it was a magical time for both of them, but always in the back of their minds was the realization that it was coming to an end. Sam's training would end in the middle of October, and he would then be shipped overseas.

Throughout his automotive mechanic training, Sam never gave up on his dream of flying. One day, in mid-October, his attention was drawn to a notice posted on his company's bulletin board. The notice called for volunteers to join a newly formed air unit to support the 5307th Composite Unit. It further explained that the 5307th was a volunteer group of experienced jungle troops under the command of Brigadier General Frank Merrill who were to undertake hazardous and dangerous operations in the jungles of Burma. Seeing his opportunity to become an aircrew member, Sam immediately volunteered and was accepted into the 5331st Air Dropping Platoon as an air traffic clerk. He had no idea at the time that he would be closely associated with a group that famously became known as Merrill's Marauders.

Events moved quickly, and within days, he received orders to proceed by train to San Francisco and from there to India by troopship. In India, he would receive on-the-job training in aerial troop supply. He was also granted a ten-day leave before his departure for San Francisco. At first, Eleanor was very dismayed when Sam told her of his new assignment. She had assumed that as a mechanic, his duties would keep him out of harm's way. She was not at all happy with the prospect of him flying around in an unarmed aircraft under combat conditions, and she told him so in no uncertain terms. Sam downplayed the dangers of his new military role by saying they would be flying far above the reach of enemy guns. After further discussion, Eleanor was somewhat satisfied with that explanation. However, Sam felt guilty knowing quite the opposite would be true. With little time to spare, Eleanor departed for home on October 30, and Sam began his leave on November 4. He knew ten days would pass quickly, but he also knew it was time to face what was before him. Like his fathers before him, he was ready to serve his country...

Sam's thoughts were interrupted again when Eleanor moved. He could feel the warmth of her body next to him. He reached over and gently placed his hand on her stomach, being careful not to awaken her. Still asleep, she placed her hand on top of his. The warmth of her body and the memories of the intimacies they shared just hours before stirred in his loins. He remembered how they put Billy to bed early and then went to their bedroom feeling a deep loneliness inside and an overpowering desire for time to stop. They were haunted by the possibility that this would be their last night together, that they might never again be able to embrace or kiss or share the physical and spiritual joys of their love. Normally, they would wear pajamas to bed, but this night, they wanted nothing to be between them. Neither had spoken a word as they completely disrobed.

Sam recalled watching her undress and marveling at the beauty of her slender body. He never tired of looking at her, and he loved her with his entire being. He was awed by the love he felt for her, by his feelings of total dedication, and his willingness to give himself completely to her. He loved her beyond anything else and with an intensity that sometimes frightened him. He had often tried to tell her how much he loved her but was never able to find the words to adequately describe the depths of his passion. Perhaps those words did not exist.

They had stood before each other in the soft light of their bedroom, silently looking into each other's eyes. Their unspoken thoughts were that if these were to be their last hours together, every second would be indelibly etched upon their souls. They went to bed feeling the urgent need and passion they had for each other. Throughout the night, they clung desperately to one another, never being able to get close enough. They made love, not once but several times, and each time was more intense and more fulfilling than the time before. Finally, the toll of physical and emotional exertion had claimed them. Upon retiring, they had made the decision not to use contraceptives, and Sam knew deep within his being that they had conceived another child this night.

The sound of the alarm clock brought Sam back to the present, and he knew it was time be begin his journey into experiences he could not even begin to imagine. Eleanor, also awakened by the alarm, put on her robe, kissed him on the cheek, and proceeded to the kitchen to prepare breakfast. Sam went into Billy's room and stared down at his peacefully sleeping son. Billy would be two years old in less than a month, and Sam wondered how much of the little guy's life he was going to miss. Sam gently woke his son and took him to the bathroom to potty. Then both of them went down stairs to be greeted by the wonderful aroma of bacon and eggs frying on the stove. Billy loved eggs and hurriedly climbed into his high chair ready to eat. Sam glanced out the window and noticed a thin layer of snow that had fallen during the night and further noted a temperature reading of twenty-five degrees Fahrenheit.

"Looks like it will be a cold one this morning," he observed.

"Yes, we will have to bundle Billy up for the trip to Tyrone," Eleanor answered as she placed the bacon and eggs on the table. "May saved her ration coupons for months so we could have bacon this morning."

"May has always been a thoughtful person," Sam responded. "She and Paul will look out for you and Billy until I get back."

Sam noticed Eleanor's slight hesitation at his words and knew she was dreading the next few hours. He knew he would have to control his own emotions and be strong for all of them. They finished their breakfast with nothing more than idle chatter, even though there was a lot he wanted to say, but as hard as he tried, words escaped him. He decided to let the events of the previous night speak for him and went upstairs to prepare for his departure.

Sam's train was scheduled to leave Tyrone at 10:00 a.m., and his sisters, May and Lynette, and May's husband, Paul, were going to the station to see him off. Lynette's husband, Chill, was not able to get time away from his job in a local coal mine to go with them. Since Lynette was the only female in the family who could drive, Sam had arranged for her to ride to the station with them and then drive his family back to Osceola Mills. May and Paul were to follow in their own car. They all departed at 8:30 a.m., thinking there would be plenty of time for the seventeen-mile drive to the train station. However, Mother Nature had other things in mind. A thin layer of snow in Osceola Mills turned into several inches on the ridge tops between there and Tyrone. Poor driving conditions on the roads delayed their progress, and they arrived at the rail station to find the train ready to depart.

With no time for appropriate goodbyes, Sam grabbed his duffle bag, gave Eleanor a quick kiss, and hurriedly jumped aboard the nearest coach. He found a window seat on the platform side of the train just as it began to move from the station. Looking out the window, he saw his family hurrying down the platform so they would have one last glimpse when his coach passed by. As they hurried, he saw Billy fall down on the snow-covered platform. Eleanor picked him up just as the coach reached them. The ensuing few seconds would be etched into Sam's memory for many years to come. May and Lynette stood waving with tears streaming down their cheeks. Paul supported May with one hand and waved goodbye with his other. Eleanor held Billy in her arms and raised his arm to wave goodbye; his little hand was as black as coal from the wet snow and soot on the platform. Sam could see tears welling in Eleanor's eyes, and in the last seconds as the train passed by, their eyes met and held just as they had during the Fourth of July parade four years ago. At that moment, he resolved that he would return to look into those eyes once again; and then they were gone. Everything had happened so quickly there had been no time for proper goodbyes. As the train picked up speed, he fought without success to hold back the tears in his own eyes.

8

NOVEMBER 18, 1943
EASTERN NEVADA

I T HAD BEEN four days since he left his family in Tyrone, and Sam was ready for this train ride to end. Even though he made his living on the railroad, spending twenty-four hours a day on a coach was not his idea of the ideal way to travel. As often as he could, he would stand and attempt to walk around, but every car was filled to capacity, and any type of movement was difficult. Sleeping was even more of a problem. Attempting to sleep in his seat had been met with only limited success, but occasionally, he found space where he could stretch out on the floor of the coach and get a few hours of rest.

In addition, there were no dining facilities available, so he had to rely on the K-rations provided by the army. Coming from a poor family, Sam had learned to eat almost anything, but K-rations were testing the limits of his unsophisticated palate. The rations were produced by the Cracker Jack Company and were designed to provide 2,800 to 3,000 calories a day. Each ration provided three courses: breakfast, lunch, and supper. The breakfast carton contained a can of chopped ham and eggs or veal loaf, four dried biscuits—which usually had to be soaked in liquid to be edible, a dried fruit or cereal bar, a packet of instant coffee, a stick of gum, and a pack of four cigarettes. Since hot water was difficult to obtain aboard the train, Sam dissolved the instant coffee in cold water and tried soaking the biscuits in the cold coffee in an effort to soften them. The result of this experiment convinced him cold coffee was not the answer.

The lunch carton was another unique experience. It contained a can of processed cheese or ham and cheese, four dried biscuits, fifteen malted milk tablets or five caramels, sugar, salt, a pack of four cigarettes, chewing gum, and a packet of powdered lemon or orange drink. Sam found that the biscuits soaked in lemon or orange drink were no more appetizing than those soaked in cold coffee.

The supper carton consisted of a can of chicken pate or beef and pork loaf, the ever-present biscuits and cigarettes, a chocolate bar, toilet paper, chewing gum, and a cube of bouillon soup. Sam tolerated the chicken pate and liked the chocolate bar, but with no hot water, he didn't even try the bouillon cube and totally gave up on the biscuits.

After four days of the ubiquitous K-rations, it was no surprise for Sam to learn that soldiers in the field were losing weight on K-rations and rarely ate the full content of the packages. He joked with those around him that the enemy would soon surrender if we dropped K-rations on them instead of bombs, but everyone agreed that it would probably be against the Geneva Conventions.

If the meals provided in the K-rations were not the highlight of his journey, the food provided by volunteer groups at stops along the way was wonderful. All the troops were amazed at the outpouring of love and friendliness they encountered. At almost every stop, they were met by local townspeople who gave freely of what they had. Sandwiches and homemade pies, cakes, cookies, and donuts were given freely. There was almost always free milk, coffee, and cold drinks, as well as magazines, newspapers, and writing supplies. When the stop was too short for the men to disembark, the welcome gifts were dispensed to the appreciative service men and women through the open windows of the coaches by volunteers pushing carts or carrying baskets. At longer stops, volunteers had erected small canteen buildings, and the troops could file through and take what they needed.

At a stop in North Platte, Nebraska, Sam asked one of the ladies handing out homemade donuts why she was spending her time and meager resources in such an effort. She told him she had lost her son at Guadalcanal and wanted to do what she could to honor his memory and help in the war effort. He came away from that brief encounter with a new understanding and appreciation of the support the American people had for their armed forces. It made him proud to be an American and a soldier serving them. Had it not been for their generosity, the journey thus far would have been a very hungry one indeed.

In spite of the discomfort he was experiencing aboard the train, Sam was amazed at the diversity of the landscape he observed as they progressed across the country. With the exception of the time he spent in rural Virginia with the CCC, he had spent his entire life in the mountains of central Pennsylvania and had never seen a large city. In just the past four days, he had been to Pittsburgh and Chicago, where he marveled at the skyscrapers and shared his wonder through postcards sent to his loved ones back home. He had traveled three quarters of the way across this great country and watched as the landscape changed from the wooded hills of Pennsylvania to the rolling farmlands of the Midwest. He was awed by the vast open expanses of Iowa and Nebraska and noted with interest the gradual change from the rich farmland to the drier, more sandy soil of the West. As they crossed the high plains of western Nebraska and eastern Colorado, he was amazed at the lack of trees and delighted at the sight of occasional herds of pronghorn antelope. He was not prepared for his first sight of the majestic snow-capped Rocky Mountains. He was totally stunned by their grandeur. When they crossed the continental divide **and** descended into Utah, the rocky desert vistas reminded him of the western movies, and he wondered what it must have been like in bygone days when masked bandits and howling bands of Indians attacked the trains.

Sam's attention was drawn to the conductor who came through the car, announcing they were about to enter the state of Nevada. He speculated on what Nevada held in store. His thoughts then turned to India. He wondered what exotic sights he would be seeing during his voyage and what strange things he would encounter in that faraway country. He realized his world was going to change, and he became apprehensive at the possibility that he would not return to his family the same man he was when he left. He didn't want to change. After the war, he wanted to pick up right where he left off, but he began to fear the experiences of war would dig into his soul and forever change the person he once was.

Sam felt uneasy with the negative direction his thoughts were taking and the uncertainty of the cause of those thoughts bothered him. Perhaps it was the long, tiring journey, or maybe it was the building indigestion he had been experiencing for the past half hour. He directed his attention to the high desert scenery of eastern Nevada, hoping his spirits would improve. He vowed to stay away from K-rations for the remainder of his journey.

In spite of his attempts at distraction, his indigestion continued to grow, and he soon found it difficult to find a body position that was comfortable. He stood to walk around but found the jarring motion of the moving train made him sick to his stomach. He immediately sat down when he realized his indigestion had turned into sharp pains near his belly button. He thought about the K-rations and couldn't help but remember how he always looked forward to the prize in a box of Cracker Jacks. As his discomfort heightened, he began to wonder what hidden prize the Cracker Jack people were putting into K-rations.

Sam's stomach pain increased along with the sick feelings.

He realized something was seriously wrong and asked a passing conductor if there was any medical help aboard. Before the conductor could respond, Sam proceeded to throw up onto the floor of the coach. Needing no further explanations, the conductor immediately hurried off shouting for medical help. By the time the conductor reappeared, Sam's pain had intensified and moved to the right side of his abdomen. Luckily, the conductor found a marine corps doctor and two army nurses.

"Hi, soldier. I'm Doctor Melbourne. Can you tell me what your problem is?"

Through jabs of severe pain, Sam explained the progression of his symptoms.

"I suspect you are having an attack of appendicitis. Hold tight while I examine you further," the doctor replied.

Further examination revealed that Sam had a fever and his lower right abdomen was extremely sensitive to touch. Realizing the seriousness of Sam's condition, the doctor turned to the conductor.

"This man will have to be removed to a medical facility as soon as possible," he said.

"We have a scheduled stop in Elko, Nevada, in about fifteen minutes. There's a hospital there, and I'll make arrangements to have him taken there," responded the conductor as he hurried toward the front of the train.

"Hang in there, soldier. You're going to be pretty uncomfortable for a while yet, but we'll get you to a hospital soon. I don't have my medical bag available, so I'm sorry I can't give you anything for the pain," the doctor explained to Sam.

Sam's pain had intensified once again, and he could only nod in response. He remembered that his sister, May, suffered the ill effects of peritonitis as a result of a ruptured appendix, so he knew firsthand how serious his condition was. With each passing mile, the severity of his pain intensified, and the fifteen minutes it took the train to reach Elko seemed like a lifetime to Sam. Doctor Melbourne and the nurses stayed by Sam's side until he was removed to an ambulance at the Elko station. By that time, Sam's pain was so intense he was not aware of much that was happening around him. He vaguely remembered the doctor telling the ambulance crew to hurry, because the appendix was about to rupture. As the ambulance sped away from the station, Sam slipped in and out of consciousness and an all-too-familiar scene invaded his mind.

The Japanese soldiers were relentless in their pursuit. Sam could hear them close behind as he raced down the jungle path. Thorns of the jungle plants and creepers clawed and tore at his clothing and exposed flesh. His heart was pounding violently in his chest, and he was near the point of total exhaustion as he looked back and caught a glimpse of his pursuers and saw the menacing long sword carried by their leader. He didn't see the vine that tripped him, and as he fell, panic overcame him, and he realized there was to be no escape. The enemy soldiers were upon him. He curled up in a fetal position, covering his face and head with his hands and arms, as the soldiers viciously kicked his body and struck him with the butts of their rifles.

The soldiers screamed at him in Japanese, and he struggled to understand what they wanted. Their words were guttural and harsh to his ear. He tried to respond, to tell them he couldn't understand, but no matter how hard he tried, words would not escape his lips. A command from their leader momentarily stopped his torment. He looked up into the face of the officer standing over him, hoping desperately to see some sign of understanding or compassion. He saw only hatred in the eyes that glared back at him. Slowly, he looked at the soldiers surrounding him. Their uniforms were mildewed and rotting and their emaciated bodies were dirty and covered with jungle sores. Without exception, their eyes revealed the malevolence and hatred they felt toward him. A cold chill ran down his spine and panic gripped his soul as he realized what was in store for him.

The officer barked another command, and two soldiers stepped forward. He could feel their rough hands as they lifted him into a kneeling position and forced his head down. The soldiers stepped back, and the officer's eyes gleamed in anticipation of the elimination of one more enemy of the Japanese empire. Clasping his sword with both hands, he stood over Sam and raised the deadly blade far above his head. Sam waited for the end to come...

"Private Huber. Can you hear me, Private? Come on, soldier, wake up. Open your eyes."

The image of the jungle and the Japanese soldiers faded, and Sam could vaguely hear the female voice addressing him. He struggled to open his eyes and saw only a long dark tunnel with a light at the end. The light grew brighter, and the tunnel widened as the darkness limiting his vision faded.

"That's good, soldier, open those eyes."

Slowly, Sam's vision cleared, and he could see the nurse standing beside his bed. Confused, he looked around the unfamiliar hospital room. Seeing the bewilderment on his face, the nurse spoke once again.

"I'm Nurse Patterson, and you are in the Elko General Hospital. You were taken off the train at eleven thirty this morning and brought here for an emergency appendectomy. Your surgeon, Dr. Pfoutz, said it's a good thing they got you here when they did because he feels you were very close to having your appendix burst. You are a very lucky man. The operation went well, and you are going to be all right."

Sam began to understand. He remembered the problems he was having aboard the train but couldn't remember being taken from the train or to the hospital. His thoughts immediately went to his family, and he knew they had to be informed of his condition.

"I need to contact my family to let them know what happened," he said.

"Dr. Pfoutz thought you might want to do that, and he instructed me to write down your message and have a telegram sent to your family," she responded as she withdrew a pad and pencil from her smock. "Where do you want it sent?"

"Send it to my wife, Eleanor, at 300 Pruner Street, Osceola Mills, Pennsylvania."

"What do you want the message to say?"

Sam thought a moment, trying to clear his mind and finally answered.

"Tell her that I was taken to the General Hospital in Elko, Nevada, for an emergency appendix operation, and I am getting along nicely. Tell her I will write soon and not to worry because everything is all right. Sign it, 'Love, Sam.'"

"I'll have our secretary get this sent out right away. In the meantime, you need to rest. By the way, your belongings were brought in the ambulance with you and are stored in the closet over there"— she pointed to a door on the left side of the room. "I'm on duty until midnight, so I'll be back to check on you shortly." With that, she left the room, and Sam, still feeling the effects of the anesthesia, slipped into a deep sleep.

He didn't know how long he slept, but when he awoke, Sam could see that it was dark outside. He remembered dictating a telegram to his family and then the thought struck him of what to do about the army. He was supposed to arrive in California on the nineteenth and sail for India on the twenty-second. He knew he was going to miss both dates and started to worry. Just then, Nurse Patterson came back into his room.

"Nurse, what day is it? I'm supposed to be in California on Friday and sail for Asia on Monday."

"Just calm yourself down, soldier. It's still Thursday the eighteenth, but you won't be in any condition to be going anywhere for a while. Dr. Pfoutz has contacted Fitzsimons Army Hospital in Denver, and as soon as you are able to travel, we will be transferring you there for recuperation."

"When do you think that will be?" Sam asked.

"We'll probably keep you here for about a week and then you should be able to withstand the one-day train ride to Denver."

Sam realized things were totally beyond his control at this point, and he decided to make the best of the situation. However, he couldn't help but wonder how his military assignment would be affected by this strange turn of events.

9

NOVEMBER 26, 1943
DENVER, COLORADO

NURSE PATTERSON HAD been correct in her estimate of Sam's stay at the Elko General Hospital. Seven days from the date of his emergency appendectomy, he was on a train bound for the Fitzsimons Army Hospital in Denver. He arrived at Fitzsimons on November 25, 1943, and was assigned a bed in the ambulatory ward and was told he would probably be at Fitzsimons for about a month. He had nothing to do but recuperate, so he decided to keep himself busy by visiting wounded servicemen throughout the hospital. Fitzsimons contained many seriously wounded veterans, but Sam was particularly drawn to the marines and sailors who fought in the Pacific. Since he too was to face the Japanese, he wanted to learn as much as he could about jungle warfare and the Japanese-fighting man. In the ensuing weeks, Sam spent many hours talking to the men who had fought against the enemy. One day, he was surprised when he met a veteran from the Burma front. When he first saw Sergeant Vince Kaminski, Sam estimated the man's age to be in his early forties and was shocked at his emaciated condition. At first, Sam hesitated to enter the room, but something drew him to the sergeant, and their ensuing conversation was one Sam would never forget.

"Hello, I'm Private Sam Huber. Do you mind if I come in and talk for a while?"

"Hello, Sam, come on in. I'd like some company. I'm Sergeant Kaminski, but please call me Vince."

Sam entered the room and sat down, feeling relieved he was not imposing.

"I'm supposed to be on my way to the India-Burma front, but I got sidelined by appendicitis, so I'm trying to keep busy by talking to you fellows about your experiences. I'm especially interested in anything I can learn about India and Burma and the Japanese."

"Well, Sam, you hit the jackpot. I was with General Stillwell during our retreat from Burma back in the spring of forty-two, so I can tell you a lot about that part of the world, but none of it will be encouraging. What will you be doing over there anyway?"

"I'll be part of an aircrew that will drop supplies to our troops on the ground," Sam explained.

"That's good. At least you won't be slogging around in the jungle. India and Burma have some extreme weather. In some parts of Burma, the temperature reaches as high as 130 degrees, and during the monsoon season, it rains as much as fifteen inches a day. Rivers can rise thirty feet overnight and when the rain stops, the temperature and humidity becomes unbearable. It was often difficult to breath and almost impossible to sleep. The monsoon season also brings some of the worst flying weather in the world."

Sam was beginning to wonder what he was getting into but continued to pursue his questions. "What can I expect if I have to bail out over the jungle?" he asked.

A mixture of sadness and pain came over the sergeant's face as he remembered his experiences in the Burmese jungle.

"I hope you never have to experience that, Sam. There are three layers of canopy in the jungle. The upper canopy reaches over a hundred feet above the ground and the middle and lower canopy are so thick sunlight seldom penetrates through them. If your chute got hung up in the upper canopy, it would be extremely difficult to reach the ground uninjured. Then there are bamboo thickets so dense you have to hack tunnels through them, and the underbrush is a thick tangle of vines and briers. If you don't have a machete, the only way to get around is by jungle trails or streams."

"It sounds pretty bad," Sam commented.

"Bad! *Bad* doesn't even begin to describe the bugs and snakes and diseases," Vince said. "After we were in the jungle for a while, we began to stink, and we all had fungus infections. Our feet and testicles and asses were raw. Everything in the jungle either bites or stings, there are wasps as big as your palm and red and white ants whose bite burn like fire. There are spiders that crawl up your legs and leave bites that swell the size of walnuts. Then there are scorpions and snakes and centipedes that like to crawl into your shoes or pocket or pant leg. If that isn't enough, there are leeches everywhere. There's the one-inch common leech, the three-inch buffalo leech, and the six-inch elephant leech. They live at different levels in the vegetation from the ground up, and they drop on you from trees or attach themselves as you cross swamps or streams. The best way to loosen them is to burn them with a cigarette, and if you don't treat their bite, it festers into ulcers that can eat clear to the bone. That's part of the reason I'm here today, that and a bad case of malaria, and I'm one of the lucky ones. Others have gotten dysentery, trench foot, jungle rot, dengue fever, and cholera to name a few."

"How about our bases in India, what are they like?" Sam inquired.

"That's a little different from Burma." Vince explained. "Most of the bases are built on tea plantations, so the area is cleared but usually surrounded by jungle. The weather is still terrifically hot and humid. The aircraft-maintenance people usually work at night to avoid the heat. During the day, the metal on the planes gets too hot to touch.

During the monsoon season, the rains make everything a muddy mess and it's difficult getting around. As far as critters go, you still have to watch out for snakes, especially cobras and kraits. The kraits are the worst. It's a small greenish snake that likes to crawl into your shoes, and its bite will kill you in a matter of minutes. There are larger animals too. Tigers and leopards, but you seldom see them. The jackals will keep you awake at night with their yipping and howling, and the damned monkeys like to get into your tent and crap on your bed. You have to be on your toes every minute over there."

Sam could see that the memories of Vince's experiences were taking their toll, and he decided not to tire the sergeant any further. He rose and extended his hand to the gallant veteran.

"Thank you for sharing your experiences with me, Vince. I won't forget what I've learned here today," Sam said.

"You're welcome, Sam. I hope you make it through all right and don't end up like me. You'd never believe I'm only twenty-six years old, would you?"

Sam nodded his head and left the room unable to respond. He had met a lot of patients at Fitzsimons, many of whom suffered terrible wounds, debilitating cases of shell shock or tropical diseases, but he would never forget Sergeant Vince Kaminski. Through it all, Sam gained a new understanding of the injustices that exist in a world, where a few individuals in leadership positions can subject millions of their fellow men and women to the horrors of war. It reminded him of how his father had fought in World War I, the war that was supposed to end all wars, and he wondered if mankind would ever change.

FEBRUARY 1, 1944
DENVER, COLORADO

Sam had spent nearly a month at Fitzsimons and was notified two days before Christmas of 1943 that he was being transferred to temporary duty in the motor pool at nearby Lowry Field. He was given no indication of when he would be sent overseas, and he figured his automotive mechanic training was the reason for the motor pool assignment. Duty in the motor pool was relaxed and easy, and he spent most of his time doing minor maintenance on vehicles. He became close friends with Tech Sergeant Steven Cornwell, who was in charge of the motor pool. Sergeant Cornwell was a native of Colorado and was born and raised in Nederland, a small town in the mountains just west of Denver. Steve was able to get access to some kind of vehicle almost every weekend, and he was delighted in showing Sam the beauty of his home state. Sam remembered vividly the trip they took from Denver through Loveland to Estes Park, Colorado.

The thirty-two-mile drive from Loveland through Big Thompson Canyon to Estes Park was one of the most beautiful drives Sam had ever taken. The road through the canyon follows the Big Thompson River and curves around towering walls of granite that rise thousands of feet into the air past timbered and grass covered slopes. Steve told Sam the river and canyon were named for David Thompson, an English engineer and astronomer, who explored many streams in Colorado in the early nineteenth century. Once they reached Estes Park, they turned south and followed mountain roads through the Roosevelt National Forest past magnificent snow-covered mountain peaks and eventually arrived at Steve's hometown of Nederland.

Nederland, with a population of only three hundred people, was smaller than Sam's hometown back in Pennsylvania. Steve explained that Nederland started as a trading post between settlers and Ute Indians during the 1850s and then boomed with the discovery of silver in 1859 and gold and tellurium in 1879. Steve's family no longer lived in Nederland, but he showed Sam his former home, and they had a wonderful meal in the rustic Pioneer Inn before returning to Lowry Field.

Sam and Steve enjoyed many trips into the Rocky Mountains and visited numerous old mining towns. They also made a trip to

Colorado Springs where Sam was introduced to the spectacular rock formations in the Garden of the Gods. His favorite spot there was the Balanced Rock where he and Steve had their picture taken beneath the rock mugging as though they were holding it up.

February 28, 1944
Denver, Colorado

The day had dawned bright and sunny with the air crisp and clear as so often happens in the mile high city of Denver. However, Sam was despondent throughout most of the day. He knew what was wrong. It was his third wedding anniversary, and he missed being home with Eleanor and his family. As the day wore on, his spirits sank lower and lower, and he had to force himself to go about his duties. Around one o'clock in the afternoon, Steve came into the motor pool and handed Sam a letter. It was from Eleanor. Sam hurriedly opened the letter and began to read. In a flash, his entire demeanor changed, and he began to hop around the motor pool like a man possessed.

"What in the world has come over you, Sam?" Steve asked.

"I'm going to be a father again," Sam responded. "Eleanor is pregnant with our second child. Dr. Flynn told her the baby is due in August, and everything is looking fine at this time."

"That's great, Sam. This calls for a celebration, and I am going to treat you a steak dinner at the Pioneer Inn in Nederland." Steve was as excited as Sam, and once again, the two friends headed into the mountains to enjoy a sumptuous meal in celebration of Sam's good news.

MARCH 1, 1944
DENVER, COLORADO

Sam was thoroughly enjoying his time in Colorado and was beginning to think he would like to spend the remainder of the war there. However, his euphoria came to abrupt end when he received orders assigning him to temporary duty with the Sixty-fourth Troop Carrier Group in Comiso, Sicily. He was ordered to proceed immediately by train to Miami, Florida, and from there by military transport plane to Sicily. Sam couldn't understand why he was being sent to Sicily instead of India, but he had learned never to question the ways of the army. When Sam showed the orders to Steve, the sergeant was genuinely stunned.

"I've come to think of you as a brother, Sam, and I'm really going to miss you. Come on, I'll help you pack your things. You have an early train to catch in the morning."

After the packing was done, Sam and Steve stood looking at each other. Both men understood the realities of war, and it was difficult for them to say goodbye.

"I know you're going into a war zone, Sam, and I wish I could go with you. But I know you can take care of yourself. Thank you for being such a good buddy the past few months," Steve said as he embraced his friend one last time.

"Thank you, Steve. You have made my stay in Denver a time I will never forget. After the war, I would like to bring my family out here to meet you."

"That would be great, Sam. You know you will always be welcome. Goodbye and good luck."

The lump in his throat made it impossible for Sam to respond as he watched his friend turn and leave the room. He wondered if they would ever see each other again.

10

MARCH 7, 1944
MIAMI, FLORIDA

T HE TRAIN RIDE from Denver to Miami had been long and arduous, but once again, the monotony of the trip was broken up by the welcome they received from volunteer groups manning canteens at numerous stops along the way. As Sam stood waiting to board his plane in the predawn darkness of the Miami airport, he had time to reflect upon the amazing outpouring of love and generosity the American people were giving to members of their armed forces, and it made him even more determined to do what he could to protect their rights and freedoms.

The approaching dawn began to lighten the eastern sky, and Sam's excitement increased as each passing moment brought him closer to the fulfillment of his dream to fly. He was seven years old when a barnstormer in a World War I vintage Curtiss Jenny came to town and gave a demonstration of aerobatics. He remembered watching the pilot put the jenny through loops and rolls and dives, and his young mind became inflamed with the idea of flight. Ever since that day, Sam had a burning desire to fly, and today he would get his first chance. His excitement grew even more when the growing light of dawn revealed the plane he would be boarding. It was a C54 Skymaster, one of the newest aircraft in the sky. The Skymaster was the military version of the Douglas DC-4 airliner and was powered by four large Pratt & Whitney engines. As Sam's eyes roamed over the impressive aircraft, he noticed a crewmember inspecting one of the engines, and he idly walked over to watch the procedure.

"How does everything look?" Sam inquired. He noticed the crewman was a staff sergeant.

The sergeant paused in his inspection and peered at Sam. "Everything looks good." He could see that Sam had a genuine interest in what he was doing. "Are you an aircrew member?"

"No, this is my first flight. I'm trained as an automotive mechanic, but these engines are much bigger than anything I've worked on. I'm Private Sam Huber," Sam replied, extending his right hand.

The sergeant grasped Sam's hand in a firm handshake and responded, "Sergeant Dan Dury, flight engineer. I'm pleased to meet you, Sam. Your first flight, huh. Well, you might be interested to know that the engines are numbered one through four from left to right as the pilot sees them and each of these engines develops 1,450 horsepower and will power the plane to a maximum speed of 275 mph. At a cruise speed of 230 mph, we can carry forty-nine passengers about 3,900 miles and climb up to twenty-two thousand feet."

"Won't we need oxygen at that altitude?" Sam asked.

"Since this aircraft is not pressurized, we would need oxygen above 12,500 feet. But on this trip, we will be flying between ten thousand and twelve thousand feet, so it won't be needed. Looks like we're ready to board. Hop on and find yourself a good window seat. I'll drop by and point out some points of interest during the flight."

"Thanks, Dan," said Sam, "I'm looking forward to that."

Sam was one of the first to board the plane, and he selected a window seat near the back of the plane where the wing would not block his view. He settled into his seat and watched as the other passengers boarded the plane. There were a total of twenty-six passengers on the flight, and Sam noticed they were all army personnel. Since there were plenty of seats available, the seat beside Sam remained empty. When everyone was aboard, the cabin door was closed, and Sam's attention was drawn to the sound of the engines starting. From his seat on the right side of the plane, he could see engines number 3 and 4 on the right wing. He watched as the propeller on the inboard engine number 3 began to slowly turn, and with a puff of black smoke from the exhaust the engine started, and the speed of the propeller increased quickly until it became a blur. In quick succession, engine number 4 went through the same procedure, and then he heard the engines on the left wing start up. Soon all four engines were running smoothly. Sam could feel the cabin vibrate from the power of the mighty engines, and he could hear their steady hum as the pilots went through their checklist and prepared to taxi. The stable drumming of the engines and the feel of their power in the seat of his pants gave Sam a surprisingly serene feeling. He felt comfortable and right at home.

A slight increase in the sound of the engines alerted Sam to the fact that they were beginning to move, and he watched from his window as the plane taxied away from the terminal building and made its way across the tarmac. Soon the big plane stopped, and one by one, the throttles of each engine were increased, while the pilots ran through their engine checklists. Sam noted the increase in noise and vibration as each engine was checked, and he wondered what it was going to be like when the throttles of all four engines were increased at the same time for takeoff. He didn't have long to wait as the pilots taxied the plane onto the active runway in preparation for takeoff. Sam could feel his heart beating faster as he realized his lifelong dream was about to come true.

The sounds of the engines increased exponentially as the pilots advanced the throttles to takeoff power, and the big plane began to roll down the runway. Sam was amazed at how quickly the aircraft picked up speed, and he felt his body being pressed into the seat as it accelerated for takeoff. He watched from his window as the runway lights sped by faster and faster, and he felt the bumps from the landing gear, as the wheels passed over imperfections in the runway. He estimated they were traveling well over a hundred miles per hour when the nose of the plane rose, the thumping of the wheels stopped, and he felt himself being lifted gracefully into the air. From his window, he observed the ground receding, and he heard the thump of the landing gear as they were retraced into the wings. He felt the power of the engines as they drove the plane higher into the sky and finally knew what it was like to fly.

Sam was fascinated as he watched objects on the ground grow smaller and smaller and marveled as distant lakes, rivers, and roads came into view. He was struck by how clean and untouched the earth appeared as they rose higher and higher. There were puffy cumulus clouds in the sky, and Sam felt the aircraft jolt as it encountered turbulence created by rising air currents. It reminded him of driving over a bumpy road. The turbulence continued until they climbed above the clouds, and then the air grew smoother. They turned on a southeasterly course out over the Atlantic Ocean, and Sam watched as the beaches of Miami disappeared behind them. When they reached their cruising altitude, Sam felt the airplane level out and heard the sound of the engines diminish as the pilots reduced the throttles to cruising power.

As the hours passed, the scenery outside his window remained relatively unchanged. Occasionally, he would spot a ship or see an island in the distance, but mostly, there was just the blue Atlantic and a few fleecy white clouds drifting by. At intervals, his eyelids became heavy, and he struggled to remain awake. Finally, lulled by the steady drone of the engines and the unchanging scenery, he succumbed to the inevitable and drifted off into a deep sleep. He didn't know how long he had been asleep when he was awakened by a change in the sound of the engines. Looking outside, he noticed small fishing boats on the ocean and realized they were descending. He saw Sergeant Dury approaching from the front of the airplane.

"I thought you might like to know we will soon be landing for fuel in San Juan, Puerto Rico. You should be able to see the island coming up on the right," Dan explained as he took the seat beside Sam.

"Oh yes, I can see land now," exclaimed Sam, "and there's a large bay filled with boats and some kind of castle overlooking the bay."

"That would be San Felipe del Morro Castle. It sits on the point of a promontory guarding the entrance to San Juan Bay," Dan explained. "Construction on the castle began in 1539, and it took hundreds of years to complete it as you see it now. The walls are eighteen feet thick."

Sam watched as the castle passed beneath them and thought how much it looked like the castles he had seen in pirate movies. In his mind's eye, he could see Errol Flynn scaling the walls, sword in hand.

"Will we have much time in San Juan?" Sam asked.

"No, we will only be there long enough to refuel. Probably about thirty to thirty-five minutes, and then we will continue on to Georgetown, British Guiana. But you will be able to get off the plane and stretch your legs," Dan responded. "I have to get back to my station. I'll see you later."

Sam observed through his window as the plane dropped closer to the ground. He felt the thump of the landing gear coming down and watched the flaps on the trailing edge of the wing as the pilots lowered them in preparation for landing. Although he could not see the approaching runway, he assumed it was close as he saw the earth rising rapidly outside his window. As they drew closer to the ground, he got a sense of the speed they were traveling, as objects outside sped by his window. He was struck with the realization that when they were cruising high in the sky with no objects close by, there had been no sense of speed, and yet they were traveling hundreds of miles per hour.

The thump of the landing gear touching down on the runway announced their arrival in San Juan. After the plane came to a stop at the terminal building, Sam disembarked to stretch his legs and was struck immediately by how hot and humid the air felt. He strolled into the terminal building, bought a soft drink from a vending machine, and purchased a few postcards with pictures of the castle he had seen from the air. He didn't have time to experience much more of Puerto Rico, because, true to Sergeant Dury's estimate, the refueling process only took thirty minutes, and they were ready to board when he went outside. Soon they were climbing into the azure skies over Puerto Rico and on their way to British Guiana.

Their flight path took them over the Eastern Caribbean and some of the islands of the Lesser Antilles. Sam was fascinated as he observed the changes in the color of the waters of the Caribbean. He marveled at the deep navy blue that marked areas of extreme depth to the light aqua of shallower areas and the many shades of blue in between. The islands they passed seemed like tiny jewels set into a vast background of blue. The serenity of the view outside his window eventually caused him to doze off.

He was awakened when Dan came by to point out their approach to the South American mainland. His first view of South America came as they neared the coast of British Guiana. He could see the dark green of the jungle and noted the many streams and rivers that drained into the ocean. He wondered what animals and people lurked in the mighty forest below.

As they approached Georgetown, their flight path paralleled the coastline of British Guiana and crossed the mouth of the Essequibo River. He was astonished at the size of the river where it emptied into the Atlantic. Dan had told him it was around twenty miles wide, and it was certainly impressive to Sam. As they neared Georgetown, he could see that it was situated along a river and was surrounded by dense jungle.

They landed one hour before sunset and were immediately taken to a mess hall for supper and then to their sleeping quarters. Sam was surprised that all the buildings of the facility were built off the ground on high wooden posts, and he surmised that this location was subject to flooding from the nearby river. The area around them was also covered by thick jungle growth. Since it was Sam's first time in a jungle environment, he decided to have a closer look at his surroundings. He walked to the edge of the jungle and was immediately impressed by how thick the jungle growth really was. He wondered how anyone could possibly make their way through the tangled mess. He was tempted to try to enter the jungle, but then he remembered the conversations about the jungle he had with Sergeant Kaminski at Fitzsimons Army Hospital. With the sergeant's warnings still vivid in his memory, he realized the jungle was no place for a small-town resident from Pennsylvania. Darkness was fast approaching as he walked back to his assigned bungalow. He entered and prepared himself for lights out. Night came quickly to the jungle, and the day's long journey took its toll. It wasn't long before all the men in Sam's bungalow were fast asleep.

MARCH 8, 1944
GEORGETOWN, BRITISH GUIANA

They were awakened at 5:00 a.m. and taken to the mess hall for breakfast, which consisted of scrambled eggs, undercooked bacon, dry toast, and coffee. Sam skipped the bacon and toast and sat down to a plate of scrambled eggs and a cup of hot coffee. He was just finishing his breakfast when Dan approached him.

"Good morning, Sam. Are you ready for another day in the sky?"

"You bet I am," Sam responded.

The sergeant sat down, and the two men chatted idly over cups of steaming coffee. During their conversation, Sam mentioned his temptation to enter the jungle the previous evening.

"My god, Sam, didn't you hear the news this morning? One of the local people was killed by a jaguar last night just a mile from here. The jungle is no place for the uninitiated."

Visibly shocked, Sam's blood turned cold as he realized how stupid he had nearly been. He thought about Billy and Eleanor and their unborn child, and he resolved never to take any unnecessary chances again. He was doubly thankful for the warnings Sergeant Kaminski had given him back in Colorado.

"You're right, Dan. I've learned a valuable lesson. It would have been stupid of me to enter the jungle. I'll be glad to get away from this place."

"I'm glad you learned a lesson, Sam. You're headed for a war zone, and if you don't think about what you are doing, it could cost you your life."

"Thanks for the advice, Dan. It looks like it is about time for us to depart. Where will be flying to today?"

"We'll be going to Natal, Brazil, today, with a stop at Belem for fuel. On our way to Belem, we'll cross the equator, so there will be a ceremony performed by the shellbacks for all the pollywogs on board. Have you crossed the equator before, Sam?"

"No, I haven't. What are shellbacks and pollywogs?" Sam asked.

"A *shellback* is someone who has crossed the equator, and a *pollywog* is someone who hasn't, so that makes you a pollywog, and you will participate in the ceremony to become a shellback," Dan explained.

"What kind of ceremony is it?" Sam inquired.

"That will be up to the captain," Dan explained. "He's an ex-navy and has considerable experience in these things from his days aboard ship. See you on board in half an hour."

From the smile on the sergeant's face as he departed, Sam got the notion that the pollywog ceremony might not be a cakewalk. He finished his coffee and went outside to board the bus that was waiting to take them to the flight line. They arrived at the C54 and boarded just as the sun was rising above the trees of the surrounding jungle. Sam took the same seat he had the day before and watched the now-familiar startup and taxi procedures. The takeoff was smooth and just as exciting to Sam as the ones he experienced the day before. The sky was completely cloudless, and visibility was unlimited as they climbed above the jungle below. About an hour and a half into their flight, Dan came back to Sam's seat. They were flying just inland of the French Guiana coast.

"If you look out the left side of the plane, you can see Devil's Island—the notorious French penal colony."

Sam shifted to the left side of the plane and peered through the window. He could see three islands in the distance.

"I see three islands. Which one is Devil's Island?" Sam asked.

"All three islands have prison facilities on them, but the one farther out is Devil's Island. The French stopped sending prisoners there in 1938, but there are still some there today. By the way, we will be crossing the equator in about two hours." Dan grinned and walked back to the front of the plane.

Sam watched until the islands disappeared and then went back to his seat on the right side of the plane. He stared at the dense jungle below and wondered what the pollywog ceremony was all about. He didn't know how long he had been daydreaming when the door to the cockpit opened and Sergeant Dury stepped into the passenger's cabin with a very serious look on his face. He had a mop head in one hand and a bucket in the other.

In a loud voice, he proclaimed to the occupants of the cabin, "Hear ye, hear ye. All pollywogs take notice. We are about to cross the equator, and the pollywog ceremony will begin. Captain Stewart, the ranking shellback, will preside."

Captain Stewart then stepped into the cabin. Sam was startled to see the captain with his jacket and hat on backwards and a mop in his left hand.

"Shellback Dury, present the pollywogs for initiation," intoned the captain.

With exaggerated ceremony, the bucket was placed beside the captain. Then with the mop head in hand, the sergeant proceeded solemnly to the rear of the plane where Sam was seated and extended the mop head to him.

"Place this on your head, private pollywog, and crawl on your hands and knees to the ranking shellback for initiation."

Sam could not believe he had been selected first for initiation, and he hesitated to accept the mop head. He noticed the other passengers were watching him with interest and decided it was best to comply. Placing the mop on his head, he crawled on his hands and knees to the front of the plane. He couldn't help but think how ridiculous he must look but took comfort in the thought that their turn would come. When he reached the captain, he stopped and waited for what seemed like minutes.

Finally, the captain spoke, "As the ranking shellback, I hereby christen this pollywog and declare him now to be an honored member of the shellbacks." He then dipped his mop into the bucket and drizzled cold water down Sam's neck and back.

As Sam shivered from the cold water, Sergeant Dury removed the mop from his head and said, "Arise, brother shellback, and return to your seat."

After Sam returned to his seat, the sergeant then proceeded to the other pollywogs on board and repeated the process. Sam noted that when the sergeant approached the officers, he addressed them as pollywog sir, but he still gave them the same instructions. Sam also noted with pleasure that none of the officers refused to be initiated, and he was delighted in the spectacle of an officer with a mop on his head and cold water running down his back. When the ceremonies were completed, Sam sat back and relaxed and thought about his old friend Kerby. He knew without a doubt that Kerby would have managed to screw things up had he been here. He chuckled at memory of his friend and wondered how he was doing. Sam's musings were interrupted when Sergeant Dury came by.

"We're just beginning to cross the mouth of the Amazon River," he explained. "It's the second longest river in the world and is about 150 miles wide here where it empties into the Atlantic. On the other side, we'll be landing at Belem for fuel. That should be in about an hour."

Sam thanked him and was once again impressed with the depth of Dan's knowledge. He then noticed the view from his window was indeed changing. The jungle was being replaced by wide areas of the Amazon River. As far as the eye could see, the river's estuary was made up of enormous expanses of river broken only by stretches of forested islands. He remembered crossing the twenty-mile-wide mouth of the Essequibo River the day before and realized it was nothing compared to what he was witnessing below him now.

Their approach and landing at Belem was uneventful, and once again everyone aboard left the plane to give their legs some much needed exercise. Sam lingered behind and could see that this airport was also surrounded by thick jungle, and as he slowly walked to the terminal building, he could once again feel the heat and humidity of their tropical location. As he approached the terminal, he noticed a tight knot of service men huddled around a radio. Dan was among the men, so Sam ambled over to see what was causing so much interest. When he neared the group, the concerned expressions on their faces became evident.

"Hey, Dan, what's going on?" Sam inquired.

"You're not headed for India, are you?" Dan asked.

"The outfit I volunteered for is in India, but I'm being temporarily assigned to a unit in Sicily. Why, what's going on?"

"It was just announced over the radio. The Japanese Fifteenth

Army has invaded India from Burma and is attacking the British Fourteenth Army at a place called Imphal. It looks like the Japs are trying to sever supply lines to General Stillwell in northern Burma and to the Hump flights into China. It's probably a good thing you're not headed for India right now, Sam. Some of the guys aboard our plane are headed there."

Sam did not respond. Instead, he turned around and walked back toward the plane. The bad news had impressed upon him for the first time that he may be heading into a very dangerous situation. When he reached the plane, he stood in the shade under the wing to escape the tropical sun and thought once again about his family back in Pennsylvania. He knew there was a distinct possibility that he may never see them again, but the more he thought about them and the freedoms they enjoyed, the more resolute he became to protect his loved ones and their freedoms. He was so engrossed in his thoughts that he didn't hear Sergeant Dury approach him from behind. The sergeant could see that Sam needed a diversion.

"How would you like to help me preflight the engines, Sam?" Dan's question startled Sam, and he turned to face the sergeant.

"I'd be glad to give you a hand, Dan. Just show me what to do," Sam said with a feeling of relief for the diversion.

The sergeant then proceeded to teach Sam how to preflight the engines, and by the time they reached the last of the four engines, Sam had become quite proficient in the procedures.

"You learn very quickly, Sam. I'll make a flight engineer out of you yet."

"You're a good teacher, Dan. I'm interested in anything that has to do with airplanes," Sam answered.

Looking at his watch, Dan responded, "It's time to get back on board and head for Natal. We'll have a few more days before we part in West Africa, so I'll have time to show you some more things about the plane. See you later."

"Thanks, Dan," Sam said with a feeling of genuine appreciation.

Sam took his usual seat aboard the C54, and they were soon airborne and on their way to Natal. As he looked at the seemingly unending jungle below, he noticed something different. As far as his eye could see, the jungle floor was covered by shallow water, and the thought came to him that as difficult as it must be to walk through the jungle, it must be that much more difficult and dangerous when it is covered by water. The thought of a forced landing down there gave him a very uneasy feeling, and he began to listen for any change in the sound of the engines that might indicate a problem, but after a half hour or so, he chided himself for worrying about such things and settled back in his seat.

Sergeant Dury sat at his station behind the pilots monitoring the operation of the engines. It was just about time to switch fuel tanks when he noticed a slight loss of power to engine number 4. At first, he thought it was a temporary situation, but the engine continued to lose power in small increments. He adjusted the fuel flow to the engine but that did not correct the problem.

"Captain, we're losing power to number 4, I've adjusted fuel flow, but it doesn't help," he announced to Captain Stewart.

The captain had also noticed a loss of rpm in the engine and was about to make throttle and manifold pressure adjustments when they all heard a muffled pop on the right side of the plane. Lieutenant Abbott, the copilot, looked out his window and saw black smoke and flames pouring from engine number 4.

"Four's on fire, Captain!" shouted the copilot.

Without hesitation, the captain began shutting down the engine and feathering the propeller. He ordered the copilot to activate the fire extinguisher in the affected engine and fought to control the aircraft, as the stopped engine induced significant drag on the right side of the plane. As the nose of the airplane yawed sharply to the right, and the right wing dipped dangerously low, Captain Stewart knew they were in danger of stalling and spinning into the ground. Both he and copilot fought the controls and applied heavy pressure to the left rudder in an attempt to control the plane. At the same time, he made frantic power adjustments to the remaining engines in an effort to divert disaster.

In the rear of the plane, Sam had just begun to relax when he also heard the muffled pop. From his window, he saw the black smoke and flames pouring out of the outboard engine on the right wing. He knew there were fuel tanks in the wing and immediately thought of the possibility of an explosion. He watched as the propeller on the flaming engine came to a stop, and he was pushed sideways in his seat as the plane slewed to the right. The ride became noticeably rougher as the right wing dipped in the direction of the ground, and he could feel his ears pop as the big C54 descended rapidly toward the jungle below. His fingernails dug deeply into the armrests of his seat, and he began to think about the possibility of his life ending in the water-covered jungle beneath them.

Slowly, the pilots leveled the wings and stopped their descent, regaining control of the airplane.

"Looks like the fire extinguisher worked, sir. I don't see any signs of fire in number four," exclaimed Lieutenant Abbott.

"Good work, Lieutenant," responded the captain. "Let's get this bird trimmed up and get her to Natal. Sergeant Dury, let our passengers know what happened."

After what seemed like an eternity, the plane leveled out, and Sam sensed they were no longer descending. He saw that the flames and smoke had stopped pouring out of the damaged engine, but the propeller was still motionless. It was then that Sergeant Dury entered the passenger cabin to make an announcement.

"I'm sure you are aware that we had a problem. A fire started in our engine number 4, and we had to shut her down. The fire is out, and everything is under control. We are currently in no danger, since this plane is capable of flying on three engines. We will be flying at a lower altitude and a slower airspeed, so our arrival at Natal will be a little later than estimated. Sit back and relax, and I will keep you informed if anything changes."

A buzz of excited conversation spread through the cabin as Sergeant Dury closed the cockpit door, and everyone took turns looking at the damaged engine. After a while, when nothing more seemed to happen, everyone took their seats and settled down. Sam was amazed that this incident did not dampen his enthusiasm for flying. It had, in fact, just the opposite effect upon him, as he experienced the adrenalin rush it provided. Nevertheless, he was just as relieved as anyone else aboard when they safely touched down in Natal.

11

MARCH 9, 1944
NATAL, BRAZIL

I N SPITE OF his harrowing experience in the air the day before, Sam had a good night's sleep and arose to another hot and humid day in the tropics. They had arrived at Parnamirim Field in Natal after dark the previous day, so this was the first opportunity for him to have a look around. As he walked from his barracks to the mess hall, he noticed that the airfield was quite large, and there were many American servicemen going about their duties. Upon reaching the mess hall, he entered and got in line for breakfast. Once again, he chose scrambled eggs and coffee, forgoing the ubiquitous greasy bacon and hash browns.

As he searched for a table to eat, he spotted Sergeant Dury talking with a group of soldiers, and he approached their table.

"Mind if I join you this morning, Dan?" Sam inquired.

The sergeant seemed genuinely pleased to see Sam, "Don't mind at all, Sam. Please join us. These are some of my friends who are stationed here at Parnamirim Field."

After a round of introductions, Sam sat down to join their conversation and eat his breakfast.

"I was just telling my friends about our drama in the sky yesterday, Sam. I found out this morning that the fire was caused by a ruptured fuel line. If the fire extinguisher hadn't worked and the flames had reached the fuel tank, it would have exploded, and we would have been bits and pieces now scattered around the Brazilian jungle. We were a very lucky bunch of guys."

"I knew it was serious. But I guess I didn't realize just how serious," Sam commented. "What's the status of the plane? Are we going to be able to continue on to Africa?"

"They're working on her now, and it looks like we'll be back in the air tomorrow. In the meantime, we have a free day in lovely Natal. My friends have access to a vehicle. Would you care to join us for a day at the beach?"

"Sounds great to me," Sam responded. "When do we leave?"

"Meet us in front of the barracks in an hour and bring your swimming suit," Dan answered.

The others left to prepare for the day. Sam finished his breakfast and walked back to the barracks. With each step he took, his anticipation of the adventures of the day grew stronger and stronger. At the appointed time, Sam met the others in front of the barracks. They had managed to procure an army six-by-six truck. The tarp had been removed from the bed, and Sam climbed aboard and took a seat on one of the benches beside Sergeant Dury. During their drive to the beach, Sam took the opportunity to ask Dan some questions.

"Why has our flight taken us so far south?" Sam inquired.

"This route was laid out when the Nazis were in control of most of Northern Africa," Dan responded. "Natal is at the easternmost part of South America and is the closest point to Africa and Europe. Because of that proximity, we've been shipping men and supplies through here to the African and Indian theaters since the early days of the war."

"That seems reasonable." observed Sam. "Why do the natives around here speak Portuguese?"

"This area was first explored by Amerigo Vespucci in 1501," Dan answered. "Then the Portuguese established the village of Natal on December 25, 1599. That was Christmas day, so they named the village *Natal*, which is the Portuguese word for Christmas."

"How come you know so much about the history of these places?" Sam asked.

"I was studying to be a history teacher at the University of Maryland before the war," Dan replied. "I hope to finish my schooling and teach history after the war."

"I hope you're successful, Dan. You really seem to know your history," Sam said as he settled back to watch the passing scenery.

The remainder of the day was spent swimming in the warm waters of the Atlantic and walking along the sandy white beaches that surround Natal. At the end of the day, they returned to Parnamirim Field and prepared for the next day's departure to Africa.

MARCH 10, 1944
NATAL, BRAZIL

Sam was up early and had his breakfast in time to join Dan for the engine preflight procedures.

"You're really taking to these preflight procedures, Sam. If I don't watch out, you'll be taking over my job," Dan joked.

"It is very interesting," Sam replied, "but I know there is a lot more to the job than just the preflight."

"You're right about that, Sam. But you seem to have a knack for it. I think you would make a good flight engineer."

"Thanks, Dan. I love everything about flying. Where is our flight plan taking us today?"

"Today we'll be leaving South America and flying across

the Atlantic to Wideawake Airfield on Ascension Island," Dan answered.

"Why is it called Wideawake Airfield, and where is Ascension Island?" Sam asked.

"Ascension Island is a very small island about halfway between here and Africa. It's only thirty-four square miles in area. I'm not sure how Wideawake got its name, but the island is so small and so remote you had better be wide awake when you fly there, or you could miss it."

"Well, Mr. History Book, I don't suppose you can tell me how Ascension got its name?" Sam chided his friend.

"As a matter of fact, I can," Dan replied. "It was named by Alfonso Albuquerque, a Portuguese navigator, when he sighted the island on Ascension Day in 1503."

"I should have known you would know the answer," Sam said, shaking his head in disbelief.

"Well, we're finished here. I'll see you on board," Dan replied with a smile.

It was times like this that made Sam wish he had paid more attention in history and geography classes while he was growing up. He watched his friend walk away and felt a pang of regret that his own education ended after the eighth grade.

Their departure from Natal was on time, and Sam noticed quite a few passengers, including himself, were watching the engines with keen interest. All four engines performed flawlessly, and they were soon on their way across the Atlantic. The flight to Ascension took a little over seven hours, and with nothing to see but the ocean, Sam slept most of the way. As they approached Wideawake Airfield, he could see the entire island from his vantage point aboard the C54. Ascension Island was indeed a very small place.

MARCH 11, 1944
ASCENSION ISLAND

Once again, Sam met Dan bright and early in the morning to help with the engine preflight procedures.

"Where are we headed today, Dan?"

"Today we have about an eight-hour flight to Dakar, French West Africa," Dan responded.

"I don't suppose you would know any of the history of Dakar?" Sam asked jokingly.

Dan grinned and replied, "Dakar is located on the Cape Verde peninsula in French West Africa. It's the westernmost city on the African continent, which has made it an important port for trade. The Portuguese established a settlement nearby in 1444 and used it as a base for their slave trade. Over the years, the area has been controlled by the Portuguese, Dutch, English, and finally the French, who still control it. The slave trade continued under each of those nations but was finally ended in 1848. It's the location of the House of Slaves. That's where the infamous Door of No Return is located. Supposedly, thousands of Africans passed through the door on their way to slavery in the western hemisphere. We're lucky we can land in Dakar now. The area was controlled by the Vichy French up until about two years ago. The Brits sent a task force to occupy the place back in September of 1940, but the Vichy repelled their efforts. It wasn't until after the invasion of Africa in 1942 that the Allies got control of Dakar."

"I'm sorry I asked," groaned Sam as he rolled his eyes in disbelief.

"Go ahead and get on board, Sam," Dan said cheerfully. "After we get in the air, how would you like to come forward and see what goes on in the cockpit?"

"That would be terrific. I'd really like that," Sam responded.

With the anticipation of seeing the cockpit area, Sam gleefully went aboard the plane and took his now-familiar seat. After takeoff, their course took them north on a heading toward Dakar and the continent of Africa. Sam saw the scenery outside was still the unchanging Atlantic Ocean, but he did note the presence of more clouds than usual along their flight path. Several hours into their flight, Sergeant Dury came back and invited him into the cockpit area. Sam was amazed when Dan showed him his workstation behind the pilots and explained the instruments he monitored and the controls he used to manage the planes fuel supply. However, Sam was totally impressed when he was allowed to enter the pilot's compartment and view the myriad array of controls, instruments, and switches that surrounded the two pilots.

"Go ahead and watch for a while, Sam. I have to attend to some fuel management, and then I'll be right back," Dan said as he returned to his station.

Sam watched as the pilots made minor adjustments to their controls, and he thought how wonderful it must be to understand everything that was arrayed before him and be able to successfully fly such a complex machine from one place to another. With each passing moment, he became more and more enamored with the idea of flight. For long moments, his eyes roamed over the instrument panel, and he was surprised when he was able to recognize and understand some of the instruments such as engine oil temperature, oil pressure, the airspeed indicator, and magnetic compass. Other instruments were completely foreign to him, but they served to whet his appetite to learn more, and he resolved to ask Dan about them when he returned.

Sam had been so wrapped up in the aircraft instruments that he hadn't bothered to look at the world in front of them through the wind shield. When he did think to look outside, he was shocked by what he saw. About twenty miles in front of them, stretching as far as he could see from left to right, was a solid mass of dark thunderstorms. He watched spellbound as lightning winked constantly from within the towering storms. He was startled when Dan appeared at his side and spoke.

"Those are storms associated with the equatorial front," Dan said.

"What's the equatorial front?" Sam asked.

"It's a zone that extends about four degrees north and south of the equator where the trade winds from the northern and southern hemispheres meet. This time of year, the storms are caused when the cold trade winds coming down from the north meet the warm trade winds coming up from the south."

"Are we going to have to fly through those things?" Sam inquired, hoping the answer would be no.

"I'm afraid so, Sam. They stretch too far east and west for us to fly around them, and the tops look like they extend up beyond forty thousand feet. That's too high for us to fly over. As you can see, storm tendrils are reaching right down to the ocean's surface, so we can't fly under them either."

"Is it safe to fly through those things?" Sam asked.

"Generally, it is pretty rough going through them, so Captain Stewart will look for a hole between the storms and try to get through them that way. We usually make it without any problems."

Before any further comments could be made, both men were startled by what sounded like hundreds of loud rifle shots being fired into the airplane. Sam immediately ducked and began looking for holes to appear in the walls of the C54. His only thought was that they were being attacked by enemy aircraft.

"It's okay, Sam," Dan explained. "We've run into some hail from the thunderstorms ahead. When you're traveling over two hundred miles an hour, they make quite a racket when they hit the plane."

Sam saw large hail stones bouncing off of the wind shield and the aluminum skin of the aircraft. Each strike sent a resounding crack through the plane. He also noticed that they were flying in clear air and were not near the thunderstorms.

"How can there be hail? We're not in the storms yet," he exclaimed.

"Some storms have such strong updrafts that they can throw hail stones out of their tops and into clear air as far as twenty miles away. Apparently, these are strong storms. You had better go back to your seat and secure yourself. We might be in for a rough ride," Dan cautioned.

By the time Sam reached his seat, the hail strikes had stopped, but when he peered from his window, he could see that the aluminum covering on the wings was dented and dimpled by the pounding it took from the impact of the hail stones. He began to realize there were hidden dangers in flying and watched anxiously as the storm front approached.

In the cockpit, the pilot, Captain Charles Stewart, and the copilot, Lieutenant Alan Abbott, were also watching the approaching storms. Unfortunately, their course to Dakar would take them directly through the line of thunderstorms. The prevailing wisdom for transiting the equatorial front was to fly parallel to the front until a break could be found in the storms and then turn ninety degrees into the break and fly perpendicular to the front and through it in the shortest amount of time. Their current heading was 355 degrees, and they drew closer and closer to the storms. The pilots could clearly see flashes of lightning and the heavy black clouds that seemed to roll and boil like a giant cauldron before them. Captain Stewart made a right turn to a heading of eighty-five degrees to fly parallel to the seething mass of storms.

"Okay, Al. Let's see if we can find a break in this mess that we can get through," the captain commanded.

"I hope we can, Captain. This looks like it could really be a rough one," answered the copilot.

They maintained their parallel course along the storm front for nearly forty minutes without finding a break. Captain Stewart was beginning to become concerned about fuel when Sergeant Dury approached.

"Captain, we've reached the point of no return on this flight. We don't have enough fuel on board to fly back to Ascension Island, so we have to continue on to Dakar," announced the sergeant.

"That settles it, gentlemen. We're going to have to fly through this monster. Al, disengage the autopilot and be ready to apply deicers at the first sign of icing," responded the captain.

Captain Stewart knew they were going to encounter severe turbulence, so he set the propellers to full pitch and adjusted the throttles to reduce their airspeed to maneuvering speed, which would give them the best chance of avoiding structural failure as they fought to control the airplane within the storm.

"Captain, it looks like there might be a break in the clouds up ahead," the copilot announced excitedly.

Both men anxiously scanned the storm front and did indeed see a break in the clouds ahead. As they reached a point directly opposite of the break, Captain Stewart made his decision and entered the opening. The way ahead looked clear as they flew through what appeared to be a narrow canyon between the thunderstorms. On both sides, they could see great masses of boiling clouds that ranged in color from black and purple to shades of blue and green. They also began to experiencing moderate turbulence, but it was nothing they couldn't handle. There was continuous lightning all around them which rendered their radio direction finder and communications radio useless due to static. They had wound their way through the cloud canyons for about five minutes when they found the route ahead blocked by a solid wall of storm clouds. Captain Stewart turned ninety degrees to the left and looked back the way they had come, only to see the storm system had closed in behind them. They were completely surrounded by the storms which were closing in rapidly. The captain turned back to his original heading and entered the seething mass of clouds.

Upon entering the storm, they were immediately surrounded by a blanket of thick black clouds. They could see nothing through the windows and were hit suddenly by extreme turbulence. The plane was tossed about like a cork in the ocean and both pilots had to fight to maintain control. They had entered the storm system at an altitude of twelve thousand feet and were immediately caught in an updraft that sucked the plane skyward at over three thousand feet per minute. The g-forces they felt were tremendous, and Captain Stewart watched as the hands on the altimeter spun up and up until it indicated twenty-one thousand feet. Just as suddenly, their ascent ended and the plane plummeted. They felt their bodies straining against their seat harnesses, and objects began flying about the cockpit. The altimeter hands now spun in the opposite direction as they fought to maintain control and stop the plane's descent. In spite of their efforts, they watched as the altimeter registered fifteen thousand feet and then ten thousand feet, and still it spun down. Finally, at five thousand feet, their wild ride downward stopped, but before they could establish a climb, the plane was tossed into a steep right turn. They fought to level the wings but were then tossed into a steep left turn causing the gyros in the artificial horizon and the directional gyro to tumble and become useless. The violent motions of the aircraft caused the magnetic compass to spin first in one direction and then in the other. They lost all indication of direction as they struggled to keep the C54 in the air.

In the rear of the plane, Sam hung on as best as he could as they were tossed around the sky. He could see nothing outside, and at times, it felt like a giant animal had the airplane in its teeth and was shaking it violently. Many of the men around him became ill and threw up. The smell in the cabin caused Sam to wretch, but he managed to keep his stomach contents in place. He had never experienced such violent motions and was amazed the airplane was still in one piece.

In the cockpit, Captain Stewart and Lieutenant Abbott were still struggling to control the aircraft when the mayhem suddenly stopped, and they found themselves in smooth air surrounded by clear sunny skies. Both pilots cheered as they looked back and saw the storm front receding behind them.

"Take us back up to twelve thousand feet and head for Dakar, Al," said the captain with a great deal of relief in his voice as he picked up the maps and papers that had been strewn around his seat.

"You had better look at this, sir," the copilot urged.

The tone in Al's voice caught the captain's attention immediately. He looked at the copilot who was pointing at the magnetic compass. The wild gyrations of the compass had finally settled down and pilot didn't see any reason for concern. It appeared to be operating normally and was indicating a heading of south.

"Shouldn't we be heading north, Captain?" asked the lieutenant.

It was then the enormity of the situation struck him. The compass should be showing a heading of north. Somehow, during the violent turbulence of the storm, the plane had been turned around, and they had flown out of the storm front on the same side that they entered it. There was a long moment of silence in the cockpit.

"Turn us around, Al. We can't go back to Ascension, so we'll have to fly back through the storms to get to Dakar," commanded the captain.

Reluctantly, but with no other alternative, they turned back toward the storm front and began searching for a point of entry. Before them and as far as they could see on either side was nothing but a solid wall of foreboding dark storm clouds.

"Sergeant Dury, how is our fuel supply?" asked the captain.

"It looks like it's going to be close, Captain. We have to get through those storms soon, or we'll be in big trouble," answered the sergeant.

Knowing their situation was becoming desperate, the captain turned the plane toward the lightest colored clouds he could see and entered the storm front for the second time. Like a predator waiting for its prey, the invisible monster within the storm immediately leapt upon them. It clawed at the plane and shook them as though it was punishing them for daring to reenter its realm. The control wheel thrashed about in the pilot's hands as if it had a life of its own. It jerked forward and backward, battering the captain's body until he called for the copilot to help him. Both pilots wrestled with the controls in an attempt to keep the aircraft upright. Once again, they were being thrown about the sky like a feather in a hurricane. Lightning flashed all about them with such frequency that the strobe effect made the propellers seem to stop, and the pilots could see ice beginning to form on the propellers and the leading edges of the wings.

"Activate the deicing equipment, Al," ordered the captain knowing they had to stop the buildup of ice before it doomed the aircraft.

At first, the deicers seemed to have no effect, and the layers of ice continued to grow, and then suddenly, the ice began to release its tenacious grip on the surfaces of the aircraft. In the rear of the C54, illumination from the lightning enabled Sam to watch as chunks of ice were swept past his window. The nerves of everyone aboard were shattered by the sharp sound of pieces of ice from the propellers being thrown against the sides of the plane. The passengers clung to their armrests as objects were thrown about the cabin, and everyone prayed that the plane would hold together. Their faces appeared ghostly white from the flashing lightning, causing the interior of the cabin to resemble a scene in a horror movie. It seemed as though some terrible beast was trying to tear its way into the airplane, when suddenly all aboard were blinded by a brilliant flash of light followed by a thunderous roar.

"Jesus, Captain. What was that?" asked the copilot as he scanned the instrument panel for signs of trouble.

"We've been struck by lightning," responded the pilot. "The engines appear okay, and we're still in the air. I don't know how much more of this we can take."

They continued to struggle in the clenches of the violent storm for what seemed like an eternity when they were suddenly spewed from its grasp into an overcast tropical sky. Once again, they saw the storm front receding behind them as they brought the plane into straight and level flight. They watched tensely as the magnetic compass settled down and were relieved when it finally indicated a northerly heading.

"Looks like me made it through, Captain," said the copilot through dry lips.

"See if you can get a fix on our location, Lieutenant," the captain responded. "Sergeant Dury, how is our fuel supply?"

"Before we entered the storm front, we were two and a half hours from Dakar, and we had four hours of fuel remaining. Finding a way through the storms cost us an hour and a half. So we have two and a half hours of fuel remaining, and until we know just exactly where we are, I can't tell if we can make it to Dakar, Captain," answered the sergeant.

"How about it, Al? Can you get a fix on Dakar radio?" asked the pilot.

"Bad news, Captain. I can't get anything on any of the radios. I think the lightning strike damaged our antennas, and with this overcast, we can't determine our location from the sun. I'm afraid there is no way of knowing our exact location, sir."

The frown on the captain's face emphasized the seriousness of their situation to the crew. "Okay, gentlemen. Let's look at this problem logically. Before we entered the storms, Dakar was due north. If the storms blew us off course to the west, a northerly course could cause us to miss the African continent completely, and we will end up ditching in the ocean. We know that Africa is due east of us, but if we fly that course, by the time we reach the coast, we probably won't have enough fuel to reach Dakar. It looks like our best chance is to fly northeast until we hit the coast and then follow it north until we reach Dakar."

"I agree that is our best option, Captain, but we are going to have to conserve as much fuel as we can. There is no telling how far from Dakar we will be when we reach the coast," responded Sergeant Dury.

"You're recommendation is duly noted, Sergeant. Keep me posted on our fuel situation at ten-minute intervals. Al, take up a heading of forty-five degrees and set the engines for the most economical cruise speed. Everyone, keep your eyes peeled for the coastline and let me know as soon as anyone spots it," commanded the captain.

The crew settled into their respective jobs and searched diligently for the first sign of the African coast. An hour passed with no sign of land, and their job was made more difficult by a layer of haze that reduced visibility to less than five miles. Another hour passed, and still there was no sign of land. They had a half hour of fuel left, and Captain Stewart knew their situation was becoming critical. He was beginning to despair that they would never reach the coast when Lieutenant Abbott sat up suddenly in his seat.

"I think I see land, Captain," the copilot exclaimed excitedly and pointed out his window on the right side of the cockpit.

Captain Stewart peered intently in the direction the copilot was pointing and finally saw the coastline appear through the haze. He immediately turned the C54 to the left to fly parallel to the coast and was relieved to see that they were on a northwesterly heading. His maps indicated the coast south of Dakar ran from southeast to northwest, so he was confident they were headed for their target. However, he had no idea how far away they were. They were down to fifteen minutes of fuel and still there was no sign of Dakar. Knowing the plane could fly on two engines and hoping to give them more time, he made a decision.

"Shut down engines number one and four, Al. We have to keep this bird in the air as long as we can."

The lieutenant immediately shut down the two outboard engines and feathered their props. Sergeant Dury watched intently as the fuel gauges sank steadily toward zero.

"We're flying on fumes, sir. I don't know how much longer the engines will run," announced the sergeant.

The captain edged the plane closer to the shore in anticipation of crash landing on the beach if the need arose.

"Sergeant, tell the passengers to prepare for an emergency landing," ordered the captain.

Sergeant Dury hurried back to the cabin and made the announcement to the stunned passengers. Sam had been expecting some kind of trouble ever since the engines were shut down, and now he joined the rest of the men aboard as they awaited their fate. He couldn't believe that having come safely through the storms they still might not make it. His thoughts were interrupted by the sound of one of the engines running rough.

The captain also heard the left engine coughing and noted a drop in rpm. He adjusted the fuel mixture to the engine and was relieved when it began to run smoothly again. However, the fuel gauges were all indicating empty, and he knew it was only a matter time before they lost both engines. He was running over the emergency-landing procedures in his mind when he noticed the coastline turn sharply to the left ahead of them. His hopes jumped immediately, because he knew that Dakar was situated on a peninsula that jutted out into the Atlantic Ocean. He quickly turned the plane to the west and began to make out the distinctive fishhook shape of the Cap-Vert peninsula. Soon, he could see the city of Dakar which rests on the southern tip of the peninsula. As they approached the city, he checked his maps and noted that the airport was on the coast five miles northwest of the city. He was straining his eyes trying to locate the airport, when the left engine suddenly quit. In a flurry of movement, he feathered the propeller and adjusted power to the remaining engine as the aircraft began to slowly sink toward the earth. He knew the plane could not maintain altitude on one engine, and he hoped they could reach the airport before they ran completely out of fuel or altitude. Slowly, through the haze before them, he could begin to see the airport.

However, at the rate they were descending, he was not sure the plane would reach the runway.

"Al, be prepared to put the landing gear down when I give you the command and not before."

The captain knew that any additional drag on the aircraft would cause it to descend faster, so he was determined to wait until the last moment before lowering the landing gear. He watched as the runway approached slowly and the ground rose steadily toward them. He felt himself lifting up on the control wheel in a subconscious effort to hold the plane aloft. He still wasn't sure they would make it when he ordered the gear down and held his breath as the additional drag caused the airplane to sink even faster. He applied full power to their sole engine and pulled back on the wheel to increase lift. The end of the runway sped toward them as he held the wheel completely back into his stomach and whispered a silent prayer. The plane stalled about a foot above the runway and settled heavily upon the landing gear. They had made it. It wasn't a landing he would brag about, but they had made it. As they rolled down the runway, their remaining engine sucked the last fumes of fuel from the tanks and sputtered to a stop. The pilots looked at each other, knowing they had been only seconds away from losing it all.

12

MARCH 12, 1944
DAKAR, FRENCH WEST AFRICA

S AM DIDN'T HAVE much of an appetite. He was sitting alone, pushing his breakfast around the plate but couldn't bring himself to eat. Like most of the passengers aboard the C54 yesterday, he wasn't able to sleep last night, and the memory of their ordeal continued to haunt him. He remembered the severity of the turbulence they encountered within the thunderstorms and wondered how the plane held together. He knew they had experienced another serious problem after they passed through the storm system when two engines were shut down and they were told to prepare for a crash landing. The image of the ground rising quickly to meet them was still vivid in his mind, and he remembered the landing gear not being lowered. He had closed his eyes and braced for the impending impact when they lost still another engine. He recalled their initial hard impact with the runway and thought it was the beginning of the end and remembered how his body shook uncontrollably from the release of tensions when he realized they were safely down. Even now, a day later, his hands were still shaking, and he didn't know if he could get back aboard another airplane. He wanted desperately to talk to Sergeant Dury but had not seen him since the landing yesterday. Then as if in answer to a prayer, the sergeant entered the mess hall and approached Sam's table.

"Good morning, Sam. You're not looking so good this morning. Are you feeling all right?"

"I'm still shook up over our flight yesterday. I'm not sure I can get back aboard an airplane," Sam responded.

"I understand how you feel, Sam. That was the closest call I've had in my flying career."

"What happened? Why did we come so close to crashing?" Sam asked.

"Well, lightning in the storms took out our antennas and a couple of the radios, so we couldn't get a fix on our position. We also used up a lot of fuel getting through the storm front. The captain took up a course he hoped would get us near Dakar, but headwinds held us back and we used up even more fuel. We shut down two engines to save fuel, but by the time we hit the African coast, our fuel situation was critical. Luckily, although we didn't know it at the time, the heading the captain selected was near perfect, and we were not far south of Dakar. The good Lord and the captain's flying skills got us safely on the ground, even though we lost one of our two remaining engines just before we touched down. When we landed, all the fuel tanks were completely empty, and our remaining engine quit during rollout. Another thirty-second delay anywhere during the flight and we would have crashed short of the runway."

"Half a minute to hell," Sam mused. "I never realized how close you can come to death. I don't know if I can do it again."

"That decision is up to you, Sam. You have your orders to be on the flight this morning. If you disobey them, you will have to answer to the army. But even more importantly, you'll have to answer to yourself and all the people depending on you."

Dan's words struck Sam hard. He remembered his family's military history and the many wonderful people he met at canteens as he traveled across America. He thought of Billy and Eleanor and the unborn child she was carrying. He knew he could never live with himself if he didn't uphold his duty, and a new determination took hold of him.

"Can I help you with the preflight this morning? Where are we flying to today anyway?" Sam asked, noticing his hands had stopped shaking.

"I would appreciate your help very much, and we're flying to Casablanca, French Morocco, today. Our radios still aren't working, but we'll be able to follow the African coastline all the way to Casablanca. We're going to be in Casablanca a couple of days while they fix the radios and antennas so I'll have time to show you around," Dan responded. "I'm glad you made the right decision, Sam. Meet me at the plane in fifteen minutes."

An hour later, they were in the air and headed for Casablanca. Sam was relieved to see that the skies were clear and the visibility unlimited. There wasn't a cloud in the sky, and it was forecast to stay that way all the way to French Morocco. As Dan had predicted, the captain was following the African coastline, and Sam was struck by the difference between the green jungles of South America and the arid terrain of the Western Sahara. The visibility was so good that Sam could see deep into the African continent, and all he could see was barren rock and desert sands. He came to the conclusion that a crash landing here would be just as perilous as one in the jungle.

As the hours crept by and the view outside changed little except to appear even more inhospitable, Sam's thoughts turned to their next destination. During his stay at Ft. McPherson, he and Eleanor had gone to the cinema to see the movie *Casablanca*. It turned out to be one of their favorite Humphrey Bogart movies. They both left the theater with the feeling that Casablanca was a faraway exotic place that only a lucky few would ever see, and now it amazed him that he was on his way to that very place. As he remembered scenes from the movie and wondered about the strange and mysterious things he would see, he drifted off into a deep slumber and didn't awaken until he felt the thump of the landing gear being lowered. Their landing at Casablanca was uneventful, and as Sam left the aircraft, the first thing that struck him was how comfortable the air temperature was. It couldn't have been more than seventy degrees. He was expecting hot, desert-like conditions and was surprised at the pleasant temperature. As he stood on the tarmac in total amazement, Sergeant Dury approached.

"You look like you just walked into fairyland, Sam."

"I'm amazed at the temperature. Shouldn't it be really hot here?" Sam asked.

"It's like this year around in Casablanca. Because of cool Atlantic currents off shore, the temperatures are seldom out of the sixties and seventies."

"I never would have guessed it," Sam responded.

"Get a good night sleep, Sam. Tomorrow I'll take you to a souk. We'll see the sights and have some gunpowder tea," Dan commented as he walked away to secure the plane.

Sam had no idea what a souk was or, for that matter, what gunpowder tea was, but he was looking forward to the experience.

MARCH 13, 1944
CASABLANCA, FRENCH MOROCCO

True to his word, Dan found Sam after breakfast. The sergeant was dressed in casual civilian clothes and appeared to be ready for the day's adventures.

"I don't have any civvies," Sam said. "Can I go into town in my uniform?"

"You'll be fine, Sam. We're going to a souk in the medina. Nobody dresses up to go there."

"What's the medina, and what's a souk?" Sam asked eagerly.

Dan laughed at Sam's childlike enthusiasm and responded, "A medina is an area of town, usually surrounded by walls, where the streets are very narrow and maze-like. They were built that way centuries ago to protect against invaders. There is no room for vehicles in the medina. A souk is a bazaar or marketplace. We'll find all sorts of things for sale there. If you want to buy something, be sure to barter for it. The merchants expect it. Start out by offering no more than one third of what they ask, and go from there. If you aren't satisfied with the final deal, don't be afraid to walk away. It's the way they do business."

"It sounds like this is going to be interesting," Sam said, "and what's this gunpowder tea you mentioned yesterday?"

Dan laughed again. "I thought you'd be curious about that. Gunpowder tea is a favorite of the locals and the Brits. It's a green tea that comes from China. They roll individual green tea leaves into small round pellets that resemble gunpowder and that's how it gets its name. I think you will like it. Are you ready to go?"

"Let's do it," Sam responded enthusiastically.

They walked to the front gate of the airbase where Dan hailed one of the many local taxis that hung around there. Sam didn't recognize the make of the vehicle. It was a small foreign-build car that looked like something out of a foreign movie. They entered the back of the cab, and Dan told the driver where they wanted to go. Before Sam could get settled, he was thrown back into his seat, as the driver floored the accelerator and sped off at breakneck speed. The ensuing ride was one Sam would never forget as the driver sped along the narrow streets. With total disregard for anyone's safety, the driver wove in and out of traffic, never braking and continually flooring the accelerator. The streets were clogged with pedestrians, donkey carts, bicycles, trucks, and cars. All the motorized vehicles constantly blew their horns, and the cab driver joined in with apparent glee. Pedestrians scattered at their approach, and several times they narrowly missed collisions with approaching vehicles. Everyone appeared to be driving in the same reckless fashion, and Sam came to the conclusion that such behavior was normal for these people. It was a great relief when they finally stopped, and Dan announced they were at the medina. They split the cost of the cab, and Sam noticed his legs were a bit wobbly when he exited the taxi.

"Tell me, we'll we be able to walk back to the airbase?" Sam asked hopefully.

"Sorry, old buddy. It's not safe to walk in parts of this city. You'll have to endure another taxi ride."

Sam groaned as they entered the even narrower streets of the medina. Besides the narrowness of the streets, the first thing he noticed about the medina was how the streets twisted and turned, forming a maze that was extremely difficult to follow. In no time at all, he became completely disoriented and had no idea where they were. He could see how an invading horde would be at a great disadvantage in such a restricted environment. Luckily, Dan seemed to know his way around, so Sam never let his friend get out of sight. Most of the two-story buildings that lined the streets were private homes with an occasional shop of one sort or another on the ground floor. There were no spaces between the buildings, and Sam noticed laundry draped over second-story window sills or hanging from ropes strung across the street from building to building. The thing that struck him the most was the uniqueness of the doorways to the houses. The doors were made of what appeared to be ancient wood and some were painted in bright vivid colors. The ironwork that adorned them also appeared to be ancient. The doorways to the shops were all open, and many of the merchants stood outside, encouraging prospective customers to enter and view their wares. Occasionally, Sam saw a shop that interested him, but Dan would not stop, having previously told him they would find the best prices and a better selection in the souk.

They walked for about fifteen minutes when they finally came to a large open square. The buildings surrounding the square all contained shops and the interior of the square was filled with hundreds of merchants displaying their wares on blankets spread on the ground or on canopy-covered tables.

"This is the souk," announced Dan. "We'll take our time and look around. I'm sure you'll find something of interest here."

As they browsed through the souk, Sam was amazed to see the great variety of goods for sale. There were items made from leather, wood, ceramic, silver, gold, and brass. There were hand-woven carpets and rugs everywhere. Handcrafted jewelry was available as well as clothing of every description. Spices of every kind were available throughout the square and were displayed in large colorful conical mounds or in wooden trays. The spice merchants encouraged them to taste their wares, and Sam accepted, sometimes to his pleasant surprise and sometimes to his regret. Many of the spices were familiar, but most were quite foreign and unpleasant to his western palate. Dan observed Sam's spice-tasting episodes with a great deal of amusement and never once offered any advice on what to avoid. It was obvious he was having too much fun watching Sam's introduction to the world of spices.

In addition to the myriad of colors in the souk, Sam was struck by the variety of aromas that permeated the air. Besides the strange and exotic odors of the spices, there were tantalizing aromas emanating from food vendors scattered throughout the souk.

"Are you getting hungry, Sam?" Dan inquired.

"I sure am," Sam answered. "What would you recommend?"

"I don't trust the food from these street vendors," Dan responded, "But I know a good restaurant that we can trust."

"Sounds good," Sam replied, "lead the way."

Sam followed Dan through the square to a small restaurant on a side street leading into the souk. They entered through a doorway draped with beaded curtains and were immediately met by the maître d' who led them to a low table surrounded by cushions. Sam followed Dan's lead and sat cross-legged on one of the cushions.

"I know what's good here, so I'll go ahead and order for both of us," Dan said.

"Go ahead," Sam responded. "It couldn't be any worse than some of those spices in the market."

The waiter spoke good English, and Dan ordered goat shish kebabs and gunpowder tea for both of them. As they waited for their meal, they talked about their experiences in the souk.

"There are so many things to buy in the souk," Sam said. "What would you recommend as a souvenir?"

"In my experience, I have found the leather goods to be the most reasonable in price and quality," Dan answered, "and if you want something really comfortable to wear, the kidskin slippers are great."

"Okay, let's look at those things after we eat," Sam replied.

Their conversation was interrupted when the waiter came with the meal. The kebabs were made with chunks of goat meat interspersed with pieces of onion and red and green peppers. They had been cooked over an open brazier and basted with a delicate combination of sauce and spices. Their aroma smelled delicious to Sam, and he attacked them with gusto. Some of the peppers and spices were unfamiliar to him, but he had to admit it was some of the finest food he had eaten since he left the States. Although he was not much of a tea drinker, Sam also found the gunpowder tea to be very good, and the waiter kept their cups full throughout the meal.

After their meal, they returned to the souk where Dan helped Sam with his first attempt at bartering. Sam noticed a leather merchant and decided to buy a wallet. The wallet was made of soft goat skin and was hand embossed with the image of a mosque, palm trees, and the words *Casablanca, Morocco*. The embossed images were highlighted with red, green, black, and gold paint. Sam asked the price, and the merchant responded $5. Sam looked at Dan who shook his head no and held up one finger. Sam offered $1 for the wallet, and the merchant immediately took on an air of indignation and extolled upon the fine workmanship that went into the making of the wallet. He then offered to sell the wallet for $4. Sam looked at Dan who again shook his head no. Deciding to test his skills, Sam then offered the merchant $1.50. Acting like he had been stabbed in the heart, the merchant then went into a tirade about how he had a wife and seven children to feed and he couldn't sell the wallet for less than $3.50. The merchant's performance was worthy of an Oscar, and Sam began to feel a little less confident. He looked to Dan for assistance, but the sergeant simply smiled and shrugged his shoulders, letting Sam know he was on his own. Deciding he was not good at haggling, Sam started to walk away, but the merchant followed, tugging at Sam's sleeve and imploring him to buy the wallet. Sam then decided to try a different approach and reached into his pocket and extracted $2.50 in cash which he offered for the wallet. The merchant immediately smiled and accepted the money in exchange for the wallet and wished all the blessings of Allah upon Sam and his family.

As they walked away from the leather vendor, Sam asked Dan how he had done at his first attempt at bartering.

"Are you satisfied with the wallet and the price you paid for it?" Dan asked.

"Yes," Sam responded.

"Then that's all that really matters," Dan replied. "However, I will tell you I bought the same wallet for $2 the last time I was here."

Both men laughed and continued on their way. Sam continued to hone his bargaining skills and purchased kidskin slippers for himself, his wife, and two sisters. At the end of the day, they endured another wild taxi ride back to the base and went to the mess hall for supper. After supper, they relaxed over cups of coffee and talked about the day's events.

"Thanks for showing me around the medina and souk today," Sam said. "I would have been in real trouble if I tried that alone."

"It helps to be with someone who has been there before," Dan replied. "You did well with the merchants. The experience should help you with the vendors you'll meet in India. They can be real rascals and like to sell fake Swiss watches and colored glass that they cut to look like real gemstones. It's best to have someone experienced with you when you deal with those scoundrels."

"I'll keep that in mind if I ever get to India," Sam responded. "What's on the agenda for tomorrow?"

"Tomorrow we continue our flight across North Africa to Tunisia. When we stop at Tunis, you'll be getting off to meet your flight to Sicily." Dan said. "I hope you can join me for the preflight in the morning."

"You don't have to hope, Dan. I'll see you on the flight line first thing in the morning."

MARCH 14, 1944
CASABLANCA, FRENCH MOROCCO

As promised, Sam was on the flight line bright and early to help with the preflight. Sam had become proficient in the preflight process and was able to complete the task under the watchful eye of his friend without assistance.

"You're a good student, Sam. I think I could make a first-rate flight engineer out of you," Dan observed.

"I'd like that," Sam responded. "I wish I could continue on with you, Dan. You've been a good friend, and I've learned a lot from you. But I guess the army has other plans for us."

"You're right about that, Sam. Let's get on board and get ready to depart. I think you'll find the flight over North Africa interesting."

Their departure from Casablanca was uneventful, and they settled into their cruising altitude above the Western Sahara Desert with only a few puffy clouds in the sky. Sam watched as the desert slipped slowly by beneath them and wondered what it would be like to traverse those vast empty expanses on the back of a camel. It all looked so inhospitable, and yet he knew men had lived there for countless centuries. The monotony of the landscape stretched for as far as he could see, and their altitude prevented him from seeing the smaller details of the terrain below. However, he did notice occasional areas containing numerous black splotches on the ground and wondered what they might be. Their flight path took them across Morocco, Algeria, and into Tunisia, where they eventually approached the city of Tunis, where the pilots began their descent for a landing at that fabled city. As they approached Tunis, Sam noticed an increase in the areas of black splotches on the ground, and as their altitude decreased, more details on the earth below became visible. He was shocked when he realized the black splotches were the burned out remains of military vehicles and equipment left behind after the fierce battles that had taken place as the Allies slowly pushed the Germans and Italians out of North Africa. It was his first sight of the ravages of war, and it was sobering to him to see the destruction and realize that many men had lost their lives in the sands below.

When they landed in Tunis, the C47 that was to take Sam to his next assignment in Comiso, Sicily, was loading on the tarmac. He gathered his belongings and then found Dan putting chocks under the wheels of the plane. He thought about the C54 and how it had brought them safely through some very challenging experiences—experiences that had helped him to grow and prepare for the road ahead.

"Well, Dan, I guess this is goodbye," Sam said, extending his hand to his friend and mentor. "Thank you for everything you've done for me."

"It's been my pleasure, Sam. I wish you good luck in this war and beyond. I hope our paths cross again somewhere," Dan responded, taking Sam's hand in a firm handshake.

"I hope we meet again too, and thanks again. You've been a great inspiration to me, and I'll miss you," Sam answered, the lump in his throat prevented him from saying more, as he turned and walked toward the waiting airplane.

Knowing that wartime friendships were often fleeting and knowing they would probably never see each other again, Dan watched as Sam climbed aboard the C47 and felt satisfied he had helped a new friend develop and become prepared for the war ahead.

13

MARCH 28, 1944
COMISO, SICILY

S AM WATCHED FROM under the wing of one of his squadron's C47s. He would soon be boarding the plane for a flight to Benghazi, Libya, where he would pick up another flight that would take him to India. As he observed, the copilot perform the preflight inspection on the C47, he thought back over his short stay in Sicily. He had arrived at the army air base in Comiso, Sicily, on the fifteenth of March and was assigned to the Seventeenth Squadron of the Sixty-fourth Troop Carrier Group. Since then, he had been learning the ins and outs of being an air traffic clerk—a job that required extensive on-the-job training. His squadron was tasked with the aerial transportation of supplies to Allied troops fighting in Italy, and he was kept busy every day learning how to properly load and secure supplies aboard a C47 in a manner that ensured the safety of the plane and the aircrew. At first, the task seemed daunting to him, but after his first week of training, his proficiency and self-confidence increased to a point where he was comfortable with the job. Because of the volume of supplies needed by the troops in Italy, there was little time available for sightseeing in Comiso. However, he did manage to get one twelve-hour pass and spent the day walking around the ancient city. During his visit to Comiso, he was able to visit many of the churches in the city. He was impressed by the colorful paintings and carvings in the Church of the Annunciation and awed by the fine wooden ceiling and marble statues in the Church of Santa Maria delle Stelle. He would have liked to have spent more time in Comiso, but his pass ended much too quickly, and he had to return to his duties at the airbase.

Sam's temporary duty in Sicily had not lasted very long. Twelve days after he arrived in Comiso, he received orders assigning him to permanent duty with the 5331st Air Dropping Platoon at Dinjan air base in the Indian state of Assam. This was his original assignment and destination before he was struck down with appendicitis back in November. He marveled that the army was finally managing to get him there. Ever since his bout with appendicitis, he had followed the events of the war in India and especially the Japanese invasion of India on the eighth of March. He had recently learned that over 160,000 soldiers of the Japanese Fifteenth Army, under the command of Lieutenant General Renya Mutaguchi, were attacking scattered units of the British Fourteenth Army around Imphal in the Indian state of Manipur. General Mutaguchi had crossed the mountainous border between India and Burma and was attacking Imphal from the north, south, and east. It appeared that his strategy was to surround and destroy the isolated British units in the Imphal area and then proceed to the railhead of the Bengal-Assam railway some 110 miles away at Dimapur. If Mutaguchi could take this railhead, he would capture large amounts of supplies stored there and block the retreat and reinforcement of the British units in the Imphal area. In addition, the capture of Dimapur would cut the lines of communications and supplies to Allied forces in Assam and Northern Burma. More importantly, it would also stop the flow of material being flown over the Hump to China. Sam had learned that the *Hump* was the term used by army pilots to describe the treacherous air route from Assam over the Himalayan Mountains of northern Burma and into China. If Mutaguchi stopped the flow of supplies to China, it would effectively remove China from the war and practically insure the success of the Japanese army in Southeast Asia. Sam didn't miss the fact that he was being assigned to a base in Assam, and his own life would be in peril if Mutaguchi succeeded. With these thoughts on his mind, Sam climbed aboard the C47 and settled into a jump seat for the flight to Benghazi.

The flight and arrival in Benghazi was uneventful, and the plane was only stopping long enough for Sam to disembark. He reluctantly said goodbye to some of his newly found friends of the Seventeenth Squadron and watched from the tarmac as the C47 taxied to the runway for takeoff. As he watched the airplane depart, he could not have guessed that he would soon be reunited with his old squadron mates in the near future.

MARCH 29, 1944
BENGHAZI, LIBYA

Sam spent the night at the transient barracks at Benghazi airport and was up bright and early to meet his flight to India. After breakfast, his belongings were thrown aboard a jeep, and he was taken to the flight line. He was surprised when the jeep stopped at a plane that looked vaguely familiar. It was a C54 like the one he had taken from Miami to Tunis. As he unloaded his gear, a familiar voice beckoned him from beneath the plane's wing.

"Are you just going to stand there, or are you going to help me with this preflight?"

Shocked, Sam spun around to be to see his friend Sergeant Dan Dury standing near the landing gear of the C54.

"I thought this plane looked awfully familiar," Sam responded as the two men met and shook hands warmly. "I never thought we would be flying together again, but I'm sure glad to see you."

"You never know what surprises Uncle Sam has in store for us," Dan replied. "It's great to see you, Sam. Go ahead and get on board. I think you will enjoy this flight. Get a window seat on the left side of the plane, there are some really interesting sights I can point out to you along the way."

"Why am I not surprised?" Sam retorted. "I'm looking forward to some more of your history lessons. See you on board Dan."

As instructed, Sam found a good window seat behind the wing on the left side of the plane and settled in for the long flight to India. He was amazed and pleasantly surprised to be on board with his friend again and decided it was a good time to write some letters to the folks back home.

Two hours into the flight, Sam heard a reduction in the sound of the engines and noticed they were descending. He was puzzled because he was told their first stop would be at Abadan, Iran, some seven hours into the flight. As they descended, he was watching the details of the desert below become clearer when the copilot appeared at the front of the plane to make an announcement.

"We are approaching Cairo, Egypt, and the captain has decided to give us all a treat. He is going to descend and circle the pyramids of Giza. You'll be able to get a great view from the left side of the plane. We'll be there in about five minutes."

The copilot reentered the cockpit, and Dan approached from his station behind the pilots.

"You're in for a real treat, Sam. The Great Pyramid of Giza is the oldest of the seven wonders of the ancient world and the only one that still exists largely intact. The captain is going to circle them from one thousand feet up so we will be about five hundred feet above the highest pyramid."

As Dan spoke, Sam watched as the pilot lowered the left wing and a magnificent view of three large pyramids spread before his eyes.

Sam's attention was riveted on the scene below as Dan continued to speak.

"Those are the Great Pyramids of Giza. The largest one you see is called the Pyramid of Khufu. It's the oldest of the pyramids and was built as tomb for Pharaoh Khufu around 2,560 BC. It's around 455 feet high and held the record as the tallest man-made structure in the world for over 3,800 years. It is estimated that the pyramid contains over two million stone blocks, the largest weighing around eighty-eight tons."

"How did the ancient Egyptians move such large blocks of stone?" Sam asked.

"Most Egyptologists believe the stones were moved from a quarry, but they can't agree on whether they were dragged or rolled into place. In any event, it took a lot of manpower," Dan explained. "The next largest pyramid is called the Pyramid of Khafre. It was built by Khufu's son, Pharaoh Khafre, and is 448 feet high. The smallest of the three pyramids is the Pyramid of Menkaure. It was built for Pharaoh Menkaure, who was the son of Khafre and the grandson of Khufu. That pyramid is about 218 feet high"

"Without modern equipment, it's hard to believe the ancient Egyptians were able to move such large stones and then erect them into pyramids," Sam commented.

"Their work is even more impressive when you learn that during the twelfth century, Saladin's son, al-Aziz Uthman, attempted to destroy the pyramids. He and his minions tried for eight months to demolish Menkaure's pyramid. They finally gave up after they were only able to remove one or two stones a day and completely tired themselves out," Dan explained.

"I certainly wouldn't want to try to tear one of those down," Sam exclaimed. "Hey, what's that giant animal statue down there?"

Dan saw that Sam was pointing to the statue of the Sphinx and responded, "That's the Sphinx. It's a statue of a mythical creature with a lion's body and a human head. It's the oldest and largest monolith statue in the world. Nobody knows for sure when it was built."

"Wow, I sure would like to see this place up close," Sam said.

"It is impressive from the ground," Dan responded. "Maybe you'll get to visit them someday."

The pilots completed their circling of the pyramids and began to climb back up to altitude.

"Well, I have to get back to work," Dan said. "Our next stop is Abadan, Iran."

"Okay, Dan, thanks for the history lesson. I'm going to try to catch a nap," Sam answered.

The remainder of the flight to Abadan was uneventful. When Sam wasn't sleeping, he read some of the *Time* and *Life* magazines aboard or watched the never ending desert scenery pass below them. They arrived at Abadan just as the sun was setting, and Sam noticed a large refinery complex as they landed. When they taxied to a stop, Dan came back to Sam's seat.

"Did you notice the large oil refinery when we landed?" Dan asked.

"Yes, I did. That's really a large installation," Sam answered.

"It should be. It's the largest oil refinery in the world. It was built by the Anglo-Persian Oil Company," Dan continued. "We're going to refuel and leave for Karachi around midnight. Get yourself something to eat and catch some sleep if you can. Then meet me back here around eleven thirty if you would like to help with the preflight."

"You got it," Sam responded as he departed to find the local chow hall.

MARCH 30, 1944
KARACHI, INDIA

The flight to Karachi took place at night, so Sam slept most of the time. They arrived at the Karachi airport at daybreak, and it felt good to be able to disembark and stretch his legs. As he looked around the airport, his attention was drawn to an enormous building nearby. At that moment, Dan approached and noticed the puzzled look on Sam's face.

"Wondering what that large building is?" Dan inquired.

"Yeah, I've never seen a building that large. It looks like a giant hangar," Sam responded.

"That's exactly what it is. Back in 1930, the Brits were trying to establish a regular airship service in these parts, so they built this hangar to house a dirigible. Its 900 feet long, 220 feet high, and 450 feet wide."

"Is there a dirigible in there now?" Sam asked.

"No, His Majesty's Airship R101 crashed on its maiden flight from England to India with the loss of forty-eight lives, so they scrapped the program, and the hangar was never used to house dirigibles."

"It looks like it's in use now," Sam observed.

"It was used to house arriving troops for a while, but droppings from birds and monkeys living in the rafters didn't make for good living conditions. Now it's used to assemble and repair combat aircraft and is big enough to hold several B24 or B17 bombers at the same time."

"Very interesting," Sam commented. "What's our schedule for the rest of the flight?"

"Well, we're scheduled to depart for Calcutta at 6:00 a.m. tomorrow, so we have the whole day to ourselves. Would you like to go see an Indian bazaar?"

"That would be okay as long as we don't have to take another crazy taxi ride," Sam responded.

"Fair enough, meet me back here in one hour, and we'll be on our way," Dan said.

The two friends met at the appointed time and walked to the exit of the terminal building. Sam looked around and saw several taxis waiting nearby.

"I thought you said we weren't going to take a taxi," Sam observed.

"We're not," replied Dan. "We're going to take a *gari*. Come on, I think this will be a unique experience for you."

Dan led the way past the waiting taxis to a group of horses standing nearby. "These are garis," he announced, pointing to unusual carts attached to the horses. "As you can see, they're two wheeled carts, usually with rubber tires, that carry two passengers and the driver. It's a horse-drawn taxi."

Sam looked at the gari, smiled, and said, "These remind me of the carts used in harness racing back home. We call them sulkies but they only carry one person."

"Exactly," Dan answered. "Climb aboard, and we'll head for the bazaar."

They took their seats on the gari; Dan told the driver where they wanted to go, and they proceeded away from the airport and down a dusty and very bumpy road.

"I'm glad this thing has rubber tires," Sam observed. "I'd hate to think what this ride would be like on ironclad wagon wheels. Don't they put shock absorbers on these things?"

"You said you didn't want another scary taxi ride," Dan retorted with a smile. "If your kidneys can stand it, we'll be there in a few more minutes."

Sam groaned and watched as they approached a large open area where a crowd of people was gathered.

"Here we are," Dan announced. "This is a typical Indian bazaar. Remember the lessons you learned about bargaining back in Casablanca."

They dismounted from the gari, paid the driver, and proceeded into the milling crowd. Sam observed that there were a few thatched-roof stalls scattered about, but for the most part, the vendors had just spread their wares out on the open ground. As they walked through the bazaar, Sam noticed quite an array of vegetables for sale and commented on the variety to Dan.

"Yes, they grow quite a few things here, but they aren't safe for westerners to eat," Dan commented. "They use human excrement as fertilizer."

Sam hurried past the vegetable vendors and came upon a man selling leaves. As they approached, the man picked up a small bundle of leaves and smilingly offered them to Sam. When the man smiled, Sam was shocked to see that the poor fellow's teeth were all rotted, and his mouth and gums appeared to be red with blood.

"Those are betel leaves," Dan explained. "They combine the leaves with areca nut and lime paste and chew it. It's supposed to be a palate cleanser and breath freshener, but as you can see, it rots the teeth and stains the mouth red."

"And I thought chewing tobacco was bad," Sam exclaimed as they hurried past the betel leaf vendor.

As they proceeded through the bazaar, Sam noticed metal smiths offering a wide variety of hooks, knives, pans, and ladles. One product that caught his eye was an oil lamp made from half of a beer can, and he began to realize that these people would not let anything go to waste. Farther on, they came upon a man with a large basin that contained an assortment of liquid-filled bottles. As they watched, a woman approached the man and spoke a few words to him. The man then filled a small bottle from various bottles in his basin, adding a drop or two from various bottles and a dash from another before shaking the whole mixture up and wrapping it in a piece of paper with writing on it.

"What's this guy doing?" Sam asked.

"That's the Indian version of a pharmacist," Dan answered. "Rather interesting, isn't it?"

"Interesting isn't the word for it," Sam responded. "I'll really appreciate the drugstores back home now."

"It's really the same principle as back home, Sam, just not as clean."

They continued their way through the bazaar and came to a section devoted to cutting hair. It was nothing like the barbershops Sam was used to. There were no hydraulic barber chairs; in fact, there were no chairs at all. The customers squatted down on their haunches, and the barbers did the same. Sam counted six barbers all plying their trade in squatting positions next to each other.

Sam's attention was drawn away from the barbers by a loud racket coming from ahead. As they approached, he saw that the noise was coming from an area containing pigs, chickens, ducks, and goats, all contributing to the overall commotion. This was obviously the livestock area, and people were walking away with chickens in woven baskets or slung over their shoulders by strings tied around their legs. Squealing piglets added to the din, as they were held up by their hind legs. The entire area was a chaotic mélange of people noisily buying, selling, or trading amid the constant cacophony of clucking chickens, squawking ducks, squealing pigs, and bleating goats. Sam looked at Dan with an expression that told his friend that he had had enough.

"Looks like we will have just enough time to get back to the airport and have some supper before lights out," Dan said, looking at his watch.

"Sounds good to me," Sam replied. "As long as we don't have to have chicken, duck, goat, pork, or vegetables."

"I guess that just leaves steak and eggs," Dan answered, "but you know cows are sacred over here so that just leaves eggs."

"I'll settle for a cup of coffee and a slice of toast," Sam countered.

MARCH 31, 1944
KARACHI, INDIA

After a good night's sleep, Sam met Dan on the flight line early in the morning. As they had done so often in the past, they performed the preflight inspection of the C54 together.

"Everything looks good, Sam. Are you ready for the flight to Calcutta?"

"I guess so," Sam answered. "That's where we part company again, isn't it?"

"Yes, you'll be catching another flight to your next assignment, and I will be taking off right away to take some British officers to New Delhi." Dan responded. "Go ahead and get aboard. Our flight path will be taking us over the Taj Mahal. I think you will really enjoy that. I'll tell you all about it when we get there."

"Okay, professor. I'll see you later," Sam retorted.

Once again, Sam found a good window seat and settled in for the long flight across India. He thought about the little bit of India he had seen so far, the crowded conditions and poverty the Indian people were living in, and wondered what the rest of India was like. He watched as the Indian countryside slipped by below them and noted that living conditions and poverty were not visible from his vantage point high in the sky.

A little over two hours into their flight, Sam realized the plane was descending, and he suspected they must be approaching the Taj Mahal. His suspicions were confirmed when Dan appeared at the front of the airplane and walked back and took a seat beside Sam.

"The pilots are going to circle the Taj Mahal from about one thousand feet. How has your flight been so far?" Dan inquired.

"Great," Sam responded. "What is this Taj Mahal anyway?"

"It's a magnificent building, a mausoleum actually, built by Mughal emperor Shah Jahan around 1632, in memory of his third wife, Mumtaz Mahal, who died during the birth of their fourteenth child." Dan explained. "Oh look, you can see it through your window now."

Sam peered out the window and at the bend of a large river saw one of the most beautiful buildings he had ever seen. He observed a large white symmetrical building topped with a magnificent dome. Each of the four sides of the building were exactly alike and consisted of large vaulted archways over an entrance with two similarly shaped arched balconies arranged vertically on either side of the archway. The building stood upon a great square base of glistening white stone with minarets placed on each corner of the base. A garden extended from the south side of the building and was laid out as a huge square which was subdivided by walkways into sixteen smaller squares.

"Wow, that's quite a complex down there," Sam exclaimed.

"Spectacular, isn't it?" Dan commented, "It's built with white marble and combines elements of Persian, Islamic, and Indian architecture. It's the tomb of both Shah Jahan and his wife Mumtaz Mahal and is considered one of the most beautiful buildings in the world."

"Have you seen it from the ground?" Sam asked.

"Yes, I managed to get there on leave last year," Dan explained. "Maybe you will be able to do the same thing someday."

"I hope so," Sam said. "It looks like it would be worth the effort."

"It's more than worth it," Dan continued. "It's even more impressive inside where there's inlay work of precious and semiprecious gemstones and intricately carved marble screens. It's hard to describe. You have to see it in person to believe it."

Sam peered in wonderment at the scene below until the pilots stopped circling and resumed their course toward Calcutta. Dan remained in the seat next to Sam, and the two men began to talk.

"I guess I never asked, Dan. Are you married?" Sam inquired.

"No, I'm not married, but I am engaged to a girl I met in college.

We were going to get married when we graduated, but the war broke out and I got drafted, so we decided to wait until the war ends."

"Are you going to finish college when you get back?" Sam asked.

"You bet," Dan responded. "I want to finish my senior year, get my degree, and find a job teaching history."

"You'll be a great teacher, Dan. I've learned a lot from you, and you make it interesting."

"How about you, Sam, what are you going to do after the war?"

"I want to go back to my job on the Pennsylvania Railroad, buy a nice house for my wife, Eleanor, and finish raising my family," Sam answered.

"Sounds nice, Sam, I want to settle down in a nice little town in Maryland and have a family too."

"Maryland is just next door to Pennsylvania," Sam responded. "I'd like to continue our friendship after the war. Maybe our families can visit once in a while."

"I'd like that too, Sam. We'll exchange addresses when we land, so we can keep in touch. I want to know how things are going for you, and I look forward to the day when I can meet your family. Well, I have to get back to work. See you on the ground."

Sam watched as Dan made his way back to his station at the front of the plane. He was happy Dan wanted to keep in touch, because he had developed a strong liking for the sergeant. Sam never had a friend he felt so strongly about. He looked upon Dan as a brother and wanted their friendship to continue after the war.

When the C54 landed at Dum Dum airport near Calcutta, Sam gathered his things and met Dan on the tarmac.

"Well, it looks like this is farewell for now, Sam. Your flight to Dinjan doesn't leave for another hour, and as soon as we refuel and load our British passengers, I'll be headed for New Delhi," Dan said sadly. "I don't have any brothers or sisters, Sam, and I feel like you are a brother to me. I know you are headed into combat, and I want you to take care of yourself, and I definitely want to know how you're doing."

"You're like a big brother to me too, Dan, and I promise to stay in touch. After this war is over, I would like our families to be very close."

They shook hands, hugged warmly, and exchanged pieces of paper containing their home addresses. No further words were needed between them. Dan went back to his preflight duties, and Sam picked up his gear and walked to the terminal building. From the doorway of the terminal, he watched his friend perform the preflight procedures that Sam had come to know so well. As he watched, he felt a true closeness toward his friend. In the short time they had known each other, he had learned a lot from Dan and was grateful his friend had helped him through the frightening flight experiences they encountered crossing the Atlantic. Because of Dan, he was prepared to meet the challenges ahead.

Sam continued to observe as the British officers Dan had mentioned climbed aboard the plane. He imagined they were on their way to New Delhi on official business or on leave. Dan followed close behind and turned as he entered the aircraft and waved. Sam returned the wave and watched as the aircraft door was closed and the engines were started one by one. Soon the C54 taxied off and stopped short of the active runway. Sam heard the engines as the pilots increased power to each one as part of the takeoff checklist, and he remembered the sound and vibration that procedure caused inside the passenger cabin. He imagined he would be experiencing those sights and sounds quite often in the coming days and reached into his pocket and retrieved the paper that contained Dan's address. He looked at the address and was comforted knowing he had a way to keep in touch with his friend. A jeep pulled up and stopped in front of him.

"Are you Private Huber?" the driver asked.

"Yes," Sam responded.

"I'm here to take you to your next flight," said the driver.

Sam tossed his gear into the back of the jeep and stopped to watch Dan's plane as it accelerated down the runway, and he remembered the feelings of acceleration and lightness associated with takeoff. He observed the C54 speed down the runway and watched the nosewheel rise in anticipation of lift off, but instead of rising gracefully into the air, the plane seemed to struggle to leave the ground. It rose momentarily and then settled back down onto the runway. Once again, the speeding aircraft attempted unsuccessfully to lift off, and then Sam saw smoke begin to billow from the wheels as the pilots applied the brakes to abort the takeoff. He watched in horror as the C54 ran off the end of the runway, the nosewheel collapsed and the right wing dug into the ground, spinning the aircraft violently around. Suddenly, a great ball of fire erupted, and the airplane began to burn before Sam's eyes. Without realizing what he was doing, he began to run toward the developing inferno. He ran, oblivious to everything around him, until the heat from the burning wreckage prevented him from getting any closer. He stood in stunned disbelief and watched as a great column of black smoke rose high into the air, and the terrible flames consumed the plane and his friend. He wept uncontrollably, not knowing how long he stood there numb with despair and grief. Finally, realizing his hands were tightly clenched into fists, he slowly opened them and saw the paper containing Dan's address. Sam folded the paper neatly and placed it in his wallet and made himself a promise that he would contact Dan's parents and fiancée to let them know how important their son had become to him and to tell them of his last moments.

14

APRIL 1, 1944
DINJAN AIRBASE, INDIA

S AM'S FLIGHT FROM Dum Dum had been delayed due to the terrible crash that took the life of his friend Dan, a loss that still weighed heavily upon him. It was in the wee hours of the morning that he eventually climbed aboard an air transport command (ATC) C47 cargo plane for the flight to his next assignment at Dinjan Airbase in the Indian state of Assam. It was the same type of aircraft he had trained on back in Sicily and one with which he would become intimately familiar in the coming months. After takeoff, Sam found it impossible to sleep, so he took paper and pen from his duffle bag and began to write...

Dear Mr. and Mrs. Dury,

You don't know me but I met your son while I was being transferred from the United States to India. Dan was the flight engineer on two of my flights and we became the best of friends. During our short time together, he taught me many things about airplanes and about facing the challenges of being a soldier during these difficult times. We shared many experiences together and his extensive knowledge of history and geography made those experiences unforgettable. Like all soldiers, we were brothers in arms but I came to know and love Dan like a true brother.

Twice during our flight to Africa we encountered serious life threatening events. In both of those situations, Dan's skill and professionalism as a flight engineer helped to bring the plane down safely and saved the lives of the 26 passengers aboard. As difficult as it is for you to lose your son, you can take comfort in the knowledge that 26 men owe their lives to him. The families of the other men on that flight may never know what they owe to Dan, but I can assure you my family will know and we will honor his memory for the rest of our lives.

I witnessed the accident that took Dan's life. He did not suffer and he died doing the job for which he was trained, a job he loved dearly. I want you to know that Dan has influenced my life profoundly. He has given me the determination and the will to face what challenges lie ahead. If I survive this war, I would like to someday meet you and Dan's fiancée. I can tell you that he loved all of you very much, and the superb job you did in his upbringing was evident in every aspect of his life. You can be eternally proud of your son.

Respectfully yours,
Pvt. Samuel Huber

They landed at Dinjan just as the sun was rising, and upon disembarking from the plane, Sam was immediately confronted with one of the realities of life in a war zone. He had no sooner stepped from the aircraft when air raid sirens began to wail, and everyone around him dropped what they were doing and scattered in all directions. Sam stood on the tarmac not knowing what to do until the lieutenant who was the copilot of the C47 grabbed him by the arm.

"Don't stand there like a love-struck ape, drop those bags and follow me. Jap bombers are five minutes away," shouted the lieutenant above the mounting confusion.

The officer's words galvanized Sam into action, and he followed the lieutenant as he raced away from the parked aircraft. They ran to the edge of the tarmac where the lieutenant dove into a slit trench, stirring up a cloud of dust. Sam followed closely behind creating his own dust storm as he landed next to the lieutenant. Sputtering and choking from the dust, Sam peered out over the edge of the slit trench as the sound of approaching aircraft grew louder.

"I can see you're a real newbie to this part of the world, Private. Get your head down if you want to keep it on your shoulders," admonished the lieutenant.

Sam slid farther down into the trench just as the first bombs exploded around them. He covered his head as the earth heaved and shook beneath him, and he could hear the sound of shrapnel as it whistled overhead. Clumps of dirt and stone fell from the sky, and for the first time, he experienced the feeling of helplessness and terror that comes from not knowing where the next bomb will fall and being helpless to change the situation. For what seemed like an eternity, the earth shook and trembled as bombs continued to explode in their vicinity. Dirt and dust cascaded down the sides of the trench until both men were covered by a layer of grime. Slowly the sounds of the enemy bombers drew farther away, and the bombing stopped. Sam stirred to look about, but the lieutenant's hand restrained him.

"Not yet, soldier," cautioned the lieutenant. "Listen."

Sam was puzzled by the lieutenant's admonition, and then as he listened intently, he heard them. The sounds reaching his ears were strange, and yet there was a vague familiarity to them. He tugged at his memory, and then in a flash of remembrance, it came to him. These were the same sounds he had heard as a child attending air shows with his father. They were the sounds the airplanes made as they dove down from the sky to perform aerobatics as they skimmed over the heads of the enthralled spectators. But these were not air show planes, and he soon heard another sound—the sound of machine gun and cannon fire as the approaching aircraft strafed the buildings and ground around them. Sam could hear the ricochet of bullets and see the explosive cannon shells as they struck nearby buildings, shattering windows and causing chunks of splintered wood to fly in all directions, and then he watched as two planes roared directly over their slit trench. From the red balls painted on their wings, he knew immediately that they were Japanese fighter planes. He wished desperately to fight back. He wanted to make them pay for the death and destruction they had caused. His ears were still ringing from the cacophony of the surrounding noise when he was startled by the sound of pistol shots coming from right beside him. He looked over to see the lieutenant emptying his .45-caliber handgun at the departing enemy planes. The lieutenant's actions brought a sense of comic relief to the situation, and Sam could feel the tension drain from his body. He watched as the empty pistol was returned to its holster, and the lieutenant turned to Sam with a satisfied look on his face and extended his hand.

"I don't get to shoot back when I'm flying an unarmed cargo plane, so I like to get my licks in when I can. Hi, I'm Lieutenant L. T. Thomas. I'm a pilot with ATC here at Dinjan. Everyone calls me LT."

The lieutenant's relaxed demeanor and his disregard for military protocol took Sam by surprise, and he grasped the lieutenant's hand in a warm handshake.

"Pleased to meet you, Lieutenant, I'm Private Sam Huber. I've just been assigned here as an air traffic clerk."

"Oh, you're a kicker. We'll probably be flying a lot together. Welcome aboard," responded the lieutenant as he released Sam's hand.

"Thank you, Lieutenant, but I don't think we'll be using that plane anymore," answered Sam as he nodded toward the crumpled ruins of the C47 they had recently flown from Dum Dum airport.

"Damn, I'm going to miss that old bird. Well, she wasn't going to last much longer anyway. She's been patched up so often I'm surprised she could still fly, but you still hate to see them go. Speaking of going, I have to go file my flight report. I'll be seeing you around, Sam. You can check in at the headquarters building behind the terminal building if there's anything left of it."

Sam took an immediate liking to the lieutenant and watched as LT dusted himself off and walked toward the control tower. Sam brushed the dirt from his own uniform and began searching for his duffel bag among the debris. He soon found the bag, dusted it off, and headed for the headquarters building.

At the headquarters building, Sam was escorted into the presence of his new commanding officer (CO), Captain George Cummings. Captain Cummings was a man of medium height with a ruddy complexion and steady hazel eyes. He wore silver pilot's wings on his left breast over an impressive row of military ribbons. Sam approached the CO's desk, stood at attention, and presented his personnel folder.

"Private Huber, Samuel D., reporting for duty, sir."

"At ease, soldier, and have a seat," said the CO, motioning toward the two chairs in front of his desk.

The captain spoke in a deep baritone voice that was pleasant to the ear and yet conveyed an air of authority. He opened Sam's folder and took a few minutes to peruse the contents. Sam sat in one of the chairs and waited for the captain to finish.

"Welcome to Dinjan, Private Huber. You've arrived at a very inauspicious time. The war is really heating up in this part of the world. I'll give you a briefing on our current mission before our company clerk gets you settled in."

The captain picked up a long wooden pointer from his desk and walked to a large map of India, Burma, and China hanging on the wall. Sam saw that the CO had a noticeable limp as he walked. Seeing that Sam noticed his limp the captain explained.

"I used to fly cargo over the Hump [Himalayan Mountains] to China," he said, pointing to one of the red lines on the map that extended from Dinjan, India, to Kunming, China.

Sam could see the line crossed over a portion of the Himalayan Mountains extending down from Tibet and into northern Burma between India and China.

"The Himalayas are not as high in Burma as they are farther north. Up north, they reach over twenty-nine thousand feet but along this route, they only extend up to eighteen thousand feet," continued the captain as he indicated a point on the map. "On my last flight over the Hump, we were jumped by Jap fighters and shot down. There were four of us aboard, and we all managed to bail out over the mountains. Unfortunately, I came down in a deep gorge, and my chute snagged on a rock. I was slammed against the rocks, and then my chute tore, sending me tumbling fifty feet to the bottom of the gorge. My leg was badly injured in the fall. Luckily, the rest of the crew landed safely nearby, and with the help of some friendly Burmese tribesmen who came to investigate the plane crash, they got me safely out of the gorge. It took the Burmese three weeks to get us back to our lines, and I had to be carried every inch of the way. As a result of my injuries, I'll be flying a desk for the rest of the war."

Sam sensed the CO's deep desire to fly and felt sorry that the man could not pursue his dreams. Still standing at the map, the captain pointed at a spot in northeastern India and continued.

"This is where you are now, Dinjan Airbase in the Indian state of Assam. Dinjan was built on a tea plantation in 1942, with the primary mission of protecting cargo aircraft flying over the Hump. However, as I alluded to earlier, with the increase in war activity in this theater, Dinjan is now one of the major hubs for the aerial supply of Allied forces in northern Burma and eastern India. We are currently tasked with supplying four different military groups." Pointing to rectangular blue boxes in northern Burma, he continued, "The first group, shown here by the blue boxes, is known as the X Force under the joint command of General Stillwell and General Sun Li-Jen. There are about thirty thousand soldiers in X Force, and their mission is to clear the way for the completion of the Ledo Road and the reopening of the Burma Road into China. They receive some supplies over the partially completed Ledo Road and the remainder from airdrops." He then pointed to three black boxes near the blue boxes in northern Burma. "The second group is Merrill's Marauders. The Marauders are made up of three battalions of American volunteers, and they total to three thousand men. Their mission is to ease the way for the X Force by attacking the enemy from behind and disrupting their supply lines. The Marauders are supplied completely from the air. The third group we are supplying entirely from the air is the twelve thousand Chindit troops under British General Wingate," he continued as he pointed to green boxes near the north-central part of Burma. "Do you have any questions to this point, Private Huber?"

"Yes, sir. What are Chindits, and what are the red boxes on the map?"

"The Chindits are commando troops recruited from throughout the British Empire. They come from all parts of the United Kingdom, Africa, Burma, Nepal, and India. You might be interested to know that they were inserted behind enemy lines aboard gliders towed by our C47s. It was the first ever operation of its kind. The Chindits job is to relieve pressure on the X Force by creating as much havoc as they can behind enemy lines. The red boxes you see are the current locations of Japanese forces."

"Thank you, sir. What is the fourth group that is being supported?"

"The fourth group is some 170,000 British troops who are currently being attacked by the Japanese at Imphal in the Indian state of Manipur." The captain pointed to a group of green boxes almost entirely surrounded by red boxes in eastern India. "As you can see, the British are in deep trouble. They are surrounded and taking a terrible beating. If the Japanese take Imphal, there is nothing to stop them from cutting our supply lines between Calcutta and here. If that happens, all our bases here in Assam could be captured, and all the groups we are supplying would be lost."

Sam realized the inherent danger everyone at Dinjan was facing. He mulled over what the captain had said and finally asked, "How can we possibly supply over 215,000 troops scattered over such a vast area, sir?"

"That's going to be part of your job, soldier. You'll be one of the aircrew members dropping supplies where they are needed. You'll be flying over hostile territory and be subjected to enemy air attacks and ground fire. Sadly, we lost two aircraft and all aboard just yesterday. The situation is desperate and the supreme Allied commander, Admiral Lord Louis Mountbatten, has ordered all available units to support the supply effort of the British forces at Imphal. In fact, the unit you just came from, the Sixty-fourth Troop Carrier Group, has been ordered to this theater from Sicily. They'll be leaving tomorrow, and some of them will arrive here in a few days. You will probably be flying with some of your old friends soon."

Sam was totally surprised by the news that he might be flying with his old unit once again, and he was concerned with the enormity of the task ahead and the dangers he would soon face.

"Welcome aboard, soldier. Our clerk, Corporal Finney, will get you settled into your quarters. Unfortunately, you are not going to have much time to look around. You will be flying your first mission tomorrow morning. Good luck," said the CO as he dismissed Sam and limped back to his desk.

Corporal Finney was waiting for Sam when he departed the Commander's office. "Follow me, Private Huber. I'll fill you in on how things work around here and show you where you're going to bunk."

Sam spent the next two hours with the corporal and was shown the facilities of the base. He noted most of the buildings on the base were quite spartan, but he was really surprised when they arrived at the area where his unit was assigned. The first building he was shown was the mess hall. It had a thatched roof and was open on three sides. There were crude tables and benches made from wood that appeared to be scavenged from whatever was available.

"If you think the mess hall looks bad, the food here is even worse," explained the corporal. "We get what's left after the troops in Europe and the Pacific are supplied, and it takes three months to get here. So you'll be seeing a lot of powdered eggs, powdered milk, powdered potatoes, powdered coffee, and Spam. We get our bread from a local British unit, and the flour they use is infested with bugs. So you either pick the bugs out of the bread or you eat them. Oh, and be sure you don't remove any food from the mess hall. There's a black crow-like bird around here called a kite. They hover in the breeze above the chow hall and swoop down and steal anything they can get from your mess kit."

Sam was beginning to wonder what he had gotten himself into when Corporal Finney led him to the shower facilities. The showers were nothing more than a ten-foot-square area surrounded by a bamboo fence for privacy. Inside was an eight-foot tower with a fifty-five-gallon drum installed at the top. Extending from the drum was a half-inch water pipe with a showerhead at the end. About six inches above the shower head, a valve had been installed with a small rope attached to the handle. Corporal Finney explained its operation.

"This is our shower. We pay an Indian houseboy a few rupees a week to keep the drum filled with water. A rupee is worth about thirty cents. The sun heats the water and you just pull the rope to activate the showerhead. As you can see, only one person at a time can shower. Sometimes you have to wait in line, and sometimes the drum runs dry before it's your turn. The best you can hope for is a semiwarm shower."

Sam was becoming completely amazed at the primitive conditions of the camp when Finney pointed out their toilet facilities. Sam had grown up using an outhouse in rural Pennsylvania, but what he saw now was totally beyond his belief. The toilet was a small building built from scrap materials and large enough for about three people at one time. It sat about three feet above the ground on stilts and in the open space underneath there were three fifty-five-gallon drums which had been cut in half lengthwise. The drums reminded Sam of watering troughs for cattle.

"You're probably wondering why the latrine is constructed in this fashion," Finney said. "Well, it has a practical function, at least for the local farmers. They come with buckets every few days and clean out the drums and then spread it on their fields for fertilizer. Needless to say, we don't eat any of the locally grown vegetables."

Sam could feel his stomach churn, and he began to feel the powdered food served in the mess hall might not be so bad after all. Corporal Finney continued his tour by leading Sam to a group of small huts nearby.

"These are our barracks. They're called *bashas*," explained the corporal as he entered one of the buildings. "The walls are made of bamboo with a layer of mud smeared over the outside. When the mud dries, it's whitewashed to reflect the daytime heat, but it still gets so hot in here it's hard to sleep."

Sam took in the primitive construction of the basha, noting the rough wooden flooring and the thatched roofing. The windows had no glass but did have screens and wooden shutters. There were six Indian beds in the basha. Finney informed him they were called charpoys. Each charpoy was the size of a single bed. They sat low to the floor and were constructed with a wooden frame and short legs. Hemp rope was stretched inside the frame to support an Indian mattress, which didn't appear to amount to much. A bamboo pole about five feet high was attached at each corner of the frame and mosquito netting was tied to the poles. Each bed had a footlocker against the wall beside it and a crude wooden clothing rack attached to the wall above.

"This will be your bunk," explained Finney as he led Sam to a bed on the right side of the basha. "The mosquitoes around here carry malaria. So when you go to bed, be sure to tuck the netting under the mattress all the way around and then spray inside with a mosquito bomb in case any have gotten in. The netting not only keeps the mosquitoes out but spiders, scorpions, and snakes as well. Oh, and its best to keep your shoes under the netting too. The scorpions and snakes like to crawl into them during the night. If you hear noises in the thatched roof during the night, it's just rats and other small critters looking for seeds in the rice thatching."

Sam was speechless as he absorbed the information presented to him and wondered how anyone could live in such conditions. He dropped his duffel bag beside his bed and looked around. All the other beds in the room had clothing hung beside them, so Sam assumed he would be sharing the basha with five other men.

"Where are the other five guys who bunk here?" Sam inquired.

"They're all currently out on missions except for Private Mitchell in that bunk over there," answered Finney, pointing to the bed directly across from Sam's. "Mitchell was one of the men lost in yesterday's missions. The other guys won't talk about it. I'll remove his things before they return tonight. It will be like he never existed. Because you never know who will return from a mission, most guys don't form close friendships. It's just the way things are."

Sam looked at Mitchell's bunk and wondered how many others would be lost before this war was over. Perhaps, he would be one of them, and the thought of never seeing his family again weighed heavily on his heart.

"I'll leave you so you can get settled in," said Finney. "If you need anything, I'll be back later to get Mitchell's things. Your Indian houseboy will bring your bedding. Check the bulletin board at headquarters after supper for tomorrow's assignments. Welcome aboard and good luck."

Sam watched the corporal leave and turned to his duffel bag. He removed pen and paper and sat down on his bunk to write a letter home.

15

APRIL 2, 1944
DINJAN AIRBASE, INDIA

SAM'S FIRST NIGHT at his new base had been an ominous taste of what was in store for him in India. He met his basha mates after supper, and while they welcomed him into their fold, he felt a sense of remoteness toward him. However, the soldier who occupied the bunk next to Sam was the exception. His name was Bobby Joe Wilson, and perhaps because they were both country boys, they formed an immediate bond of friendship. Bobby Joe was a tall, lanky Texan who grew up on his parent's ranch near Waco. He stood six feet four inches tall, had sandy blonde hair and blue eyes. The most noticeable feature of the young man was his skin, which had the tanned, leathery look of someone who spent most of their life outdoors. When Sam asked Bobby Joe about his rather cool reception from the other men in the basha, the Texan explained that because of the loss of so many of their comrades, the others were reluctant to form close friendships. He assured him it was nothing personal. It was just the way things were in war time. Sam was relieved by Bobby Joe's assurances and was doubly relieved to learn that Bobby Joe would be mentoring him on his first airdropping mission the following morning.

After lights out, Sam had dutifully tucked his mosquito net under his mattress and made sure his shoes were inside the netting. However, he soon discovered that sleep was nearly impossible. He expected the stifling heat of the day to abate at night, but that was not the case, and he soon discovered his bedclothes were completely soaked with sweat. In addition to the unpleasant heat, his rest was disturbed by the almost constant rustling of critters in the thatched roof. At one point, he had almost fallen asleep when he was jerked upright in bed by the sounds of ungodly howling and yipping coming from the surrounding jungle. Awakened by Sam's movements, Bobby Joe explained it was just the nightly serenade of the local jackals and was nothing to worry about. The news did nothing to assuage Sam's sleeplessness. As the long hours of the night wore on, he noticed the other men in the basha were having no trouble sleeping. He assumed he would someday be able to join them in restful slumber and was just getting comfortable with the thought when the roar of a nearby big jungle cat destroyed any hope of sleep for the remainder of the night.

Dawn found Sam still sleepless in his sweat-soaked bed when the call to reveille woke the camp. He stirred listlessly from his charpoy and stared at Bobby Joe through bloodshot eyes.

"Partner, y'all look like ya been rode hard, bucked off, and stomped on," exclaimed Bobby Joe.

"I don't know how anyone can sleep with the heat and racket that goes on around here at night," Sam moaned.

"Y'all git used to it," Bobby Joe responded, "Come on, let's grab us some breakfast vittles 'fore all them powdered eggs is gone."

The two men dressed and walked to the mess hall under a blazing morning sun that held the promise of another uncomfortable day. Sam ate a meager breakfast of powdered eggs, powdered coffee, and fried Spam. Bobby Joe enjoyed large portions of the same things including several slices of the insect laden bread. They finished eating and were cleaning out their mess kits when Lt. L. T. Thomas approached carrying a mess kit laden with eggs and bread.

"Private Huber, the CO wants his breakfast delivered to him. Take this to him in the headquarters building," commanded the lieutenant.

Somewhat confused, Sam looked at Bobby Joe who simply shrugged and nodded his head.

"Yes, sir," Sam responded, taking the mess kit from the lieutenant.

Thinking that this must be standard operating procedure, Sam dutifully walked out of the mess hall and headed toward the nearby headquarters building, intent on safely delivering the CO's breakfast. However, he was not to succeed in his mission. He no sooner stepped into the open air when he was assailed by a swarm of screeching black birds that swooped from the sky picking at the food in the mess kit. Startled and overwhelmed, Sam dropped the mess kit and ran back to the safety of the mess hall, as the birds frantically swarmed to get at the CO's breakfast. Stunned and panting from the experience, Sam watched as the last of the birds flew off, leaving a completely clean mess kit lying on the ground. It was then that he heard the snickers and muffled laughter of the men around him, and he realized he'd been had. He turned to face the men as the snickering erupted into uproarious laughter.

"LT done got ya good," Bobby Joe explained with a smile. "Welcome ta Dinjan, Sam. Now we better git on over to our preflight briefing."

Even though he was chagrinned by the experience, Sam had to chuckle to himself as they walked to the briefing room, and he made a mental note to watch out for Lieutenant Thomas in the future. They arrived at the briefing room just as Captain Cummings was placing a large map of Burma on an easel. They sat down and waited for the remaining flight crew members to arrive. Turning from his map, Captain Cummings noticed Sam seated in the first row and smiled.

"I understand Lieutenant Thomas introduced you to our local kite population this morning. I hope it wasn't too much of a traumatic experience," the captain said to Sam.

"Yes, sir, he certainly did. It was an experience I'll never forget," responded Sam.

"I'm afraid you're in for lots of unforgettable experiences, Private. Starting with today's mission," cautioned the captain as he noted that all of the flight crews had arrived. Picking up a sheaf of papers from the table before him, he began the mission briefing.

"Good morning, gentlemen, we have an urgent mission for you this morning. The entire Second Battalion of Merrill's Marauders, eleven hundred men in all, are completely surrounded by an estimated four thousand Japanese soldiers in the small Burmese village of Nhpum Ga," the captain announced pointing to a small dot in north central Burma.

"The village consists of about five bashas and is not currently occupied by the Burmese. The only source of water for the village is a small spring which has been captured by the enemy. Needless to say, they are in a desperate situation, and your mission today will be to drop fresh water to them. As you can see on this map, Nhpum Ga is located on top of a narrow ridge between the Tanai River to the east and the Hkuma River to the west. The village is located in rugged terrain and sits fourteen hundred feet above the river valleys. You are going to have to be very precise in your drops today, because the Marauders are confined to an area four hundred yards long and only two hundred feet wide. As I stated earlier, they are completely surrounded, so you can expect to receive considerable ground fire from all directions as you make your approach to the drop zone. You will be dropping a total of five hundred gallons of water, and in order to minimize your time over the target, we are splitting the load between two planes. This is not going to be an easy mission, and it will require all your concentration and skills as airmen. Good luck and Godspeed, gentlemen."

With the completion of the briefing, everyone rose and departed from the briefing room. Sam followed Bobby Joe as he led the way toward two C47s parked on the tarmac under the scorching sun. When they reached their assigned aircraft, Bobby Joe climbed aboard and motioned Sam to follow. Upon entering the plane through the portside cargo doors, Sam was immediately struck by the extreme heat in the cargo bay. It felt like an oven and must have been at least 130 degrees inside. Bobby Joe immediately removed his shirt and t-shirt, revealing a well-tanned muscular body. Beads of sweat were already forming on his brow and streaming down his chest and back.

"Y'all better git that shirt off 'fore ya melt," Bobby Joe instructed Sam.

Sam found it difficult to remove his own sweat-soaked clothing as it tended to stick to his body. After a struggle, he finally completed the job but didn't feel any cooler in the steaming cargo bay.

"It'll git cooler in here after we takeoff and climb up ta cruisin' altitude," Bobby Joe said.

As they settled in for the flight, the third member of their kicking crew arrived. His name was Delbert Swanson, and he came from Ames, Iowa. Delbert was about the same height as Sam but couldn't have weighed more than 135 pounds, and as it turned out it was Delbert's first mission too. Introductions were made all around, and Bobby Joe, as the senior airman of the crew, explained the procedures that would be followed.

"We got 250 gallons a water aboard in five-gallon plastic bags. That's a full ton a water. Each chutes got five bags attached, so each loads gonna weigh two hundred pounds. Before each pass, we'll put three loads at the door and shove 'em out when the pilot turns on the green signal light," Bobby Joe explained, pointing to a light at the entrance to the cockpit. "Y'all gotta be quick, so we kin hit the target.

We don't want them Japs gittin any a this water. It's gonna take three passes ta unload everythin', so y'all gonna be busy."

Sam noticed the cargo doors had been removed from the plane and asked, "How come there are no doors on the plane?"

"They're too much trouble ta open durin' flight, and it heps ta reduce the weight of the plane," explained Bobby Joe.

Their conversation was interrupted by the sounds of the aircraft engines starting, so the men took a seat on the floor of the cargo bay. Sam chose to sit near the open cargo doors so he could have a good view of the ground during the mission. The pilots didn't waste time getting airborne, and they were soon climbing into cooler air above the Indian landscape. The weather was clear with only a few puffy cumulus clouds floating in the bright blue sky. From his vantage point, Sam watched as the tea plantations and forests around Dinjan gave way to a thick carpet of verdant jungle growth. As they flew higher, the air became much cooler, and Sam noted that the ground below had changed to jungle-covered mountains. He saw streams in the mountain valleys that fed into rivers and observed an occasional native village along the river banks. Bobby Joe joined Sam near the doorway as the mountains became steeper and more rugged.

"How can the Marauders cross such rugged terrain let alone fight a battle in it?" Sam asked.

"It ain't easy," Bobby Joe responded. "They got pack mules and horses ta hep carry their supplies. Mostly they foller jungle trails and streams, but sometimes they got ta hack through thick jungle and they kin only cover 'bout a mile or less a day."

"How can they do that and still have the strength to fight?" Sam inquired.

"Well, they're losin' more men ta exhaustion and disease than ta the Japs," Bobby Joe explained as the sound of the engines decreased and the plane began to descend. "We must be approachin' the drop zone. We'll circle couple a times ta git the lay a the land and then we'll go in for the drops. Jus foller my lead and we'll git the job done."

The plane continued to descend and began a wide circle at an altitude of about five thousand feet. Sam could see a narrow ridge with river valleys on either side, but he could not make out the drop zone. He was beginning to think they were at the wrong location when his attention was drawn to a very small area on the ridge by puffs of smoke.

"That, there's the drop zone," explained Bobby Joe. "Them puffs a smoke is Jap artillery poundin' our guys."

The pilots circled in closer to the target area, and Sam could begin to make out more detail in the scene below. He could see more bursts of artillery shells and could begin to recognize the small perimeter of the Marauder's position, which appeared to be outlined by hundreds of dead bodies.

"Them bodies is dead Japs that's been kilt chargin' at the Marauders," Bobby Joe said.

Sam could see live men within the perimeter who were waving at them in anticipation of the airdrop. He knew they were in desperate need of water, and it made him feel good that he would be instrumental in helping them. His attention was then drawn to the sight of the bloated carcasses of hundreds of dead mules and horses within the Marauder's perimeter.

"Them pack animals don't stand much of a chance when artillery shells explode in the trees above them," Bobby Joe said sadly. "Let's git our first load ready ta drop. We'll be makin' our first pass soon."

Sam and Delbert followed Bobby Joe's lead and carried three of the two-hundred-pound clusters of water containers to the doorway. Each cluster had a parachute attached to it, and Bobby Joe went about affixing a static line from a cable inside the plane to the rip cord on chute. The pilots stopped circling and were setting the plane up for the first drop. They lined the C47 up on a north-south heading along the ridge, descended to an altitude just two hundred feet above the ground and slowed their airspeed to 120 knots.

"Okay, y'all, when the pilot turns on the green drop light, we gotta git this water outta here pronto," instructed Bobby Joe. "Y'all stand in the door and push the loads out, and I'll feed 'em ta ya quick as I kin."

Sam and Delbert stood in the doorway with the first cluster of water between them. They held on to the doorsill with one hand and grasped the parachute harness with the other. Bobby Joe positioned the other two clusters close behind. Sam felt exposed as he stood in the open doorway with the ground whizzing by just two hundred feet below. He had an unobstructed view of the ridge top and could see the Japanese emplacements below as they sped toward the drop zone. He could also see individual Japanese soldiers, many of whom were pointing their rifles at the plane as it approached. It wasn't until he heard the metallic ping of bullets striking the plane and saw holes appear in the side of the fuselage that he realize they were being fired upon. A bullet struck the door sill near Sam's head and another tore through one of the plastic water bags at his feet, spilling water on the floor of the cargo bay. Sam's first reaction was to seek cover in the interior of the airplane, but he stood fast, knowing they had to deliver the desperately needed water to the Marauders. He could feel a knot beginning to form in his stomach as he observed puffs of smoke coming from the rifles below. Finally, Bobby Joe gave the command to unload. In quick succession, they pushed the first three clusters of water into the air. Sam was amazed at the strength and speed Bobby Joe exhibited in getting the two-hundred-pound clusters into the doorway. Just as the third cluster was jettisoned, Sam's nostrils were assailed by an ungodly stench coming through the doorway. He reeled back from the open door, gagging and trying to keep the contents of his stomach down.

"That's the smell a the rottin' corpses from the men and pack animals below," said Bobby Joe. "Think how bad it must be fer our guys down there."

Getting his stomach under control, Sam returned to the doorway and with the others, observed as the last chute opened. The five-gallon plastic bags dangling below the parachutes reminded him of giant sausages suspended in the air. As they watched the chutes float slowly toward the ground, they saw another water bag hit by ground fire. The ruptured bag exploded spraying its precious contents into the air. The prism effect of sunlight shining through the water droplets formed a beautiful rainbow which proved to be a good omen because all three clusters of water landed safely within the Marauder's perimeter. As they circled around for their second approach, the men watched and cheered as the other C47 also delivered its first load safely to the Marauders.

Bobby Joe and his crew repeated the airdropping process two more times, and each time the water reached the Marauders safely, but each time, their aircraft took multiple hits from enemy ground fire. The same was true of the other C47, and as the aircraft climbed away after their last pass, the men watched from above as the thirsty Marauders, still under fire, crawled from their foxholes to retrieve the precious lifesaving liquid. When they were out of sight of the drop zone, Sam sat on the floor of the cargo bay and, with a sigh of relief, let the tension of his recent experience drain from his body. Bobby Joe and Delbert sat down beside him, and for the longest time, no one spoke.

"Y'all done good," Bobby Joe finally said. "We been droppin' up ta twenty-five tons a supplies a day ta the three Marauder battalions, but this is one drop they ain't gonna fergit."

The men remained seated and enjoyed the cool air as the C47 took up a course for home. However, their reverie did not last long. The copilot appeared in the cargo bay with a message for all of them.

"The day isn't over yet, gentlemen. We just received a radio message from headquarters directing us to Chabua Airbase where we will take on a load of howitzers and ammo. Then we will proceed right back here, where we will drop the artillery to the Marauder's third battalion, who are trying to break through and rescue the men trapped at Nhpum Ga. We should be arriving at Chabua in about an hour," explained the copilot.

"Dang, I'm gonna miss lunch agin. Oh well, it was probably gonna be Spam sandwiches agin anyway. Ya know, I think ya git more protein from the buggy bread than ya do from the Spam," Bobby Joe said stoically as he sat mulling the thought over in his head.

Sam's stomach could take no more. Between the smells from Nhpum Ga and the images aroused in his mind of the buggy bread, his stomach churned, and he thrust his head out of the doorway and heaved into the open air. Unfortunately, the slipstream from the moving aircraft distributed the contents of his stomach all along the side and bottom of the plane.

"Whoa, Nellie, the ground crew sure ain't gonna like cleanin' that up," Bobby Joe observed flatly.

Sam rolled back into the plane and gave Bobby Joe the evil eye. Little was said during the remainder of the flight to Chabua.

APRIL 2, 1944
NHPUM GA, BURMA

Sergeant Bill Wesley lay in his hastily dug foxhole, awaiting the enemy attack he knew was coming. They knew of the enemy's plans, because during the night, his best friend, Sergeant Roy Matamoto, an American citizen born of Japanese parents, had crawled toward the Japanese lines and listened as the enemy made plans for their attack the next morning. When Roy reported his findings to their platoon leader, the entire platoon was ordered to booby-trap their foxholes and establish new positions fifteen yards to the rear. It was from these positions that the weary Marauders awaited the next enemy onslaught. Sergeant Wesley had lost count of the number of attacks they had endured. Over the past few days, the Japs had come at them in waves screaming "Banzai!" and "Die, Joe, Die!" At times, they overran the Marauders outer defenses, and the combat turned to savage hand-to-hand killing. Sergeant Wesley had personally killed three enemy soldiers with his bayonet and one by strangulation. The area in front of them was covered with the bloated corpses of dead Japanese, and behind them lay the rotting, fly-infested bodies of over half of their two hundred pack mules. The hot, moist climate of the Burmese jungle hastened the decomposition process, and the stench surrounding the Marauders was almost unbearable. The men began calling their little piece of the ridge Maggot Hill.

"I'd give anything for cool drink of water," Bill said to his buddy, Sergeant Matamoto, who was hunkered down beside him. "You got any water in your canteen?"

"I got about one swallow of that slop we got from the elephant tracks yesterday," Roy responded. "But even with halazone and lemonade tables added, it still tastes like stagnant mud."

"No, thanks," Bill answered. "I sure hope that airdrop of water the colonel called for gets here soon." The enemy had captured the only water supply for Nhpum Ga three days ago, and the entire Second Division of the Marauders was in desperate need of drinking water. "When do you think the Japs will attack?"

"From what I heard them saying last night, it should be any time now," answered Roy.

Bill admired the courage of his friend. He knew Roy was a Nisei, a second-generation Japanese, and he knew Roy's parents were in an internment camp back in California, and yet the young soldier fought with as much tenacity as the rest of them. "I wish they would attack and get this over with, I hate the waiting part. I hated it on Guadalcanal, and I hate it here."

"Was the fighting on Guadalcanal worse than here?" Roy asked.

"It was very bad, but I think overall it's worse here," Bill answered.

Their conversation was brought to an abrupt halt when the jungle before them erupted with cries of "Banzai," and hoards of Japanese soldiers poured from their concealed positions and charged up the ridge toward Bill's platoon. The Marauders withheld their fire until the enemy was within fifteen yards, and then they let loose with every gun they had. Japanese soldiers leading the attack were killed instantly by the withering gunfire, and those behind sought shelter by jumping into the deserted foxholes, only to be blown apart by the booby traps left behind by the Marauders. The remaining Japanese took cover wherever they could.

Seeing a golden opportunity, Sergeant Matamoto began yelling to them in Japanese. "Charge! Charge!" he yelled above the din of battle and the remaining enemy soldiers obeyed his orders, jumped to their feet, and were immediately cut down by the withering fire laid down by the Marauders. When no further enemy soldiers were left standing, fifty-four of them lay dead in and around the foxholes Bill's platoon had evacuated.

"Dang, that was some pretty smart thinking," Bill said to Roy.

"Sometimes it's an advantage to speak Japanese," Roy responded.

Their conversation was interrupted by the sound of approaching aircraft, and their spirits were raised as they watched the C47 supply planes begin to circle their small ridge top position.

"Man, I hope them flyboys are bringing us some water," Bill exclaimed.

"Me too," Roy responded. "I just hope they can drop it on us and not on the Japs."

They watched as the first plane approached and heard the enemy firing at the defenseless aircraft. The Marauders began shooting into the surrounding jungle in hopes of lessening the fire on the approaching airplanes. The first plane came in very low, and Bill could see the crewmen in the doorway as they shoved their cargo out of the door. He watched as the first parachutes opened and saw the long plastic appendages containing water float lazily to the ground behind them. The lifesaving water had no sooner touched down when several men from each platoon were dispatched to retrieve it. Under fire from the enemy in the surrounding jungle, the men raced to the water containers, cut them free from their parachutes, and carried them back to their respective platoons. The process was repeated each time the supply planes passed overhead until all of the water had been delivered.

"I've got to hand it to those flyboys," Roy said. "Not a single parachute landed in enemy hands."

"You and me both," Bill exclaimed between gulps of fresh water. "Someday I hope I can do something to repay them."

16

APRIL 3, 1944
DINJAN AIRBASE, INDIA

GLANCING AT HIS watch, Sam saw that is was only one o'clock in the morning. It seemed as if he had been lying in his charpoy for a week, and yet it had only been three hours since lights out. Once again, the oppressive heat and countless sounds of insects and animals in the surrounding jungle joined forces to deprive him of the sleep he so desperately wanted. Lying there in the dark, he thought about the two missions he had flown the previous day. He felt good about being part of the effort to provide much-needed water to the trapped soldiers of the Marauders Second Division, and he fervently hoped the howitzers they delivered to the Third Division just north of Nhpum Ga would enable them to break the stranglehold the Japanese had on their besieged brethren. He replayed in his mind the scenes he had witnessed of dead bodies stacked three and four deep around the perimeter of the Marauder's defenses and the bloated corpses of the pack animals in the midst of the chaos below. His stomach churned once again at the memory of the stench that rose from the battle field, and he wondered how anyone was able to tolerate it day and night. He remembered the panic he felt the first time he saw and heard bullets tearing into their aircraft and wondered what it must be like for the soldiers on the ground. He came to the conclusion that for them war was worse than hell.

Finally, his eyes began to grow heavy, and as he began to drift off into sleep, he hoped the coming day would bring mail from home. He had not received any mail since leaving Sicily, and he prayed it would soon catch up with him. The blessings of restful sleep were just beginning to take hold when he was jerked awake by the cough of a large jungle cat.

The sound came from just outside their basha, and Sam's senses came to full alert when he heard a scuffing noise outside the window near his head. He waited tensely for five minutes, but no further sounds could be heard. He looked around, envying the other men in the basha, who continued to sleep oblivious to what had happened. Eventually, sheer exhaustion took over, and he finally fell asleep. However, it was not a restful sleep, because he was visited once again by his recurring nightmare of being chased and caught by Japanese soldiers in the jungle.

Bobby Joe was already up and half-dressed when reveille came. Sam reluctantly hauled himself out of bed to face another day.

"Did you hear that big cat outside the basha last night?" Sam asked his friend.

"I didn't hear a thing. Y'all musta been dreamin'."

"You have to be asleep to dream, and I definitely wasn't asleep. It sounded like it was right outside the window. I'm going to check," said Sam as he finished tying his shoes.

Both men exited the basha and walked around to the side where Sam's window was located. They carefully scanned the ground as they walked, and there in the loose dirt under the window, they found the paw prints of a large cat.

"Whoa, Nellie, y'all weren't dreamin' t' all. Look at the size a that print. It must be seven inches across. That's gotta be a tiger and a big feller ta boot. I seen cougar tracks in West Texas, but I ain't never seen anythin' that big."

"Well, what can we do about it? I don't feel comfortable with a cat that size prowling around," Sam said.

"He ain't done no harm yet, but we'll report it ta the CO after breakfast and let him ponder over it," Bobby Joe replied as they walked toward the mess hall.

After a standard breakfast of powdered eggs, Spam, and powdered coffee, they went to the company headquarters building for the day's briefing. Upon entering the briefing room, they could tell immediately from the map hanging on the wall that they were going to be returning to Nhpum Ga. A chill settled over Sam as he remembered yesterday's missions, and he took a seat just as Captain Cummings entered to begin the briefing.

"Good morning, gentlemen. Before I get into the details of today's mission, I would like to commend you on your excellent performance yesterday. You hit your target dead on and not an ounce of water was lost to the enemy. That was quite a feat, considering two of you were on your first mission. You will get a chance to repeat that performance today with a little twist. You are once again going to deliver supplies to the Second Division at Nhpum Ga. The loads will contain their regular provisions plus some reading materials, but you will also be dropping a special container to the Japs. That container is set up with a few regular supplies of K-rations, some extraneous reading material, and a dummy message addressed to Lieutenant Colonel McGee, the commander of the Second Division. The message conveys false information about a paratroop drop tomorrow behind the Japanese forces surrounding Nhpum Ga. The Third Division is going to make a push tomorrow to break through to the Second, and we are hoping the Japs believe the ruse and withdraw some troops from Nhpum Ga to meet the false threat. If they do, it will make the Third Division's job easier. After your drop at Nhpum Ga, you will proceed to Ledo for another load to be delivered to General Wingate and his Chindit troops. They have a secure drop zone ready for you, so you shouldn't receive any enemy fire there. You have your work cut out for you today, gentlemen. Good luck."

"Well, doggie," said Bobby Joe, "this is gonna be an interestin' day. Let's go git saddled up, Sam."

They checked the crew assignments for the day and were pleased to see that Delbert would be flying with them once again. Together, the three men walked to their assigned aircraft and began checking that the load was secured for flight. They found the specially marked container that was to be dropped to the enemy, and Bobby Joe then proceeded to instruct them on the procedure that would be used for this drop.

"These containers weigh 'bout 250 pounds apiece, so we're gonna kick 'em out rather than toss 'em out. I'll show ya how it's done," said Bobby Joe, "Y'all move one a them containers in front a the door."

Sam and Delbert moved a container in front of the door, and Bobby Joe lay down on his back behind the container facing the open door. He brought his knees up and placed his feet firmly on the center of the container.

"When we git ta the target, I'll take up a position like this, and y'all will put containers in front a the door. When the pilot turns on the green light over the cockpit door, I'll kick the containers out as fast as y'all kin put them in the doorway. We should be able ta kick out three containers on each pass. I figger it'll take bout seven passes ta git everythin' kicked out," explained Bobby Joe. "Y'all got any questions?"

"How are we going to handle that special container with the dummy message for the Japs?" Sam asked.

"Well, I figger durin' our first pass that'll be the last container we kick out, but I'll delay kickin' it 'til I'm sure it'll land in Jap hands."

Everyone was satisfied with the procedures, and they were soon on their way back to Nhpum Ga. Sam and Delbert spent the time en route talking about their families, and Bobby Joe stretched out on top of the canisters and slept until they arrived over the target area. The situation on the ground didn't look any different to Sam as they circled overhead. He could still see the dead bodies of men and animals strewn around the battleground, and his stomach tensed at the memories of the smells they had encountered the day before. The fact that they could expect to receive ground fire again today didn't do much for his nerves either. However, he didn't have long to think about those things, because the pilot began his descent for their first pass over the drop zone.

"Okay, y'all git those first three loads up ta the doorway and be sure the special canister is the third one," ordered Bobby Joe.

Sam and Delbert wrestled the first container into the doorway and moved the other two into positions where they could be quickly shoved into place. Bobby Joe took up the kicker position behind the first container and waited for the pilot to give the green light. As they approached the drop zone, the familiar ping of bullets ripping into their aircraft could be heard. At that moment, the pilot turned on the green light, and Bobby Joe kicked the first container out. Sam and Delbert immediately shoved the second container into place, and it was instantly kicked out. In quick succession, the third container was positioned, but Bobby Joe waited ten seconds before kicking it out of the aircraft. The three men watched as the parachutes opened and the first two containers drifted down for perfect landings among the waiting Marauders. The third container drifted beyond the Marauders' perimeter and landed in the jungle, where they could see Japanese soldiers scurrying to retrieve it.

The aircraft made two more passes with Bobby Joe in the kicker position, and then he announced it was time for Delbert and Sam to get some experience kicking. Delbert was first to assume the kicking duties, but due to his light weight, he was not able to kick the containers out as quickly as needed on his first attempt. This resulted in two of his first three loads landing in enemy hands.

"Aw cripes, Bobby Joe," Delbert exclaimed. "You better do this, I'm dumping half the supplies in Jap hands."

"No, y'all stay right there," Bobby Joe commanded. "The only way yer gonna learn ta do this right is by doin' it."

The next pass over the target, Delbert delivered all three loads on target. Needless to say, he felt much better about his performance, and then Bobby Joe announced it was Sam's turn. Delbert and Bobby Joe positioned three canisters for the next drop, and Sam assumed the kicker position. The floor of the cargo bay felt hard and cold against his back, and he could feel the vibration of the engines throughout his body. He shifted position and placed his feet firmly against the first canister. At first, he felt uncomfortable in the kicker position but soon forgot about his discomfort as he felt the C47 begin to descend for the drop. He tensed his leg muscles and pressed his feet tightly against the canister in anticipation of the kick. He was determined to get all three loads into the hands of the Marauders and turned his head to the right so he could see the green light the moment it came on.

As he waited for the light to come on, his attention was drawn to a line of holes suddenly appearing in the floor of the cargo bay to his right. He watched in fascination as the holes progressed steadily toward the spot where he was lying. They took on the appearance of a living thing as they moved toward him, and then, just as abruptly as they started, the holes stopping only three inches from his head. Sam's fascination with the holes quickly turned into mind-numbing fear when he realized the holes had been made by high-caliber machine gun bullets passing through the aircraft floor.

Sam had missed being killed by just three inches. His immediate reaction was to roll away from the evil holes; but before he could move, the green light came on. Putting his fear aside, Sam pushed with all his strength against the canister. To his amazement, the load disappeared out the door and another took its place in the blink of an eye. He quickly repositioned his feet and pushed again and then again as a third canister was placed in front of him. Before he realized it, he had kicked his first three loads from the aircraft, and he watched with a great deal of satisfaction as all three loads drifted gently into the waiting hands of the Marauders below.

"Y'all done a good job, Sam," Bobby Joe said, "I don't think I coulda laid there with them bullet holes approachin' my head."

Sam could only give Bobby Joe a weak smile, and then all three men prepared for their last pass over the drop zone. The final drop went smoothly, and the remaining supplies were delivered on target to the Marauders. As the C47 winged its way toward Ledo, all three crewmen stretched out for some much-needed rest. However, Sam's eyes kept straying to the line of bullet holes that stretched across the empty cargo bay floor.

APRIL 3, 1944
NHPUM GA, BURMA

The situation for Sergeants Wesley and Matamoto and the rest of the Second Division had not changed much. They were still surrounded and outnumbered four to one by the Japanese. More of their pack animals had been killed and lay rotting within their perimeter, and perhaps twice as many dead Japanese were strewn all about in front of them. They were thirsty, hungry, and suffering from the stifling heat of the jungle, and to add to their misery, the putrid stench of decaying flesh all around them was almost unbearable. Because of the enormous amount of labor it would take and the limited space within their confines, they found it nearly impossible to bury the bodies of the pack animals. They tried to bury a few of the animals at night, but the enemy crept close to their lines under the cover of darkness and threw hand grenades at the sound of scraping shovels.

Bill and Roy were clearing debris from their foxhole. The usual morning attack by the Japanese had just been repelled, and the number of dead bodies in front of them had increased significantly.

"You would think the Japs would realize these attacks are costing them a lot of men," Bill said as he shoved loose dirt from the foxhole with his helmet.

"They have more men to lose than we do, and sooner or later they're going to find a weakness in our defenses, and then it will be all over for us," Roy responded as he peered through the smoke and haze created by the recent conflict. "Hey, am I seeing what I think I'm seeing?" Roy whispered.

Bill looked up and saw a Japanese soldier walking toward their foxhole. The soldier seemed dazed and was mumbling to himself, apparently totally unaware of where he was. The soldier approached and was about to step into their foxhole when Roy raised his rifle and shot him.

"Do you think he was coming for morning coffee?" Bill asked in disbelief.

"I don't know," answered Roy, "but I wasn't going to wait around to find out."

Their attention was drawn away from the dead soldier by the sound of an approaching aircraft.

"Hey, looks like the flyboys are bringing us some more supplies," Bill observed.

"Yeah, it's always nice to get fresh supplies even if it is only K- and C-rations," Roy responded.

The two men observed the C47 approaching and noted the usual gunfire directed at the plane by the enemy. As the aircraft zoomed overhead, they watched as three bundles were ejected from the plane. They saw the parachutes open and waited expectantly as the bundles floated down toward them. Two of the bundles landed safely in the interior of their perimeter just a few feet from their foxhole, but the third came down in the area occupied by the Japanese.

"It looks like we're in luck today, Roy. We get first pick from these canisters," Bill exclaimed as he crawled quickly toward the nearest canister. He tore into the bundle with his combat knife and began unloading the ever present packages of K- and C-rations. Finally, with a whoop of joy, he held a package up in the air and yelled, "Looks like they sent us some reading material." And he tossed the package to his friend.

Roy ripped into the package eager to see what reading materials had been delivered. By the time Bill returned to the foxhole, he found Roy sitting there with a look of total disbelief on his face.

"What's up? Is something wrong with the reading material?" Bill inquired.

"*Wrong* isn't the word for it," Roy answered as he held up three novels written in French and an English language manual titled *Symposium on Gynecology.*

After a brief moment of silence, Bill exclaimed, "This is great, they sent us a secret weapon."

"What the hell are you talking about?" Roy lamented.

"Well, we'll just show the Japs what the army sends us to read, and they'll laugh themselves to death. The war will be over in no time," Bill explained with a straight face.

Roy threw the manual at his buddy and turned his attention to a package of K-rations.

APRIL 3, 1944
THE SKIES OVER NORTHERN BURMA

Sam and the rest of the crew picked up their next load at Ledo Airbase and were now on their way to deliver it to General Wingate who was operating with his force of Chindits behind enemy lines in Burma. The load consisted of crates of various types of ammunition, food, and water for Wingate's troops. The crates were heavier than normal, and each one weighed approximately 250 pounds. On the way to the drop zone, they were encountering early monsoon thunderstorms, so the visibility outside was poor and the air was rough. Before they took off, Bobby Joe had them lash the crates securely to the front and central sections of the cargo bay. This was done to ensure a proper center of gravity so the pilots could fly the aircraft safely. During training, the importance of maintaining a proper center of gravity had been drummed into all flight crew members. An airplane could become unstable and crash if the center of gravity was not kept within certain limits. The rough weather they were currently experiencing was putting a strain on the lashings, and Bobby Joe had a concerned look on his face.

"Y'all check the lashings on the crates up front, and I'll check 'em back here," Bobby Joe instructed.

Due to the bouncing of the airplane, Sam and Delbert had some difficulty making their way to the front of the cargo bay. Once there, they began inspecting and tightening the ropes that held the crates in place. They were almost done with their inspection when the plane encountered a particularly severe area of turbulence. The C47 pitched and yawed violently, and the men were thrown to the floor. In the back of the plane, they heard a warning shout from Bobby Joe and looked up in time to see the lashings on three crates break loose. The three heavy crates began sliding toward the back of the plane. Bobby Joe was lying helplessly against the rear bulkhead and was in danger of being crushed by the runaway crates.

In the cockpit, both pilots were applying all their strength to control the wild gyrations of the airplane. The sudden shift of 750 pounds of cargo toward the back of the plane caught them completely by surprise as the center of gravity shifted toward the rear. The nose of the plane rose, and their airspeed dropped quickly, threatening a stall and complete loss of control. They applied full power to both engines and tried to push the nose down, but their efforts were futile. The C47 shuddered as it continued to lose airspeed and approached an imminent stall.

Back in the cargo bay, Sam and Delbert were unable to regain their feet and lie helpless as the increased pitch of the airplane accelerated the crates toward Bobby Joe who was also unable to move. Sam looked into Bobby Joe's eyes and saw not fear but acceptance of the fate that was fast approaching.

Knowing he could not help, Sam reached out his hand toward his friend. Bobby Joe watched as the crates approached, and he felt every muscle in his body tense in anticipation of the impact. However, fate is a fickle thing and so are thunderstorms. Just as the crates were about to crush him against the bulkhead, an updraft caught the tail of the plane, causing the nose to pitch steeply down. Miraculously, the crates stopped just inches from his body. They then reversed direction and slid back toward the front of the airplane where they crashed into the crates that were still secured. Fortunately for everyone aboard, the shift in weight toward the front of the plane placed the center of gravity of the C47 back into normal range, and the pilots were finally able regain control and avoid a stall.

Sam, Delbert, and a much-relieved Bobby Joe hastily set about securing the rogue crates, and they soon had everything tied down and safe once again.

"I guess ole Saint Pete's gonna hafta wait another day fer me," Bobby Joe said as they all sat down to rest.

The remainder of the flight to the drop zone was uneventful, and the skies began to clear as they reached their target. As they circled above, they could see the drop zone was delineated by white panels, which they assumed were made from used parachute material. Bobby Joe had them unlash the first crate and position it in the doorway, while he attached the static line to the parachute rip cord. As the plane set up for the first drop, Sam stood on the left side of the doorway, and Delbert stood on the right side. Both men were ready to help shove the crate from the aircraft, while Bobby Joe took up the kicker position. Perhaps because of his recent close call with death or just the frenzy of preparing for the drop, Bobby Joe failed to tell Sam and Delbert about the special maneuver the pilots would use to discharge heavy loads.

The air was still a little rough as they approached the drop zone, and in order to maintain their balance, Sam and Delbert held on to the door sill with one hand, keeping the other hand free to help eject the crate. When they reached the drop point, the pilot turned on the green light and executed his special maneuver by lowering the left wing slightly, applying right rudder to keep the aircraft from turning and pushing forward on the control wheel to raise the tail of the plane slightly. This had the effect of slanting the load toward the doorway and lightening it momentarily. Bobby Joe was ready for the maneuver and kicked the crate easily out of the plane. When Sam felt the unusual movement of the aircraft, he immediately let go of the crate and held on to the door sill with both hands. However, Delbert was not so quick to react and lost his balance while still hanging on to the crate. To his surprise and everyone else's, he was jerked from the airplane and found himself plummeting toward the ground.

"My god, Delbert fell out," Sam shouted in disbelief.

After the shock of falling from the plane, Delbert realized he was still holding on to the straps around the crate with his left hand. In desperation, he immediately grabbed hold of the strap with his right hand and clung to the crate for dear life. When the parachute snapped open, the jolt caused him to lose his grip with his right hand, and he felt the strap beginning to slide from his left hand. He struggled to maintain his tenuous hold as the ground rose rapidly to meet him, but it was no use. He could not hang on.

Back in the plane, Bobby Joe scrambled to the doorway, and both men looked out. They could not see Delbert anywhere, and their hearts fell in the belief they had lost their friend.

"There. There he is hanging from the bottom of the crate by one hand," shouted Sam just as their view was blocked by the descending parachute.

"I hope that crate didn't land on top a him," Bobby Joe said as he hurried toward the cockpit to tell the pilots what happened.

Sam remained in the doorway, hoping he could see what happened to Delbert. The plane continued to circle, and in a little while, Bobby Joe came back to give Sam the news.

"The pilots talked ta the troops on the ground, and they told him Delbert's okay. He let go just a foot above the ground, and the crate missed him by inches. He did break his leg in the landing though. They're gonna patch him up and send him back in one a them light recon planes. They also said the next time y'all send replacements ta pick a better way a doin' it."

Relieved that their crew had cheated death twice in one day, Bobby Joe and Sam set about delivering the remainder of the crates. Both men knew they may not always be so lucky.

17

APRIL 3, 1944
MOSHANNON VALLEY, PENNSYLVANIA

EVERY MORNING, AT ten o'clock, Eleanor stood at her living room window and watched as their mailman, Ed Fleagle, delivered mail on her street. As in most small towns, the mail carrier was well-known, and everyone knew and liked Ed. Eleanor liked Ed too, but ever since Sam had been shipped overseas, she always experienced a mixture anticipation and fear when the mailman approached her house. She felt anticipation at the prospect that he would deliver a letter from Sam and fear that he would deliver a letter from the government announcing that her beloved husband was missing in action or worse. She faithfully wrote to Sam three or four times a week, and she would usually receive a couple of letters a week from him. Understandably, his letters had come less often during the period he was being shipped overseas, but they increased once again when he arrived in Africa. Because his mail was censored, she never knew exactly where he was, but his last letter had indicated he was training for combat missions and would be flying real missions soon. That was almost two weeks ago, and she had not heard from him since.

The sounds of Billy playing in the next room and the occasional movement of the unborn child in her womb did nothing to ease the apprehension she felt this morning as the mailman approached her front porch. Deep down, she knew something had changed in Sam's world, and she sensed he was in danger. Her anxiety was further heightened when, instead of placing letters in her mailbox as he usually did, Ed came to the door and knocked. She hurried to the door and then stood paralyzed with her hand on the doorknob. It couldn't be good news; the mailman never came to the door. She couldn't bring herself to open the door, and Ed knocked again a little louder.

"Mama, door," she heard Billy say.

"I know, Billy, Mommy's going to answer it."

Mustering all her courage, Eleanor opened the door and was relieved to see Ed standing there with a package in his hands.

"Good morning, Mrs. Huber, I have a package for you all the way from Casablanca, Morocco," he said with a smile. "It looks like Sam picked something up for you in his travels."

"Thank you, Ed," she said as she accepted the package.

"I noticed you had a worried look on your face when you opened the door. Is everything okay with Sam?" he asked.

"I haven't heard from him in about two weeks, and I'm afraid of receiving bad news," Eleanor responded.

"Oh, don't let that bother you," he said, "I see it happen all the time. The army isn't the most efficient mail processor, and letters can get delayed anywhere along the line. I'm sure he's all right."

"Thanks, Ed, that makes me feel better. Have a good day."

"The same to you, Mrs. Huber. I'm sure you'll be getting a letter from Sam soon," Ed responded as he continued on his way.

Eleanor closed the door and hurried to the kitchen to open the package. Her anxiety was now replaced by the excitement of receiving a package from Sam.

"What's that, Mama?" Billy asked.

"A package from Daddy," she replied as she took a paring knife and began cutting the wrapping paper around the parcel.

"Daddy come home?" Billy inquired.

"Not for a while, Billy, but Daddy sent us a present," she answered as she removed the last of wrapping paper and opened the box inside.

The contents of the box were wrapped in pages from a newspaper, which was printed in letters that appeared to be Arabic. She looked at the strange symbols and wondered what they meant. Her memory flashed back to the time in Atlanta that she and Sam went to see the movie *Casablanca*. At the time, Casablanca seemed such a faraway and inaccessible place, and now Sam had been there. Her excitement mounted even more with the realization she was holding in her hands things from that very city. Her excitement grew even more when she discovered a note from Sam among the wrapped items. She hurriedly opened it and began to read.

Dearest Eleanor,

Enclosed are a few things I picked up in Casablanca. The slippers are for you, May, and Lynette. They're made of kidskin and are very comfortable. The toy airplane is for Billy. It's a handmade wooden model of a C47. That's the type of airplane I will be flying in. There's also something for the new baby when he comes. Tell everyone I said hello and I will write soon.

Love,
Sam

Tears came to Eleanor's eyes as she carefully removed the contents of the package. She had received letters from Sam since he was in Casablanca, but he never wrote anything about sending a package. She removed the wrapping from the slippers and set them aside, admiring their delicate workmanship and the softness of the leather.

Next, she picked up the package containing the model airplane and removed it from its wrapping. It was an exquisitely crafted model painted in the colors and markings used by the army. It was authentic in every detail, including a name painted on the nose. The name read Billy Boy. Eleanor cradled the toy in her hands. Tightness gripped her heart as the model airplane reminded her of the dangers Sam would be facing in the real thing. She said a silent prayer that he would always be safe, especially when he was flying.

"What's that, Mama?" Billy asked as he tugged on his mother's dress.

"It's a toy airplane Daddy sent to you. Isn't it nice?" she said as she handed the airplane to him.

The look of happiness on Billy's face made Eleanor feel warm inside, and she watched her son as he took the airplane and sat down on the floor to play with it. He held it up in the air and made motor sounds like it was flying. She knew Billy had an affinity for airplanes, just as his father did, but she hoped that love would never lead her son into war.

As Billy played with his airplane, she removed the final package from the box. When she picked it up, she heard a slight rattling sound emanating from it. At that exact moment, the child in her womb moved. Removing the newspaper wrapping, she found a small dried gourd that was painted in wonderfully bright colors and exotic symbols. The neck of the gourd was just the right size for a baby's hand, and the seeds inside rattled with the slightest movement. She placed the gourd against her swollen stomach and moved it so that it rattled. Once again, her unborn child moved as if in response to the noise of the rattle.

Still holding the rattle, she walked into the living room and saw her sister-in-law approaching from her home across the street. Before May could knock, Eleanor opened the door and greeted her with a smile and a big hug.

"I saw the mailman deliver a package, and from the smile on your face, it must be from Sam," May said excitedly.

"Oh yes, he sent some beautiful things. Come and see."

May followed Eleanor into the kitchen where Billy was still playing contentedly with his new airplane.

"And what have you got there, young man?" May asked Billy.

"Zoom," Billy replied as he held the airplane up for her to see.

"Sam had that made for him, and it even has his name on it," Eleanor explained.

"What a nice thought," May said, "and what is that in your hand?"

"It's a rattle for the new baby. It's made from a gourd. Watch," Eleanor answered as she placed the gourd against her stomach and rattled it.

Once again, the unborn child moved in response to the sound of the rattle, and this time, Eleanor could not only feel the movement, but both women could see it move through Eleanor's dress.

"My goodness," exclaimed May, "it's as if he knows the rattle is for him. Oh my, I guess I shouldn't call it him since we don't know what sex it will be."

"That's okay, May. Whatever it is, it will be welcome. Sam sent something for you and Lynette too," Eleanor said as she retrieved a pair of slippers and presented them to May.

"Oh, how delicately made and soft they are," May said as she slipped them on her feet. "They're so comfortable. Do you know what kind of leather this is?"

"Sam's note says they are kidskin," Eleanor responded, handing the note to May.

"This was sent from Casablanca, and we've heard from Sam since he left there. I guess that doesn't explain why we haven't heard from him recently," May said.

"No, it doesn't, but the mailman said it isn't unusual for the mail from overseas to get delayed," Eleanor replied, trying to sound convincing.

May could see the tears forming in the corners of Eleanor's eyes, and she walked over put her arm around her. "What's the matter, Eleanor? Tell me what's bothering you."

"Oh, May, it's so hard not knowing from one moment to the next where he is, what he's doing, if he's well or maybe hurt and suffering. He could be dead right now, and we wouldn't even know it," sobbed Eleanor.

"Don't even think those things, Eleanor. You have enough to worry about with Billy and your pregnancy. Sometimes it's better not knowing what Sam's going through. You know he can't be in danger every minute of the day, so just have faith that God is watching over him and everything will be okay."

"You're right, May. My nerves have been on edge lately. I guess being pregnant at a time like this doesn't help either."

"I was getting ready to go to the grocery store when I saw the mailman. Why don't you put a jacket on Billy and come with me. It will do you good to get out," May said.

"That's a good idea, May. Would you put Billy's jacket on him while I get my rationing books? I hope there's something available that I can use this week."

"I know what you mean," replied May, "I saw in the paper that they have reduced the amount of sugar that we can buy. I wonder what is going on now."

"I recently read that there is a shortage of sugar, because the ships that normally haul it have been diverted to hauling war supplies," Eleanor explained. "The article also said that soldiers use about twice as much sugar as we civilians do and that last year people applied for more canning sugar than they really needed."

"I guess that make sense," May responded. "Speaking of canning, Paul and I have decided to double the size of our victory garden this year. We'll be able to can more. We know you won't be able to garden in your condition, so we are going to grow more to share with you."

"You and Paul have been so good to me. I don't know how I can ever repay you."

"Letting us watch Billy while you work nights in the sewing factory is payment enough," May explained. "How are things going at the factory anyway?"

"Well, since I don't know how to drive, it's been a big help working on the same shift with Lynette and being able to ride to the factory with her," Eleanor answered. "The work doesn't bother me until we begin sewing combat clothing for the army. Then I wonder whether the pieces I'm sewing will be something Sam will use someday. It's a constant reminder that he isn't here."

"Remember what I just told you about having faith," May cautioned. "Now let's get to the A&P before everything is gone."

The A&P was only a block away, and it was a nice spring day, so the two women walked slowly with Billy between them, each holding one of his hands. Occasionally, he would lift his feet off the ground and hang suspended between them, giggling and saying "Zoom, Billy, fly." His youthful exuberance brought a smile to their faces and comments from the people they met along the way.

Eventually, they reached the grocery store, and Eleanor picked up a shopping basket and took Billy firmly by the hand. The women scanned the list put out by the Office of Price Administration that detailed the items their ration stamps enabled them to purchase for the week and then proceeded to search the store for the things they wanted. Eleanor was careful to keep Billy in the center of the aisle and well away from the stocked shelves. She knew all too well what those busy little hands could do if he could reach those shelves.

The women shopped and commented on the change in ration points required for many items. At one point, Eleanor picked up a can of peaches but put it back on the shelf when she saw it required ration stamps worth sixteen points. May picked the can up and put it in her cart.

"I know Billy likes peaches, and I have enough points, so I'll get them for you," May explained.

"Thank you, May. Things are either not available or they take too many points to buy," Eleanor lamented. "Instead of canned soup, I did get some Aunt Jemima green pea-flavored dry-soup mix. At least it doesn't require any ration stamps."

"I got some of that too, only I got the navy bean flavor," May said. "Looks like we're done here. Let's go check out."

They got in line at the checkout counter and waited their turn. As they waited, Eleanor thought about the rationing process, and she took out the set of instructions that came with her rationing book and read once again:

> *Your first ration book has been issued to you, originally containing 28 war ration stamps. Other books may be issued at later dates. The following instructions apply to your first book and will apply to any later books, unless otherwise ordered by the Office of Price Administration. In order to obtain a later book, the first book must be turned in. You should preserve War Rations Books with the greatest possible care.*
>
> *1 – From the time to time the Office of Price Administration may issue orders rationing certain products. After the dates indicated by such orders, these products can be purchased only through the use of War Rations Books containing valid War Ration Stamps.*
>
> *2 – The orders of the Office of Price Administration will designate the stamps to be used for the purchase of a particular rationed product, the period during which*

each of these stamps may be used, and the amounts which may be bought with each stamp.

3 – Stamps become valid for use only when and as directed by the orders of the Office of Price Administration.

4 – Unless otherwise announced, the Ration Week is from Saturday midnight to the following Saturday midnight.

5 – War Ration Stamps may be used in any retail store in the United States.

6 – War Ration Stamps may be used only by or for the person named and described in the War Ration Book.

7 – Every person must see that this War Ration Book is kept in a safe place and properly used. Parents are responsible for the safekeeping and use of their children's War Ration Book.

8 – When you buy any rationed product, the proper stamp must be detached in the presence of the storekeeper, his employee, or the person making the delivery on his behalf. If a stamp is torn out of the War Ration Book in any other way than above indicated, it becomes void. If a stamp is partly torn or mutilated and more than one half of it remains in the book, it is valid. Otherwise it becomes void.

9- If your War Ration Book is lost, destroyed, stolen or mutilated, you should report that fact to the local Ration Board.

10 – If you enter a hospital, or other institution, and expect to be there for more than 10 days, you must turn your War Ration Book over to the person in charge. It will be returned to you upon your request when you leave.

11 – When a person dies, his War Ration Book must be returned to the local Ration Board, in accordance with the regulations.

12 – If you have any complaints, questions, or difficulties regarding your War Ration Book, consult your local Ration Board.

May noticed what Eleanor was doing and commented, "The whole process is complicated and mind boggling, isn't it?"

"Yes, it is," Eleanor answered, "The war has certainly made our life more difficult, but at least we haven't been subjected to the evil and destruction that is taking place in Europe and Asia."

Their turn came to checkout, and they unloaded their groceries onto the counter. In accordance with the law, they tore the necessary stamps from their ration books in the presence of the clerk and handed her the cash needed to purchase the items. The clerk packed their purchases into the cloth shopping bags that each woman had brought along, and with their groceries and Billy in tow, they returned to May's house where they sat down to talk over a relaxing cup of tea.

"It's so depressing to go grocery shopping anymore," Eleanor complained.

"Yes, and with never knowing what you can buy from week to week or how much you can buy, it's difficult to plan meals ahead of time," May responded.

"It's not only food that's a problem, but clothing too," Eleanor continued. "Silk and nylon items are really hard to get, and Billy is growing so fast I'm having a problem finding shoes for him."

"Rationing is affecting every part of our life," May lamented. "With gasoline limited to only four gallons a week, we can't even go for a Sunday drive anymore. After a hard week in the shop, Paul used to look forward to those Sunday drives."

"With me on night shift and Paul on days, I don't seem much of him anymore," Eleanor said. "How are things going for him at the machine shop?"

"With the government collecting every possible ounce of metal for the war, it's been difficult keeping the machines going. Most of their work now is repairing machinery for the coal mines. Since the mines are essential to the war effort, they can get what they need to keep things running," May explained.

At that moment, May's phone rang, and she excused herself to go into the living room to answer it. Eleanor sat sipping her tea in the kitchen, and she could see May as she answered the phone in the next room. She watched as May listened to the person on the phone and then she saw May's body stiffen and knew immediately that something was terribly wrong. Hurrying into the living room, Eleanor caught her sister-in-law just as she dropped the phone and began to swoon.

"What's wrong, May?" Eleanor asked as she helped her into a chair.

May could not answer. Her complexion was pasty white, and her heart was racing. Finally, she recovered enough to speak.

"There's been an accident at the machine shop. Paul's been taken to the hospital in Philipsburg. It's serious, Eleanor, very serious."

"We've got to get you to the hospital," Eleanor exclaimed, "but neither of us knows how to drive."

"Paul's boss is coming to pick me up now. Will you go with me, Eleanor?"

"Of course I will. We'll have to take Billy. I'll get him ready."

Eleanor had Billy and May ready by the time Paul's supervisor, Frank Hanson, arrived. He helped them into the back seat of the car and began the five-mile trip to the Philipsburg hospital.

"What happened, Frank? Is Paul going to be all right?" May asked.

"He was turning a large piece of steel on our biggest lathe when the sleeve of his coveralls got caught in the spinning machine. His upper body was pulled into the machine."

"Is he dead, Frank?" May asked, her voice wavering.

"He was still alive when we got him out of the machine, but he was pretty badly injured, and he's lost a lot of blood."

May could ask no more questions and buried her head in Eleanor's shoulder and wept until they arrived at the hospital. Eleanor didn't know what to do and kept telling her everything would be okay, even though she wasn't sure it would be. Frank dropped them off at the emergency room entrance and then went to park the car. When they entered the emergency room door, they knew immediately by the way the nurses and orderlies were scurrying about that an emergency was in progress. The walk down the long hallway to the emergency waiting room was the longest either woman could remember. They took a seat and waited and soon Frank came in and sat with them.

"You don't have to wait, Frank," May said. "I know you have a shop to run, and you're a busy man."

"I've worked with Paul for over fifteen years, May. I couldn't leave him or you now. I'll be here if you need anything."

At that moment, a nurse came by. "Are you Mrs. Miller?" she asked.

"Yes, do you know how my husband is doing?" May asked pleadingly.

"I'm sorry I don't know. I just wanted to tell you that he is in the emergency operating room, and Dr. Flynn is attending him. I'll let you know the minute we learn something."

May was somewhat relieved to hear that her uncle was working on Paul. She knew he was an excellent surgeon, and she had a lot of faith in him. As the minutes ticked by, May settled in to wait, and Eleanor kept Billy busy, showing him pictures in the waiting room's magazines. The minutes turned into an hour and one hour into two hours, and still there was no word from the operating room. Billy had long since fallen asleep, and the women sat lost in their own thoughts. Frank had gotten them coffee from the cafeteria and periodically excused himself to use the pay phone to check on the machine shop. Time dragged on.

Finally, Dr. Flynn appeared at the waiting room door. His smock was smeared with blood, and his face showed the weariness he felt inside. They all waited in silence as he approached them.

"I don't know how or why, May, but I think he's going to make it. By all rights, he should be dead. His right arm and shoulder were broken when he was pulled into the machine. He has a couple of broken ribs and lots of bruising and contusions on his body. His worst injuries were caused by trauma to his head. He lost a lot of blood from his head wounds and suffered a severe concussion. I stitched up a large section of his scalp and reattached his right ear. I'm afraid that ear won't look very pretty, but at least it will support the stem of his glasses. His biggest threat now is from the concussion, and we're monitoring that closely."

"Can we see him?" May asked.

"He's in the recovery room and heavily sedated, but you can go in for a few minutes. Just keep it short."

"How long do you think he will be hospitalized?" Frank inquired.

"If the concussion doesn't cause problems, he will probably be here about a week, and then it will take six to eight weeks before he can go back to work."

Frank could see the concern in May's face at the prospect of an extended period without pay. "It will be all right, May," he said. "Since he was hurt on the job, our insurance will cover the hospital bills, and we'll give him half pay until he can come back to work."

"Thank you, Frank, and thank you, Doctor. I'll go in and see him now," May said.

"You go with her, Eleanor," Frank said. "I'll watch over Billy until you come out."

Eleanor took May's hand as they walked to the recovery room. She could feel May's hand trembling. "Remember what you told me earlier about having faith," she said.

"I know," May responded, "but you know how difficult that can be."

Eleanor knew. She knew all too well as her thoughts turned to Sam. He was so far away, and she realized she could not be there if he was injured and maybe dying. She couldn't be there to comfort him and let him know how much she loved him. It tormented her that he was surrounded by the evil and tyranny of war, and she couldn't be there.

18

APRIL 4, 1944

DINJAN AIRBASE, INDIA

S AM AND BOBBY Joe were totally exhausted when they crawled into their charpoys. The harrowing events of the day had taken its toll on them physically and mentally. In spite of the heat and noise of the jungle, Sam felt the blessed relief of sleep approaching soon after his head hit the pillow. However, as he drifted off, a feeling of unease came over him. It was a feeling that something was wrong, not here in India, but at home. He didn't know if he felt uneasy because he still hadn't received mail from home or because of some unknown reason, but the feeling stayed with him until he finally succumbed to his exhaustion and slipped into a deep sleep.

Thankfully, his slumber was not disturbed by his recurring nightmare, and he slept soundly until the wee hours of the morning when he suddenly awoke not knowing what had disturbed him. A light rain was falling outside, and except for an occasional flash of distant lightning, the basha was pitching black. He lay very still, listening to the sounds around him. He strained his hearing, but no sound came except for the steady breathing of the sleeping men around him. After several minutes, he relaxed, thinking his imagination was playing tricks on him. He was almost asleep again when he thought he detected a faint unfamiliar sound coming from somewhere in the basha. Once again, he listened intently, not sure he had heard anything; but then he heard the sound again—only this time it seemed closer, and he was sure it came from within the basha. He couldn't quite place the sound, but it seemed like something soft brushing against an object. He listened closely, but all was silent. None of the other men in the basha stirred, and after an extended period of silence, he relaxed once again in anticipation of sleep.

He was in that dreamy state just before slumber when he felt the presence of something or someone nearby. Once again, his senses came to full alert, and he made a conscious effort not to move. He listened carefully, bringing all his senses to bear. He could see or hear nothing, and yet he was sure something was there. He was startled when someone at the other end of the room moved, but then all was silent once again. He was lying on his back, so he slowly moved his head to the right and scanned the darkness.

At first he saw nothing, but then attention was drawn to a slight movement at the foot of his bed. He couldn't make out what it was. It appeared to be an undistinguishable shadow against the darker background of the room. As he watched, the shadow moved, and he held his breath as it silently glided along the side of his bed. There was no sound as it moved, and it slowly drew nearer and stopped near the head of his bed. He could tell that it was something large, but due to the extreme darkness, he was unable to see what it was. His instincts told him this was something dangerous and evil, and the hairs on the nape of his neck stood erect. At that moment, a distant flash of lightning faintly illuminated the scene, and in that instant of light, Sam could see the large form of a tiger standing beside him.

The animal's head was enormous. Its eyes, momentarily reflecting light from the faraway lightning, gave the beast an evil, devil-like appearance. This was death incarnate staring directly at him.

Sam was frozen with fear, and his heart seemed to stop. His .45-caliber pistol hung on the wall not three feet away, and he cursed himself for not keeping it inside the mosquito netting with him. He knew the tiger could see that he was awake, and he feared any movement would cause it to attack. The animal stepped closer, and Sam could see its dim outline and smell its damp fur and the fetid odor of its breath. The tiger appeared to know its victim was helpless. The great beast took its time as it sniffed the mosquito netting as if testing its strength. Slowly it raised a huge paw and placed it against the puny impediment. The tiger's claws caught in the netting, and with a mighty swipe, it ripped the flimsy material away from the bed.

Luckily for Sam, the tiger became momentarily confused when the netting fell on top of the beast. This gave Sam time to roll out of the opposite side of his bed, but he was still not within reach of his pistol. The tiger roared and thrashed angrily beneath the netting as it lashed out with mighty paws in an attempt to free itself. The noise and commotion instantly aroused the other men in the basha, and shouts of confusion came from every direction. Sam was struggling to keep his charpoy between himself and the tiger when a shot rang out. Taking the nearest avenue of escape, the angry tiger, still shrouded in mosquito netting, leapt through the screening of the open window beside Sam's bed. He could hear the angry beast crashing through the jungle as it made its escape.

Confusion reigned within the basha, and someone finally lit a kerosene lantern, illuminating the scene inside of the room. Bobby Joe stood in the middle of the room with a smoking pistol aimed at the ceiling. Rain slowly dripped through the hole he had blown in the roof. Sam struggled to crawl out from under the shambles of his overturned bed, and the other three men stood around with bewildered looks on their faces.

"What happened? What were you shooting at Bobby Joe?" one of the men asked.

"Danged if I know," Bobby Joe answered. "I heard this god-awful commotion and roar right by my bed. I figgered it was some kind a animal so I grabbed my pistol from under my pillow and fired a shot inta the roof. Did y'all git a look at it, Sam?"

"It was a big tiger," Sam answered shakily. "It was trying to get at me through the mosquito netting, but thankfully, your shot scared it away."

"Hey, y'all looka the tracks on the floor," Bobby Joe exclaimed as he pointed his pistol at the floor.

The men gathered around and could plainly see large wet footprints on the floor. The prints clearly indicated that the tiger entered through the open door of the basha and then meandered from one side of the room to the other until it reached the foot of Sam's bed. It then continued along Sam's bed where it stopped. Everyone shuddered when they realized that any one of them could have been a victim of the animal.

"Well, doggie, by the looks a them tracks, that was one big cat," Bobby Joe commented. "Dad gum, I wish I coulda got a clear shot at it."

"I'm glad you couldn't," Sam responded. "All we would have needed was a wounded tiger in here. Do you think it was the same cat that was outside the other night?"

"I would guess it was," Bobby Joe said as he looked at his watch. "It's almost time for reveille so we might as well git on up ta headquarters and report this ta the CO."

Everyone agreed, and they hurriedly got dressed. After helping Sam straighten up his bed, the five men armed themselves and stepped into the darkness outside their basha. It was immediately evident that Bobby Joe's shot had aroused most of the camp, because lights were burning in all the bashas and the men inside were calling back and forth trying to determine what had happened. When Sam and his roommates reached the headquarters building, the CO was already there.

"Do any of you men know what's going on?" Captain Cummings asked.

"Yes, sir," Sam answered. "We had a tiger in our basha, and we think it was the same one we reported yesterday."

"Are you sure it was a tiger?" queried the captain.

"Yes, sir. It tried to get at me through my mosquito netting. I got as close a look as I ever want to get of a tiger, sir," Sam responded.

"I spoke with the local plantation owner about your report yesterday," continued the captain. "He told me there have been reports of a tiger killing domestic animals in the area. So far, there have been no human killings, but with this morning's events, I don't think we can take any chances. I'll talk to our British hosts about organizing a tiger hunt right away."

"Whee, doggie sir, I sure would like to git a crack at that critter," Bobby Joe chimed in.

"We'll see private," Captain Cummings answered, "but for now I want you all to go get some breakfast and then report back here for the morning briefing."

With that, the men headed for the mess hall with Bobby Joe talking excitedly about a tiger hunt. After breakfast, Sam and Bobby Joe returned to the briefing room and sat waiting for their mission assignments. Sam noticed the map on the wall was indicating further missions to supply the Marauders at Nhpum Ga. He surmised from the map that the Second Division was still trapped, and he wondered how many of them had survived the night. His thoughts were interrupted when Captain Cummings entered the room.

"Good morning, men," the captain began, "As you can see from the map, we still have a critical situation at Nhpum Ga. The Second Division is still trapped and the Third and First Divisions are going to attempt to break through to them today. We have three basic missions today. First, we will be dropping dummy supplies to a make-believe force behind the enemy, in hopes of drawing some of them away from Nhpum Ga. Secondly, we will be dropping regular supplies and ammunition to all of the Marauder divisions. Both of these missions will originate here at Dinjan. The third mission will originate out of Ledo Airbase, and I currently have no idea what it involves. I can only tell you that it was requested by General Stillwell himself. Check the bulletin board for your mission assignments, and good luck, men."

Sam and Bobby Joe exited the briefing room and went to check the bulletin board. When they found their names on the mission list, they saw that Bobby Joe was assigned to the dummy supply mission, and Sam was assigned to the Ledo mission. Sam noted he was assigned to aircraft number 300 and took that as a good omen, since his house number back in Pennsylvania was 300.

"Whoa, nelly," Bobby Joe said. "Y'all got a double whammy today."

"What do you mean?" asked Sam.

"Well, y'all not only got a mission that nobody knows anythin' about, but y'all got plane number 400. That's Lieutenant Thomas's airplane."

"Besides being a practical joker, what's wrong with Lieutenant Thomas?" Sam asked.

"He's a joker fer sure, but he don't take kindly ta being shot at in a unarmed airplane." Bobby Joe continued.

"What do you mean by that?"

"Well, he's been known ta come back inta the cargo bay and shoot at the Japs with a Thompson submachine gun, and once, he brought a case a hand grenades aboard and tossed them at 'em."

"I can hardly blame him for that," Sam said. "Sometimes I'd like to shoot back too."

"Y'all just be ready fer anythin'," responded Bobby Joe, "and I'll see y'all tonight. Good luck."

Sam walked to the flight line and located the C47 number 300. Lieutenant Thomas and the copilot were already aboard and had the starboard engine running. When Sam climbed aboard, he was met by his fellow crew member Corporal Virgil "Wimpy" Hutton. Wimpy was quite a sight. He already had his shirt off, and he was so thin you could see every bone in his body. He had a Spam sandwich in his right hand while he munched on another one in his left hand.

"Hey there, I'm Wimpy. My real name's Virgil, but everyone calls me Wimpy," the corporal announced as he took another bite from the Spam sandwich.

"Hi Wimpy, I'm Sam," responded Sam as he offered his right hand in greeting.

Wimpy looked at the sandwich in his right hand as if perplexed. Then he crammed the sandwich into his pants pocket and took Sam's hand in a firm handshake.

"Glad to meet you, Sam. Would you like a sandwich?" he said as he pulled the crumpled sandwich from his pocket and offered it to Sam.

Sam could see that the sandwich was made with the bug-infested bread from the mess hall, and his stomach churned. "No thanks, Wimpy. I just had breakfast."

"So did I," responded Wimpy, "but I just can't get enough to eat. Especially hamburgers. I love hamburgers. That's why they call me Wimpy. You know, like Wimpy in the *Popeye* comic strip," he continued as he polished off the sandwich in his left hand and started on the one in his right.

"Yes, I've seen that character in the comic strips," Sam said, wondering how his new friend could eat so much and remain so thin. "Do you know what we'll be dropping today?"

"No, I sure don't, but I hope it's a short mission, so we get back in time for lunch," Wimpy answered. "I did bring along a couple of extra sandwiches though. If you get hungry, just let me know."

"I'll be sure to do that," Sam responded as he heard the pilots start up the port engine. "Better get settled in. It looks like we're on our way to Ledo for our mystery cargo."

The flight to Ledo was a short one, and Wimpy kept Sam entertained with stories about all his favorite restaurants and favorite foods. By the time they landed at Ledo, Wimpy had eaten two more sandwiches, and Sam was convinced that the man was totally obsessed with food. When the plane rolled to a stop on the tarmac, both men disembarked.

"Hey, Sam, can you supervise the loading of the plane? I'd like to hustle on over to the chow hall and see what I can find to eat."

"Sure, Wimpy, I'll take care of things here."

"Thanks, Sam. Can I bring anything back for you?"

"No, thanks, Wimpy, I'm okay," Sam answered as he watched the corporal hurry toward the mess hall.

Lieutenant Thomas disembarked and stood beside Sam as Wimpy disappeared into the mess hall.

"What do you think he will scrounge up to eat this time?" asked the lieutenant.

"I'm sure he'll find something, sir," Sam said. "I've never seen anyone so obsessed with food."

"You only have to call me sir in the presence of other officers Sam. Just call me LT," the lieutenant responded, "If you think Wimpy's obsessed now, wait until we take on our mystery load."

"What do you mean, sir, ah I mean, LT?"

"I found out on the flight over that the cooks here at Ledo heard about the plight of the guys at Nhpum Ga, so they cooked up a bunch of fried chicken and apple turnovers for us to deliver to them."

"Oh my god, lieutenant, I mean, LT. How are we going to keep Wimpy away from it?"

"That's going to be your job, Sam. Here comes the truck with the goodies now," LT answered.

Sam watched as the truck backed up to the open cargo doors and then helped to unload and stow its precious contents aboard the plane. By the time they were finished, the inside of the C47 was filled with the aromas of fried chicken and apple turnovers. Sam watched as the empty truck pulled away and braced himself when he saw

Wimpy approaching from the mess hall empty-handed. He jumped down from the aircraft and met him outside the plane.

"What a bunch of rotten guys those cooks are," Wimpy lamented. "They wouldn't give me anything to eat, and I know they have fried chicken in there. I could smell it, and I could smell cooked apples too. Oh man, what I wouldn't give for some fried chicken. I haven't had fried chicken since I left the States."

Before Sam could stop him, Wimpy scrambled aboard the plane and then stood dead still as Sam hurried aboard behind him.

"Sam, there's chicken in here, and something made with apples too. The whole plane's filled with it. Oh Lord, I think I've died and gone to heaven," Wimpy shouted as he began to tear into one of the containers.

"Attention, soldier," shouted Lieutenant Thomas as he appeared in the cockpit doorway. "Keep your paws off of those containers. They're to be delivered untouched to the Marauders at Nhpum Ga. Do you understand, Corporal?"

"Yes, sir," Wimpy responded with downcast eyes, "but couldn't we open just one package lieutenant?"

"You heard my orders, Corporal. Now get everything secured for takeoff."

Sam and Wimpy set about their duties as the pilots started the engines, and they were soon on their way to the beleaguered men at Nhpum Ga. The flight to Nhpum Ga was pure torture for Wimpy. He kept looking at their cargo with longing eyes, and Sam could see the torment on his face. Sam could occasionally hear the poor man's stomach rumble with hunger as they winged their way across northern Burma.

When they arrived at Nhpum Ga, Sam could see that the Marauders were under artillery attack. Puffs of smoke from exploding shells erupted within their perimeter. Some of the enemy shells exploded in treetops, sending deadly shrapnel in all directions. Sam and Wimpy prepared the first containers of chicken and turnovers for ejection and waited as their plane approached for the first drop. When the green light came on, they quickly pushed the food-laden containers out of the plane, and Wimpy moaned as each one left the aircraft. They continued making passes ejecting the precious food, and with each pass, Wimpy's moans grew louder. On one pass, an enemy bullet hit a descending container, splitting it open and spilling its contents to the earth below. Wimpy was beside himself with rage.

"Did you see that, Sam?" he shouted. "I always thought them Japs were barbarians, but to waste food like that is just plain wrong."

Sam didn't say anything and continued to prepare the remaining canisters for the last drop. When the time came to eject the last container, Wimpy watched it until it reached the Marauders on the ground. He could see numerous soldiers racing to the canisters in spite of the shelling they were enduring.

"Them lucky bums," Wimpy lamented. "I almost wish I was down there with them, but even then, I'm not that hungry."

April 4, 1944
Nhpum Ga, Burma

Sergeants Wesley and Matamoto were hunkered down in their foxhole. The enemy had been shelling them steadily for the past hour, and a few shells had come close to their position. They hated the shelling because they never knew when a shell was going to make a direct hit on their position. Their foxhole afforded them reasonable cover from nearby ground explosions, but it offered them little protection from the deadly shrapnel that rained down from above when a shell exploded in the treetops. So far, there had been no treetop explosions in their vicinity.

Both men took turns peering over the edge of their foxhole at the jungle in front of them. Often, the enemy would launch an attack in conjunction with artillery shelling, and they didn't want to be caught unprepared. Their field of view was clear now, but after yesterday's attacks, enemy bodies were stacked five and six deep in front of them, and their view of the jungle was blocked. They had remedied the situation last night when they slipped out of their foxhole under the cover of darkness and pushed the piled bodies aside. As they watched and waited, they heard an aircraft approaching, and when they looked up, they saw that it was a lone C47.

"What do you make of that?" Bill asked, pointing to the airplane.

"I don't know," Roy responded. "Usually there are three or four C47s when we get an airdrop. We just had a drop yesterday, so I can't believe they have anything for us today."

The two men observed with interest as the plane circled and then approached in the manner customary for an airdrop. They ducked quickly when an artillery shell burst thirty feet away from them and then watched curiously as the aircraft passed overhead and bundles tumbled out. The first parachutes drifted slowly to the ground and landed about twenty yards to their rear as the C47 circled in preparation for another pass.

"I can't imagine what the fly boys are bringing us now," Bill said. "I hope in ain't more of that stupid reading material."

"I know what you mean," Roy exclaimed. "I wish they'd drop us an iron lid for this foxhole or, better yet, a big juicy steak."

Both men laughed at the ridiculous thought and ducked when another shell burst nearby.

"What do you suppose is in those bundles?" Roy asked. "Nobody seems to be willing to risk their skin to go find out."

"I don't know, but it must be important for them to send out a single plane. I'm going to find out," Bill said as he slithered out of the foxhole and began to crawl toward the nearest bundle.

Roy watched as his friend crept slowly through the dirt. Bill made steady progress toward the bundle, stopping only when an artillery shell exploded nearby. When he reached the bundle, he took out his combat knife and slashed it open, revealing about one hundred seven-by-four-by-three-inch boxes inside. Roy's interest was piqued when he saw his buddy open one of the boxes, immediately grab another box, and make a mad dash back toward their foxhole. Bill was almost blown off his feet when a shell burst nearby, but he made it safely back to the foxhole with both boxes intact.

"Are you nuts?" Roy inquired. "What's so important in those boxes that you would risk your life for it?"

"This," Bill answered simply as he opened one of the boxes, revealing three pieces of golden brown fried chicken and a sumptuous apple turnover.

Roy couldn't believe his eyes but became a believer when his friend eagerly bit into a piece of the chicken. Bill tossed the other box to his friend and shouted to the other men around them to pass the word that the airdrop was fried chicken and apple turnovers. Roy and Bill hungrily dug into their treasure while the word was passed along. Soon, other men were braving the shelling to get their share of the manna from heaven. Each time the plane passed overhead, the men below cheered as the parachutes unerringly landed in their midst.

"That's the best chicken I've ever eaten," Roy exclaimed as he tossed the last bone away.

"That makes two of us," Bill said. "Someday I'm going to pay them flyboys back for this."

"Amen," responded Roy.

APRIL 4, 1944
THE SKIES OVER NORTHERN BURMA

Wimpy sat glumly in the back of the plane, thinking of all the tasty chicken that had passed untouched through his hands. Even the thought of the Spam sandwich he had squirreled away couldn't pull him out of his depression. Sam sat silently beside him, listening to the rumbling noises coming from the dejected fellow's stomach. Their musings were interrupted when they witnessed LT toss an object from the cockpit onto the floor about midway between them and the cockpit doorway. Neither man moved, but then LT tossed another object back that landed at Wimpy's feet. When Wimpy picked the object up, he looked at Sam in disbelief.

"It's a drumstick bone, Sam. Them SOBs have chicken up there," he shouted in consternation.

Before the exasperated corporal could say another word, LT appeared in the cargo bay carrying three boxes. He walked to the rear of the plane, sat down beside the two enlisted men, and handed each of them a box.

"You don't think I would let your hard work go unrewarded, do you?" LT said. "Eat up, boys! There's chicken and turnovers for everyone."

The copilot, enjoying his own chicken dinner, flew the plane on autopilot back toward Dinjan, while LT, Sam, and the elated Wimpy sat feasting in the back of the plane. Each time one of them finished a piece of chicken, they would toss the bones out the door and laugh as the slipstream whisked it away.

✶ ✶ ✶ ✶ ✶

Lieutenant Kosuke Shimura was flying alone in his Nakajima KI-43 fighter plane over northern Burma. He was on his first combat mission, and his squadron had been jumped by a group of American P-51 fighter planes. In the ensuing chaos, he used the superior maneuverability of his aircraft to escape from the Americans, but he had gotten separated from the rest of his squadron. His radio wasn't working, so he was unable to regroup with his fellow Japanese airmen. He was now returning to his base at Myitkyina, Burma.

The encounter with the American fighters had made Kosuke very nervous, and he was especially vigilant as he flew toward his home base. His watchfulness paid off, and he couldn't believe his luck when he spotted an unarmed American cargo plane several thousand feet below him. Kosuke scanned the skies all around to see if the cargo plane had a fighter escort, but he saw no other aircraft in the vicinity.

Excited with the anticipation of his first kill, Kosuke put his plane into a dive and pulled out a few thousand feet behind the American plane. He adjusted his speed so that he slowly closed the gap between the two aircrafts and stopped his closure rate when he was thirty yards behind the American. He saw that it was a C47, the type of plane the Americans were using to supply their ground troops. Holding his position behind the C47, he armed the twin machine guns on his cowling and turned on his reflector gun sight. He couldn't believe how easy this kill was going to be as he aligned his gun sight behind the engine on the left wing of the cargo plane. He knew the fuel tanks were in that area, and he hoped to ignite an explosion that would bring the American down in flames.

He moved his finger to the firing button and was about to press it when he was startled by the sharp crack of something bouncing off of his canopy. He looked around quickly, but seeing no bullet holes in the canopy, he lined his gun sight up once again and prepared to fire. Just as before, he was interrupted by something hitting his canopy. Puzzled by these strange occurrences, Kosuke knew the unarmed American plane could not elude him, so he decided to investigate further. He climbed slightly above and to the left of the American and noticed that the number painted on the tail of the C47 was 300, the same number that was painted on the tail of his aircraft.

Emboldened by the lack of evasive movement by the American, Kosuke maneuvered his plane just off the left-wing tip of the C47, where he could see into the cargo plane through its open doors. To his surprise he could see three American soldiers who appeared to be eating something and throwing small objects out of the door. Just as he came to the conclusion that the small objects had been the things that were bouncing off his canopy, the Americans noticed his plane flying beside them.

* * * * *

Wimpy had finished his chicken first and was trying to mooch a piece from Sam when he noticed an airplane flying in formation right off their left-wing tip.

"What the hell is that?" he exclaimed pointing out the door.

LT's blood ran cold when he recognized the situation they were in. It was the first time he had seen a Japanese fighter plane up close, but there was no mistaking the dark green paint of the Japanese Army Air Force and the large red circles painted on the fuselage and wings. He could plainly see the Japanese pilot looking at them.

"That's a Jap fighter plane we call an Oscar," he said, "Don't make any sudden moves. He seems curious at the moment."

LT stepped to the open doorway and waved at the Japanese pilot. The pilot raised the goggles from his eyes, slid his canopy open, smiled a toothy grin, and waved back.

"Sam, where's your pistol?" LT asked as he moved to the right side of the doorway and positioned his right hand where the Japanese pilot couldn't see it.

"It's hanging with my chute by the cockpit door," Sam answered.

"Don't make any sudden moves, just ease on over there and get your gun, bring it back here, cock it, and place it in my right hand," LT ordered.

Sam did as he was told as LT waved once again to the Japanese pilot. The pilot waved back and then pointed at LT with his index finger and then made a thumbs-down gesture. Stalling for time, LT made a thumbs-up gesture, but the fighter pilot shook his head no and gave the thumbs-down gesture once again. There was no misunderstanding his intentions.

LT heard Sam jack a round into the chamber of the .45 and felt its hefty weight as it was placed in his right hand. Without hesitation, LT brought the weapon to bear on the enemy pilot and fired off six rounds as quickly as he could pull the trigger.

LT's shots seemed to have missed, but the reaction of the enemy pilot was immediate as he banked the Oscar steeply to the left and dove away behind the C47.

"Wimpy, keep watching out the door to see if you can see where he went," LT ordered as he raced to the cockpit. "Sam, get up in the navigation dome and see if you can spot him from there.

LT jumped into the pilot's seat and immediately put the C47 into a steep dive. He knew their plane would be harder to spot if they flew close to the ground with dense jungle as a background. Sam climbed up to the navigation dome behind the pilot and peered in every direction.

"Do you see anything, Sam?" LT asked.

"Not a thing, Lieutenant. I'll keep watching," Sam responded.

LT flew a zigzag course just a few feet above the tree tops as they headed west toward Dinjan. After fifteen minutes with no further sighting of the enemy plane, he took up a direct heading for Dinjan but ordered the crew to keep a close watch. Finally, when they were in sight of their airbase, he relaxed. They made a good landing and taxied to a stop on the ramp where the entire crew disembarked and stood talking.

"I wonder why that Jap didn't make any further passes at us," LT commented, "and I wonder why he didn't just shoot us down to begin with. We weren't even aware he was there. We were sitting ducks."

"We'll probably never know, sir," Sam answered. "I'm just grateful it turned out as well as it did."

"Me too," Wimpy chimed in, "and I'm glad we had time to finish our chicken."

Everyone laughed and watched as a jeep carrying their company commander pulled up. The crew stood at attention and saluted as Captain Cummings stepped out of the jeep.

"At ease, men," he commanded. "Lieutenant Thomas, did you have a close encounter with a Jap Oscar during your flight?"

"Yes, sir, but how did you know about that?"

"An OSS detachment observed the whole incident from the ground. They thought it was odd when they saw a Jap fighter plane flying in formation with a C47. They said the Jap fighter peeled off and descended in circles until it crash-landed not far from where they were. They went to investigate and found the wreckage and the pilot with a single gunshot wound to the throat. They figure he slowly died of blood loss and was able to control the plane until almost the end. Your plane was the only C47 in the vicinity. Do you know how that pilot received the gunshot wound, Lieutenant?"

"Yes, sir, I emptied Private Huber's .45 at him as he flew beside us."

"Well, congratulations to you and your crew, Lieutenant. You're the first unarmed aircraft to shoot down an enemy plane. You can paint a Jap flag on the side of your cockpit."

Everyone was elated and congratulated each other roundly. When they were through, Captain Cummings had one more thing to say.

"Private Huber, you and Private Wilson report to the headquarters building tomorrow morning at 0500. I've arranged for you two to take part in a tiger hunt."

The captain departed in his jeep, leaving Sam stunned and speechless.

"Can you make hamburgers out of tiger meat?" Wimpy was heard asking as they walked toward the mess hall.

19

APRIL 5, 1944
DINJAN AIRBASE, INDIA

THE MEN IN Sam's basha had decided to sleep with the door closed and the windows shuttered. They knew this would make the basha extremely stuffy and uncomfortable, but no one wanted to take the chance that the tiger would pay them another visit. Sam had told Bobby Joe about the tiger hunt when the two men got together for supper the previous evening, and their excitement over the upcoming hunt, combined with the stifling conditions in the basha, resulted in neither man getting much sleep during the night. However, they were up at 4:55 a.m. and were waiting for Captain Cummings's arrival at the headquarters building. The captain arrived promptly at 5:00 a.m.

"Good morning, men," the captain said cordially.

"Good morning, sir," they responded in unison.

"The Brits informed me yesterday that they have arranged for the local tea plantation owner, Sir Ian McGregor, to put on a hunt for the tiger that's been prowling around the area lately. Since you men have somewhat of a vested interest in the animal, I thought it would be a nice reward for the good work you've done on your missions lately if you could participate in the hunt. Is that agreeable to you?"

"Yes, sir," responded Bobby Joe.

"I sure would like ta git a crack at that critter," Sam also responded affirmatively.

"Good, I spoke with Mr. McGregor yesterday and made all the arrangements. My driver is waiting outside. He will take you to the plantation where you will join the McGregors for breakfast followed by the hunt. Enjoy your day, gentlemen."

"Thank you, sir," both men responded as they hurried out the door to the waiting jeep.

The McGregors had donated part of their plantation for the construction of the Dinjan Airbase, so the ride to the plantation was a short one. Sam and Bobby Joe had seen the plantation from the air, but this was the first time either man had viewed it from the ground. As they rode along, their interest was drawn to the tea bushes, which stretched for vast distances across the rolling hills. Most of the bushes seemed to be about waist high; however, there were sections where the plants were much smaller and appeared to be newer. The scene reminded them of a vast green ocean stretching to the distant jungle.

The captain's driver wound his way through the vast plantation and eventually arrived at the McGregors' estate. The main house of the estate was a large two-story wooden structure which was painted white to reflect the intense daytime heat. It had a verandah on the ground floor that completely circled the house and provided shade for the downstairs windows. Lacy curtains could be seen in every window, and colorful flowers were planted along the edges of the verandah. Numerous wooden outbuildings also painted white gave the complex a clean and tidy look.

When their jeep pulled up to the main house, Mr. McGregor immediately came out to greet them. He was wearing a khaki bush jacket with long pants tucked into sturdy riding boots, and there was a wide-brimmed bush hat perched jauntily atop his head. He was a tall man with piercing gray eyes and a ruddy outdoor complexion. As he strode purposefully toward them, he gave off an air of authority, and Sam got the distinct impression that this was someone who was used to wielding authority.

"Good morning, gentlemen. I'm Ian McGregor, your host for the day. Welcome to my home," he announced as he removed his hat, revealing a full head of snow-white hair.

"Howdy, your lordship? I'm Private Bobby Joe Wilson, and this here's Private Sam Huber," Bobby Joe drawled.

A twinkle came to Ian's eyes. "By the sound of your accent, I take it you are from America's Wild West," he said as he shook hands with Bobby Joe and then Sam.

"Yes, sir, I'm from the great state a Texas, and my partner here's from Pennsylvania," Bobby Joe responded proudly.

"Wonderful," said Ian. "Please come in. We have breakfast all ready for you."

Mr. McGregor led them up onto the verandah and to the entrance of his home. The entrance consisted of two large ornately carved teak doors. Sam was enthralled with the carvings on the doors and brass knockers in the shape of a lion's head attached to each door.

"Teak is one of the most durable woods in the world. These doors were crafted by local artisans and are over fifty years old," Ian explained as he opened the doors to reveal the interior of the home.

The entrance hallway was two stories high with a grand staircase in the center leading to the second floor. The staircase appeared to be constructed of shiny dark mahogany with ornately turned spindles on the banisters. On each side of the staircase, hallways led to the rear of the house, and along each hallway, huge mahogany doorways led to what appeared to be a large sitting room on the right and a library on the left. Pedestals were positioned along the hallways, and each pedestal held a vase containing a brightly colored arrangement of fresh flowers. The parquet wooden floor of the grand entranceway was laid out in an intricate geometric design and polished to a high sheen. Above it all hung a magnificent crystal chandelier that reflected all the colors of the rainbow in the morning light.

"Follow me please, gentlemen," Ian continued as he led them down the hallway to the left of the staircase.

Sam and Bobby Joe were completely in awe as they followed the plantation owner down the hallway. A quick peek into the library as they passed revealed floor-to-ceiling bookshelves teeming with books, a large teak desk, and assorted furniture designed for comfortable reading. At the end of the hallway, they were met by Mrs. McGregor, who was dressed in a white cotton dress. She was a petite woman with sparkling blue eyes and a fair complexion. Her hair was pulled back in a bun, and despite the overwhelming gray in it, you could still see traces of the blonde hair she once possessed.

"Gentlemen, may I introduce you to my wife, Mary McGregor. Mary, these are our guests, Bobby Joe Wilson and Sam Huber," Ian said.

"Welcome to our home, gentlemen," she responded in a soft voice.

"Thank you, ma'am, It's a pleasure to meet you," Sam said.

"Ah, reckon the pleasure's all mine, ma'am," Bobby Joe echoed.

"You men must be famished," she said. "Please come into the breakfast room. I hope you don't mind, but we are just having a typical English breakfast this morning."

As she led the way into the breakfast room, they were immediately assailed by a myriad of delicious aromas. They saw a table set for four with silver flatware and china dishes. A large vase of fresh flowers decorated the center of the table, which was covered by a white linen tablecloth. The eastern wall of the room was completely constructed of large windows with French doors leading to the veranda. The windows and doors had beveled glass window panes, and the morning sunlight streaming through the windows gave the room a warm, cheery feeling. Along the opposite wall stood a large mahogany sideboard that was laden with silver tureens piled with steaming food.

"There are warm plates on the sideboard, gentlemen," said Mrs. McGregor. "Please help yourself to whatever you would like and then have a seat at the table. Our houseboy, Basu, will pour whatever you wish to drink. We have coffee, tea, fresh milk, and mango juice."

Sam and Bobby Joe, following Ian's example, took a plate from the sideboard and proceeded to fill it from the array of foods before them. They couldn't believe the variety of food that made up a typical English breakfast. There were fried eggs, ham, baked beans, fried tomatoes, fried mushrooms, kippers, black pudding sausage, what appeared to be fried bread, and another greenish-colored dish that they didn't recognize. After the powdered eggs and Spam that the army had been providing, the fresh food before them was indeed a treat.

Bobby Joe placed some of everything on his plate, but Sam was a little more selective and chose fried eggs, ham, fried tomatoes, and some of the black sausage, before hesitating over the greenish-colored dish.

"That's bubble and squeak," explained Ian. "Try some, it's quite delicious." Seeing the confusion on Sam's face, he further explained, "Bubble and squeak is simply fried cabbage and potatoes. I like mine cooked with some onion too."

Deciding to try it, Sam put some bubble and squeak on his plate and then proceeded to the breakfast table. Mary was already seated at one end of the table, and Ian sat at the opposite end. Sam and Bobby Joe took seats across from each other at the sides of the table. When they were all seated, Basu brought in warm sliced homemade bread, butter, and a selection jams and jellies. Sam was overjoyed to see that the bread was free of bugs. Basu poured Mary and Ian hot tea and a glass of mango juice, while Sam and Bobby Joe selected coffee and mango juice. Since powdered milk was all they could get on base, both soldiers asked if they could also have a glass of fresh milk.

Sam and Bobby Joe thoroughly enjoyed the fresh food and ate heartily, although Sam didn't really care for the sausage, thinking it was not spicy enough for his American taste. Mrs. McGregor asked about their life in the United States, and they told her about their families and the states where they lived. The conversation was pleasant and eventually got around to the tea plantation.

"I noticed while we were driving over here that almost all of your tea bushes are the same height and there were lots of leaves on them. Don't you pick the leaves to make the tea?" Sam asked.

"We keep the bushes trimmed waist high for easy picking," Ian explained, "and we don't pick all the leaves from the plant. We only pick the two leaves and bud from the tip of a branch. That's where the best tea comes from."

"How often do y'all pick the tea?" Bobby Joe inquired.

"We get two pickings a year," Ian responded. "What we call the first flush is usually picked in March, and then about two weeks or so later, we pick the second flush. Second-flush tea is more full bodied and sweeter and is considered a better tea."

"How long have you been in the tea business?" Sam asked

"My grandfather started this plantation in 1860, and it's been in the family ever since."

"Do you have children who will take over from you?" Sam continued.

"Yes, we have two sons," Ian said. "Phillip is a captain in the British army and is currently a prisoner of the Japanese. He was captured when Rangoon fell. Nigel, our youngest son, is also in the army. He's fighting with General Wingate in Burma right now. If they survive the war, they will take over the plantation."

"I'm sorry to hear about Phillip, I sincerely hope he survives prison camp," Sam replied, "and the next time we drop supplies to General Wingate's troops, it will have a special meaning for me."

"Thank you, lad," Ian responded. "I hear you boys have been

doing a superb job up there. Well, I guess it's time to get ready for the hunt. Please follow me, gentlemen."

The men thanked Mrs. McGregor for her hospitality and followed Ian out of the breakfast room. He led them across the hall to what he described as his den. Upon entering the room, Sam and Bobby Joe were confronted with what could only be described as a man's hideaway. Three walls were covered with rich dark mahogany paneling, and the room was furnished with a large sofa and two overstuffed chairs upholstered in fine leather. There was a large coffee table and two end tables made of rosewood that had deepened with age to a lustrous reddish brown color. The wall facing the sofa was covered in natural stone and contained a huge fireplace. In front of the fireplace, a large tiger skin rug was spread across the teakwood floor. The wall opposite the fireplace contained built-in gun cases that displayed a great variety of Ian's hunting rifles and handguns. All about the room were examples of his hunting prowess. Over the fireplace, the head of a large stag was displayed. Its fur was yellow-brown in color, and the antlers were long and slender with one tine at the base of the each antler and two tines at each tip.

"That's a sambar deer," Ian announced. "Those antlers are almost four feet long, and he weighed in at a little over twelve hundred pounds. I shot him ten years ago right here on the plantation."

On each side of the Sambar deer hung the heads of two smaller but still impressive stags. "Those two are chital deer," Ian explained. "As you can see, their antlers are shaped similar to those of the Sambar but are only two and half feet long. The chital only weighs in at around 180 to 200 pounds."

"That's impressive," Sam said. "The deer in Pennsylvania usually have more tines but the antlers aren't as big, and they generally average around 150 pounds."

"We got them critters in Texas too, only they're usually a little smaller in weight," Bobby Joe chimed in as he looked around the room. His attention was drawn to the head of a large water buffalo. "Did y'all shoot that monster? How much did he weigh?" he asked.

"Yes, I shot him not far from here along the Brahmaputra River. He weighed around a ton and a half, but there's a bigger animal than that over there," Ian responded pointing to the head of an Indian Rhino on the opposite wall. "That rhino weighed two and a half tons. When he charged, it took three shots to bring him down. He was only three feet from me when he finally dropped."

Sam and Bobby Joe both whistled in awe as they visualized an animal that big bearing down on them.

"But I imagine you men are more interested in the tiger rug over here," Ian said as he walked to the fire place. "This tiger was a man eater. I shot him fifteen years ago at a spot where your airbase is now located. He measured ten feet from head to tail and weighed nearly six hundred pounds."

"Lord-a-mighty, looka the teeth on that feller," Bobby Joe exclaimed.

"Those canines are three inches long," Ian explained, "but pay attention to the front claws. They are four inches long."

"That there's one big kitty," Bobby Joe muttered.

"Yes, it was," Ian continued, "but I must tell you the cat we are going after today is reported to be even bigger."

Sam and Bobby Joe looked at each other in disbelief as Ian walked to the gun cabinets and removed a rifle. "This is perhaps one of the best big-game rifles around. It's a Holland and Holland .375 bolt-action magnum. It has great stopping power and low recoil, so I think it will be the best rifle for you two to use today."

He handed the rifle to Bobby Joe and removed an identical rifle from the rack and handed it to Sam along with ammunition for both men. He then removed another bolt-action rifle and held it in his hands.

"This is my favorite big-game gun, and I'll be using it today. It's a .416 Rigby and has superb stopping power. Well, we have a bit of a way to go to where the tiger's been located, so let's get the hunt on, gentlemen. Our transportation is waiting outside."

With those words, Ian strode from the room carrying his rifle. Sam and Bobby Joe followed closely behind. Ian led them to the rear exit of the house, and when they stepped outside, they were surprised to see two Indian elephants patiently waiting for them. The elephants were each attended by a handler, and on the back of each elephant was a large box-shaped framework open at the top and on the sides.

"These are our transportation, gentlemen. You'll be using the elephant on the right. Her name is Shirley, and she is the gentlest animal we have. Your mahout's name is Deepak, which means 'exciting' in the Indian language," Ian explained.

"I hope he doesn't live up to the meaning of his name too much today," Sam said.

"What's a mahout, and what's that there contraption on the elephant's back?" Bobby Joe asked.

"A mahout is the name for an elephant handler, and that contraption, as you call it, on the elephant's back is a howdah. That's where you and Sam will be riding during the hunt."

Bobby Joe walked to the side of the elephant and looked up at howdah, which was resting on the elephant's back a good ten feet above the ground.

"I don't see no stirrups or anythin' on this critter," Bobby Joe exclaimed. "How do y'all git up there?"

"I'll demonstrate for you," Ian responded as he strode to the side of his elephant and handed his rifle to Johar, his mahout.

Johar began tapping the elephant on the side with his open palm while issuing a command in Indian at the same time. The elephant responded by slowly kneeling on its right hind leg and then lowering its entire body so that its stomach rested on the ground with its left hind leg extended outward. The howdah was now at eye level, and Ian used the animal's extended hind leg as a step and gingerly climbed atop the elephant and into the howdah. He sat down on the padded floor of the howdah and extended his legs through the open sides with one leg on each side of the left-front upright of the framework. He took his rifle from Johar and rested it upon the top railing of the howdah. Johar then clambered up the elephant's front shoulder and sat down on the animal's neck. He then issued another command in Indian, and the elephant slowly rose from the ground with both men securely aboard.

Sam and Bobby Joe looked at each other, shrugged, and nodded to their mahout. Deepak repeated the process Johar had demonstrated, and soon Shirley was resting on the ground. They handed their rifles to Deepak and then each in turn climbed aboard the elephant and took a seat in the howdah. They sat side by side in the same fashion Ian had demonstrated, with Bobby Joe on the left and Sam on the right. Deepak returned their rifles, took his seat on the neck of the elephant, and issued the command for the elephant to stand up. Shirley obediently rose while Sam and Bobby Joe clung to the railing of the howdah.

"Excellent, gentlemen," Ian proclaimed. "We have about a four-kilometer ride to where the tiger is hiding. Enjoy the ride."

The mahouts issued commands, and the elephants began walking with a gentle gait that produced a slight side-to-side motion that neither Sam nor Bobby Joe found uncomfortable. Ian directed them to the west away from his home and into the surrounding tea fields. After traveling for about an hour, they came to a small pond surrounded by elephant grass at the edge of the jungle. The elephant grass stood six feet tall in most places but was beaten down around the edges of the pond. The carcass of a half-eaten goat could be seen at the edge of the pond nearest the jungle. Several Indian men were waiting for them when they arrived, and Ian spoke to them in their native tongue and then turned to his hunting guests.

"These men have informed me that the tiger is hiding in the jungle in front of us. They have surrounded the area on three sides with beaters, and in twenty minutes, they will begin beating drums and creating a lot of noise as they close in on the tiger's hiding place. If all goes well, they will drive the tiger out into the open at this pond where we can get a shot at it. Aim behind the front leg and slightly low on the chest where the heart is located or if you get a frontal shot, aim between the eyes or at the chest under the chin."

Sam and Bobby Joe checked that their rifles were loaded and on safety, while the mahouts positioned the elephants on either side of the pond. Ian's elephant was on the right, while Sam and Bobby Joe were on the left. They settled in to wait as the Indian sun climbed higher in the morning sky.

"I sure hope that critter comes out so Mr. McGregor gits the first shot," Bobby Joe commented.

"So do I," Sam answered as he remembered his encounter with the tiger in his basha. "I wouldn't want to just wound an animal like that."

"Me neither," Bobby Joe responded. "We might be ten feet off the ground, but I got a feelin' that ain't gonna be high enough."

Their conversation was interrupted by the sound of distant drums as the beaters began their drive. The sound of the drums slowly drew nearer, and they could begin to hear the shouts of the beaters as they closed in on the tiger. The hunters intently watched the edge of the jungle, waiting for the tiger to appear.

The drums and shouting grew louder, and Sam and Bobby Joe could now hear the thrashing sounds some of the beaters were making as they beat the bush with sticks. Sam nervously fingered the safety on his rifle as the tension mounted. He looked over at Ian and saw that he had his full attention on the jungle to their right. Sam turned his attention to the edge of the jungle in front of him when he was startled by a whisper from Bobby Joe.

"Sam, I saw somethin' move over ta the left."

Sam looked to his left past Bobby Joe and at first saw nothing, but then he too saw some movement just inside the edge of the jungle. They watched the spot attentively as the beaters drew even closer, and their efforts were rewarded when a large tiger slowly emerged from the underbrush about fifty yards away. It stood sideways to them as it nervously looked back into the jungle.

"You're the only one with a clear shot," Sam whispered to Bobby Joe.

Sam could see Bobby Joe swallow hard as he released the safety on his rifle and raise it to his shoulder. The tiger turned its head and looked directly at them. Sam saw those yellow eyes and froze in remembrance of their evil glare. His trance was suddenly broken by the report from Bobby Joe's rifle.

They watched as the tiger leapt into the air at shock of the bullet entering its body. However, the beast was not fatally wounded. It regained its feet and with a mighty roar charged directly at them. Bobby Joe pulled the trigger again, but nothing happened. Realizing he had not ejected the empty shell, he frantically tried to work the bolt of the rifle, but it seemed to be jammed. He looked up in time to see that the tiger had covered the distance between them in a few great bounds. He shrieked in horror and pulled his feet up as the tiger leapt, its claws raking the side of the elephant just inches from his shoes. With the tiger clinging to her side, Shirley moved quickly to get out of the way, causing Sam to lose his balance and begin to fall from the howdah. Frantically, he grabbed the railing of the howdah and hung dangling from the side as Shirley continued to spin to shake off the tiger. Ian was not able to get a clear shot at the tiger and shouted for Johar to move them to a better position.

The tiger finally slid to the ground and gathered its legs beneath itself in preparation for another leap at the man-thing that had caused it such much pain. Before the tiger could leap again, one of the drum beaters emerged from the jungle just five yards away. In a single bound, the tiger was upon the poor man, driving him to the ground. With the drum between them, the tiger stood over its victim as the man screamed in terror. At that moment, Ian shot at the wounded beast. The tiger spun around and charged at the new threat.

Sam clambered back into the howdah, and he and Bobby Joe watched as the beast closed the distance to Ian's elephant. Just as the tiger was about to leap, Ian fired again. This time, his aim was true, and the beast fell to the ground just ten feet from the elephant. Ian slid to the ground and approached the tiger cautiously. He was ready for another shot as he poked the animal's eye with the end of the rifle's barrel. There was no reaction from the beast.

"Looks like he's dead, lads," Ian called. "Come on down, and we'll measure him up."

Sam and Bobby Joe slid to the ground as Ian saw to the injured beater. Aside from some scratches and bruises, the frightened man was thankfully okay. Some of his fellow beaters led him away to their nearby village, while the remainder gathered around Ian, who was inspecting the dead tiger.

"Your shot was a good one, Bobby Joe," Ian said. "You missed the heart by an inch, and the beast would have died soon. Even with a shot through the heart, these beasts have been known to go on for fifteen to twenty seconds, and they can do a lot of damage in that time."

"Y'all kin keep tiger huntin'," Bobby Joe responded. "That dadgum critter almost got ta me."

"The critter, as you put it, did put on quite a show," Ian observed. "I estimate he weighs close to six hundred pounds. Let's measure him."

With the help of the beaters, the tiger was stretched out, and Ian measured it from the tip of its nose to the end of its tail.

"Eleven feet exactly," Ian announced. "This fellow will make a fine addition to my trophy room. It's been a good hunt, gentlemen. Let's load this beast up and be on our way."

Sam and Bobby Joe watched in fascination as the beaters cut limbs and poles from the surrounding jungle and lashed them together with vines to construct a sturdy travois. They attached the device to Ian's elephant and then tied the carcass of the tiger to it. When the work was finally done to Ian's satisfaction, the hunters remounted their elephants and began the journey back. Along the way, there was a great deal of talk about the excitement of the day's hunt, and Ian regaled them with tall tales of his past hunting experiences. He liked and enjoyed these American soldiers, and he had one more surprise in store for them.

Instead of proceeding back to his home, Ian directed the mahouts to take them to the front gate of Dinjan Airbase. Their arrival at Dinjan surprised Sam and Bobby Joe and drew a great deal of attention. Word spread throughout the base, and soon a great throng of soldiers arrived to view the tiger and ask questions of the great hunters. Sam and Bobby Joe were instant celebrities, and by the time Ian departed with the tiger and the elephants, he had to chuckle to himself at the embellishments Bobby Joe was adding to the description of the hunt.

20

APRIL 7, 1944
THE HUMP, BURMA

THE PAST TWO days had brought a lot of changes to Sam's world. After their successful tiger hunt, he and Bobby Joe had become overnight celebrities on the base. Their names were now well known, and everyone was sleeping much easier since the tiger had been eliminated from their midst. In addition, planes from the Seventeenth Squadron of the Sixty-fourth Troop Carrier Group had arrived from Comiso, Sicily, and Sam was able to renew some old acquaintances from when he was stationed with them. The arrival of the Sixty-fourth had come just in time to meet an increased demand for aircraft to supply the embattled British Fourteenth Army around Imphal. The Japanese Fifteenth Army was attacking the widely separated British units around Imphal from several directions, and it was recently learned that the Japanese were being helped by units of the Indian National Army, who were fighting for independence from England. If the situation around Imphal wasn't bad enough, yesterday, twenty thousand men of the Japanese Thirty-first Division laid siege to 2,500 British troops at Kohima, creating another Nhpum

Ga situation for the allies. Kohima was only thirty miles south of the vital and unprotected supply base at Dimapur. If Dimapur was taken, the Japanese would not only capture vast amounts of critical supplies but also cut the only land-supply lines to the air bases in the state of Assam. If that happened, it would threaten the lives of Sam and his fellow soldiers in Assam and effectively end the supply of materials to China over the Hump.

When Sam checked his mission assignment this morning, he had been surprised to see that he was scheduled to make his first flight over the Hump. He was assigned to supervise the loading and unloading of a C47 carrying a cargo of lend-lease materials to Kunming, China. He had been equally surprised to find out that the plane was to be piloted by his friend Lt. L. T. Thomas. The loading of the airplane went well except for the fact that they were five hundred pounds overweight. Sam brought this to the attention of LT, and the lieutenant explained that there was a maximum effort to increase the amount of supplies being flown to China, and it was not unusual to be overloaded. With LT's assurances that the C47 could handle the load, they had taken off and were now headed over the Hump.

It was an unusually clear day for Hump flying, and Sam stood in the doorway between the pilot and copilot where he could view the world through the windshield. LT was providing a running commentary as the flight progressed.

"We're currently flying over the Naga Hills," he told Sam, "They're named for the head-hunting people who live down there. They supposedly only take heads from neighboring tribes now, but you can never be sure. If you have to bail out, some of them are friendly to American flyers, and some will sell you to the Japs."

"That's a comforting thought," Sam responded. "Hey, it doesn't look like we're high enough to get over that peak up ahead."

"Yeah, we're approaching the W pass. You can see that the central mountain and the mountains on either side of it form the shape of a W. We call the mountain in the middle 'gun sight peak' because it resembles what you see when you look down the barrel of a rifle," LT explained. "Sometimes when we're heavily loaded, like today, we can't get enough altitude to fly over the peak, so we have to navigate through the pass on either side."

Sam was watching as they approached the pass on the right side of gun sight peak when a question occurred to him. "What happens if it's cloudy and you can't see the peaks?"

"Well, we get as high as we can get. Sometimes we have to throw some cargo out to lighten the load, and then we plot a course that should take us through the pass and hope for the best." LT answered as they neared the pass. "If you look below, you can see the results of miscalculating."

As they entered the pass, the mountains on either side towered above them and the floor of the pass grew closer and closer. At first, Sam saw only rocks and patches of snow, and then he saw the wreckage of a plane scattered across the ground below. A short distance further on, he spotted the remains of another plane, and, soon after that, another.

"Did any of those crews get out alive?" Sam asked with a feeling of dread.

"No," answered LT, "Very few men survive crashes in these mountains. It's clear enough today that you'll see the remains of many planes between here and Kunming. Some were brought down by the Japs, but most were caused by bad weather. There have been so many that this route has become known as the Aluminum Trail."

Sam remained silent as they continued their flight over the deep valleys of the Irrawaddy, Salween, and Mekong rivers and the fifteen-thousand-foot mountain ranges that separated them. LT kept up his commentary, and as they crossed each mountain range, Sam could see the sunlight glistening off the scattered remains of wrecked airplanes. By the time they crossed the last ridge and began their descent into Kunming, he had become convinced of the dangers of flying over the Hump.

"We've been cleared to land," LT announced, "but I've just been informed that the airfield is under a one-ball alert."

"What's a one-ball alert?" Sam asked.

"The Chinese have a quite effective air-raid warning system that is spread across China," LT explained. "They use telephone, telegraph, radio, and any other forms of communication to warn of impending air raids. Here at Kunming, there's a pole on a hill overlooking the airbase. When Jap planes are airborne and headed this way, one red ball is hoisted up the pole. That's the situation on the ground right now. When the Jap planes are twenty minutes away, a second red ball is hoisted up the pole, and everyone is supposed to take cover. When the Jap planes are in sight, a third red ball is hoisted, and you had better be in a bomb shelter."

"Let me get this straight," Sam observed. "Right now Jap planes are headed this way, but they are still more than twenty minutes away. Is that right?"

"That's right," LT answered, "and the situation could change at any minute."

Sam thought the situation over as LT aligned the C47 with the runway and began preparations for landing. Sam watched through the windshield as they approached the ground, and he marveled at the skills of the pilots as they deftly brought the airplane in over the runway. Just as their wheels touched gently down, his attention was drawn to the right side of the runway ahead of them where a Chinese coolie was running at full speed toward the runway. Sam expected the man to stop when he saw the approaching aircraft, but instead of stopping, he continued to run onto the runway in front of the speeding C47. LT also saw the coolie and knew that at their current speed, he could not swerve to miss him without risking the aircraft and all aboard. Instead, he applied the brakes as hard as he could, and everyone held their breath as the coolie continued his mad dash and disappeared under the nose of the aircraft.

Sam braced himself expecting to feel a thump as the tires ran over the coolie or the propeller blades cut him to pieces. However, the thump never came, and the airplane continued to slow down as it proceeded down the runway. Sam ran to a window on the left side of the plane and peered out. A short distance behind them he saw the Chinese coolie standing at the edge of the runway and waving merrily back at the C47 that had nearly killed him.

As the airplane slowed and taxied off the runway, Sam returned to the cockpit doorway.

"I can't believe what I just witnessed. What do you suppose that was all about?" Sam asked.

"That, my friend, was an example of Chinese superstition," LT answered. "The Chinese believe they are followed by evil spirits, and they think they can get rid of the spirits by running in front of our planes where the propellers will chop the evil spirits to pieces."

"That's got to be the craziest thing I've ever seen," Sam said. "Do any of them ever get killed?"

"Yes, a few have been killed, and we've lost a couple of planes in the process too," LT responded.

"Their belief in evil spirits must be awfully strong," Sam mused.

"It is, and you'll see signs of it everywhere," LT continued. "They believe evil spirits only travel in straight lines, so you will see walls built across paths leading to villages to stop the spirits. Their homes are also built that way so that you have to turn right or left immediately upon entering."

"I can hardly wait to see more of this country," Sam commented.

"Well, the only part you're going to see right now is from an air raid shelter," LT said pointing to a nearby hill. "They just raised a second red ball."

As LT brought the C47 to a halt on the apron, Sam could distinctly see the hill and the pole with two red balls dangling from it. He also noticed the frenzied activity around them as everyone rushed to the safety of air-raid shelters.

"Come on, we've got to get to safety," LT ordered as he unbuckled his harness.

Sam followed the pilots as they rushed to the rear of the C47 and jumped to the tarmac. They began running toward a nearby bomb shelter when a jeep pulled up beside them.

"Hey LT, do you and your crew want to view the fireworks from the cheap seats?" asked the driver as he pointed to a hill overlooking the airbase.

Without hesitation, LT jumped into the passenger seat of the jeep and motioned for Sam and the copilot to get in the back. With everyone barely aboard, the driver gunned the jeep's engine and sped off toward the nearby hill. Sam hung on for dear life as the jeep careened across unpaved surfaces as it made a beeline toward the cheap seats.

"Gentlemen, I would like you to meet Lieutenant Waldo "Biggie" Biggins, an old friend and drinking buddy of mine," LT announced. motioning toward the driver. "Biggie got his nickname, not from his last name, but from his legendary prowess with the women."

"Hi, guys, welcome aboard," Biggie said as he swerved to avoid a large stone as they neared the top of the hill. "You're going to love the view from up here."

Reaching the top of the hill, Biggie slammed on the brakes, bringing the jeep to a skidding stop amid a cloud of dust. As the air cleared, a splendid view of the buildings of the air base and numerous parked aircraft was revealed below them. The hill with the air-raid warning pole was also clearly visible, and as they watched, a third red ball was hoisted up the pole, and the sound of distant aircraft engines became discernable.

"Here they come. Get ready for some fireworks," Biggie announced, pointing in the direction of the approaching aircraft.

Sam could clearly see five twin-engine Japanese bombers as they started their bombing run on the airbase. "Is it safe to be out here in the open?" He asked nervously.

"The Nips are notoriously poor bombers, and they usually miss their target, but they've never bombed this hill," Biggie explained.

Biggie's assurances didn't comfort Sam as he observed the Japanese planes draw nearer. He could plainly see the enemy planes now, and he watched as tiny black sticks began to fall from them. It took him a moment to realize that the sticks were bombs, and then he watched as they began to explode on the airbase below. Biggie was right about the accuracy of the Japanese bombardiers as most of the bombs fell in the empty space along the runway. Great clouds of dirt and smoke arose as the bombs exploded, and Sam could hear the blasts and feel the ground tremble beneath his feet. However, not all the enemy bombs missed their target. He saw several small buildings disintegrate as they were struck, and he watched in awe as a C46 laden with fifty-five-gallon drums of gasoline exploded in a great ball of fire that rose hundreds of feet into the air.

As the enemy bombing run ended, a new sound came to their ears. It was the sound of high performance single-engine aircraft.

"That's our P40 fighter planes," Biggie explained. "Now we're going to give those Nips some hell."

The men watched as the P40s dove into the Japanese formation. The enemy bombers split up and began to take evasive action; however, their efforts were of no avail. One bomber exploded in midair and smoking pieces of it cascaded to the ground. Cheers arose from those on the hill, as two more bombers began trailing smoke and slowly spiraled out of the sky. A few parachutes could be seen, as some of the enemy crewmen were able to escape their crippled aircraft. They watched as the parachutes descended into the fields surrounding the base.

"What will happen to those Jap airmen?" Sam asked.

"If the Chinese Army doesn't get to them first, the local farmers will hack and beat them to death," Biggie explained, "and if the army does get to them, they probably won't survive the torture they'll endure during questioning."

"The Chinese have no love for the Japs," LT added. "They've suffered under the Japanese invaders for quite a few years now."

The remaining two bombers were nowhere in sight as the air raid ended, and the men climbed back aboard their jeep and headed down the hill. When they arrived back on the base, the unloading of their aircraft had already begun.

"You men go to the mess hall and get some fried eggs and coffee," LT said to his crew. "I'll check to see what kind of load we'll be taking back to Dinjan and then I'll join you later."

"You mean they have fresh eggs here?" Sam asked.

"Yes, the Chinese seem to have plenty of chickens," LT answered. "Enjoy them, and I'll see you soon."

Sam and the rest of the crew hurried off to the mess hall where they enjoyed the luxury of fresh eggs cooked any way they desired. Sam was relishing his second helping of eggs over easy when LT joined them.

"Everything going okay?" the lieutenant asked.

"The eggs are great," Sam responded, "Did you find out what cargo we're taking back to India?"

"Yes, we'll be taking three dozen Chinese recruits back to Chabua for infantry training. Luckily, they will be escorted by an English-speaking officer from the regular Chinese Army." LT answered, "We'll be taking off as soon as we get back to the plane."

The crew finished their meal and headed for the flight line. When they arrived at their C47, they found the Chinese recruits were already waiting for them. Sam had never seen a sorrier-looking group of men. Most were dressed in ragged peasant clothing, and all of them looked to be malnourished. They stood in a group away from the airplane, and they seemed to be reluctant to approach the C47. A sense of overall fear hung over the motley throng. A lieutenant in the Chinese Army and several Chinese soldiers armed with rifles surrounded the group. The lieutenant stepped forward as the crew approached.

"I am Lieutenant Wu Cheng at your service," he said in excellent English as he saluted LT and the copilot.

"I'm Lieutenant Thomas," LT responded as he returned the salute. "Your English is very good, Lieutenant. You must have studied in the United States."

"Yes, I graduated from Stanford University," replied Wu Cheng. "I enjoyed your country very much."

"It's a pleasure to meet you Lieutenant Wu," LT continued. "Your recruits seem to be very nervous. Is there a problem?"

"These men have been conscripted from the peasant population of a remote area of China," Lieutenant Wu explained. "This is the first time they have seen an airplane, and they fear it is some evil beast that will devour them."

"We'll get aboard to show its safe, and then Private Huber will help you get them on board," LT responded, nodding toward Sam.

"I will do my best, Lieutenant," Wu answered.

LT turned to Sam. "It looks like you are going to have your hands full with this bunch, Sam. Get them loaded and stay close to the cockpit door during the flight."

"Yes, sir," Sam responded. "Uh, LT, I noticed while you were talking to Lieutenant Wu that the ground crew was draining fuel from our wing tanks. What's going on with that?"

"Oh, that. That's standard procedure on flights returning to India. They need every drop of gasoline they can get to fight the war here in China. So they drain our tanks and only leave us enough fuel to get back to India."

"Isn't that a little risky?" Sam asked. "What if something unexpected happens on the way back?"

"It is risky, Sam, and we've lost some planes when their fuel ran out due to unexpected weather conditions. But the orders come from the top, and we have to live with them. Now see if you can get this mob safely aboard and then report to me in the cockpit."

"Yes, sir," Sam responded as he turned toward the Chinese recruits.

Lieutenant Wu pointed to the American crewmen as they entered the C47 and cajoled the recruits in soothing tones in an attempt to get them to enter the aircraft. His efforts were met with looks of sheer terror from the distraught Chinese. He continued to plead and reason with the men, but they would not approach the airplane. Finally, Sam climbed aboard and stood in the open doorway smiling broadly and motioning for them to follow. Still, none of the frightened peasants would go near the aircraft. Finally reaching the limits of his patients, Lieutenant Wu drew his pistol and angrily issued a command to the armed soldiers surrounding the recruits. The soldiers raised their rifles and aimed at the horrified men. Realizing that the uncertainty of getting into the airplane was better than the certainty of being shot, the terrified men began to board the C47.

There were no seats in the cargo plane, so Sam had to devise a scheme to get all of the Chinese aboard. He seated the first three on the floor in the rear of the aircraft with their backs against the aft bulkhead and then had Lieutenant Wu instruct them to pull their knees up against their chests. Then as the remainder of the recruits filed aboard, he placed them in similar positions in front of the men already aboard with their backs against the knees of the men behind them. In this fashion, he formed three rows of twelve men inside the cargo bay, leaving a narrow walkway from the open cargo doors to the cockpit entrance. Lieutenant Wu dismissed the armed soldiers that had accompanied him, and then he and Sam walked to the front of the C47 and stood in front of the cockpit entrance, facing their passengers.

"I see a lot of fear on the faces of these men," Sam said to Lieutenant Wu. "And we haven't even started the engines yet. Are you sure everything will be okay?"

"Once we are in the air, there will be no place for them to go, and they will have to settle down. If they don't, I always have this," responded Lieutenant Wu as he patted the pistol hanging from his belt.

"You're the boss," Sam said. "I'll tell Lieutenant Thomas everything is secure back here."

Sam turned and told LT that they were ready to go, and the lieutenant immediately began the engine start-up procedures. Sam watched the faces of the recruits as first the starboard and then the portside engine were started. He could see the fear in their faces begin to deepen as the throb of the engines increased, sending vibrations through the floor of the cargo bay. Some of the men struggled to rise, but they stopped immediately when Lieutenant Wu shouted a command in Chinese and withdrew his pistol from its holster. When the C47 began to taxi, another wave of disquiet erupted among the frightened passengers, but Wu's stern commands and menacing pistol once again restored order. As they taxied to the runway, Sam could see fear and hatred under the lowered brows of the recruits as they watched Lieutenant Wu.

Sam notified LT of the ominous mood of their passengers, and so the pilot did not hesitate when they reached the runway, and he applied full power to the engines for takeoff. The engines roared, and the C47 immediately began to accelerate down the runway as panic gripped first one and then another of the terrified recruits. Lieutenant Wu tried shouting commands over the din of the engines, but it was of no avail. As the aircraft approached liftoff speed, several panicked men scrambled to their feet and leapt out of the open cargo door. More rose to follow, but they stopped when Lieutenant Wu fired a shot into the floor in front of the door.

Hearing the gunshot behind him, LT immediately aborted the takeoff and brought the C47 to a stop at the end of the runway.

"What the hell is going on back there?" he shouted as he taxied from the runway.

"Several of the Chinese jumped out of the airplane during

takeoff, and Lieutenant Wu fired a shot to keep the rest in place," Sam explained.

"Well, tell him no more shooting for God's sake," LT ordered. "I'll get on the radio and find out what happened to the men who jumped out."

Lieutenant Wu stood guard over the restless recruits as Sam went to a window to look out. He could see several trucks and an ambulance picking up bodies from the runway, but he had no way of telling how badly the men were hurt. It was several minutes before word of their fate came over the radio.

"Two of the men are dead, and the third isn't expected to live," LT sorrowfully announced. "You just don't survive jumping out of an airplane going seventy miles an hour. There's nothing more we can do for them, so we've been ordered to taxi back for takeoff."

"I sincerely apologize, Lieutenant Thomas. These are primitive people," Wu said. "I will do my utmost to prevent this from happening again."

As they taxied back to the runway, Lieutenant Wu and Sam got the recruits reseated, and with much shouting and waving of his pistol, Wu enforced a semblance of order among them. Under the watchful eye of Wu, a second takeoff was completed successfully, and they were soon climbing toward the distant mountain ranges of Burma. The frightened recruits continued to cast sidelong glances out the open door, but when the plane entered a thick layer of clouds, they could no longer see the ground, and they settled down.

An hour into the flight, they were still in the clouds when the plane began to encounter some light turbulence. At first it was not too bad, but as they continued on over the mountains of Burma, the turbulence became worse. Sam could see the fear return to the faces of the Chinese recruits as they began to plead with Lieutenant Wu.

"What are they saying?" Sam asked the lieutenant.

"They say the plane is in the teeth of an evil spirit, and they want out," Wu replied.

"Did you explain to them that it's impossible to get out?" Sam asked.

"I tried to explain, but they have no concept of flying. They are threatening to revolt, and I don't think I can stop them," Wu answered.

"Try to keep them calm while I talk to Lieutenant Thomas," Sam said.

Lieutenant Wu tried once again to reason with the recruits, but the only thing that was keeping them at bay was his pistol. With each passing minute, their mood became uglier.

"We have a problem, LT," Sam said to the pilot. "Our passengers believe we are in the grip of an evil spirit, and they want out. Lieutenant Wu says he doesn't think he can control them much longer. It looks like they are about to rush the cockpit and take matters into their own hands."

"Okay, get Wu into the cockpit area with you as quickly as possible and then close and lock the cockpit door. Whatever you do keep them from breaking in here. I'll climb as high as this crate can go, and hopefully lack of oxygen will knock them out," LT commanded.

Sam returned to the cargo bay and relayed LT's message to Lieutenant Wu. Several of the recruits were now on their feet trying to convince the others to rush the cockpit. As Sam and Wu backed toward the cockpit door, others joined the instigators, and it became obvious a riot was about to break out. Sam pushed Lieutenant Wu into the cockpit area and followed close behind. He just managed to close and lock the cockpit door as the first wave of angry recruits rushed forward. Sam stood with his shoulder braced against the door when the first surge struck. The door held, but he could feel it give a little as the terrified men beat upon it from the opposite side. The pounding stopped as the men regrouped, and then they threw themselves against the door with renewed fury. This time, the door gave a little more, and Sam knew it would not be able to withstand much more.

"I don't think the door will hold much longer, LT," Sam shouted.

"Okay, I'll try to keep them off balance," LT answered as he banked the plane steeply to the right and then to the left. "We're almost up to twenty thousand feet, so everyone get their oxygen masks on."

Sam could hear the men in the cargo bay being thrown about by LT's maneuvers, and the assault on the door stopped momentarily. During the lull, Sam and Lieutenant Wu donned oxygen masks and then returned to their positions at the door. Sam hadn't realized how much the lack of oxygen had affected him until he started breathing the oxygen. The dull headache he was experiencing and the fogginess he felt in his head began to clear. He almost felt sorry for the men in the cargo bay until another wave assaulted the door. This time, their efforts did not feel as strong, and the door held once again.

"I think the altitude is beginning to affect them," Lieutenant Wu said. "Fewer of them seem to be shouting, and the speech of those that are yelling is slurred."

"Good, a few more minutes at this altitude, and most of them should be unconscious," LT announced.

As Sam and Wu listened, fewer and fewer sounds could be heard from the cargo bay, and finally, no sound at all came from beyond the door. Sam cautiously unlocked the door and peered into the cargo bay. The floor from the cockpit door to the aft bulkhead was strewn with the bodies of the recruits. Most were totally unconscious, but a few were still conscious but unable to speak or rise.

"It looks like everything is under control, LT," Sam said.

"Great, I'll take us down to a lower altitude so they can recover," LT answered, "but you better tie up as many of them as you can."

Sam and Wu immediately set about tying up the men who were not unconscious, and then they used whatever material they could find to bind some of the unconscious recruits. When they had exhausted all materials at hand, there were still about fifteen men who were not tied up, so they placed them against the rear bulkhead and wedged them in with the men who were bound. By the time Sam and Wu were finished, they had descended to a lower altitude, and the once-riotous recruits began to regain consciousness. Suffering from the effects of hypoxia, none of the men were in any condition to cause further trouble. The fact that they had flown out of the turbulence also helped their situation.

With everything now under control, Lieutenant Wu had a chance to access the condition of his charges. He counted the men once and then counted them again before turning to Sam.

"The men are in good physical condition," he announced, "but we lost an additional seven men back there. They either jumped or accidentally fell from the plane."

The import of what Lieutenant Wu said fell heavily upon Sam. They had started out with thirty-six recruits, and ten of them had lost their lives due to ignorance and superstition. He felt sorry for those lost lives, but he realized they would all be dead if the door to the cockpit had not held.

The remainder of the flight was uneventful, and as they day ended, Sam had completed his first flight over the Hump. It was a day he knew he would never forget even though he wished he could.

21

APRIL 11, 1944
SOOKERATING AIRBASE, INDIA

S AM COULD HEAR the hiss of the samurai sword as it arched down toward his exposed neck, but once again, he awoke just before the sharp blade cut into his flesh. Sweat trickled down the side of his face, and his heart pounded within his chest as he opened his eyes, realizing he had once again experienced the nightmare that had been plaguing him for months. Total exhaustion seemed to permeate his body as he slowly looked around. He was shocked when the scene that met his gaze was totally unfamiliar. He was lying on the ground under the wing of a C47 at an airbase he had never seen before. Activity bustled all around as aircrews readied their planes for flight, and cargoes were loaded on board. As he slowly rose from the cold ground that had served as his bed, he struggled to remember how he got here.

"Howdy, partner. Y'all look like somethin' the cat dragged in and the dog won't eat," a familiar voice said from behind.

Sam turned to see Bobby Joe Wilson grinning at him from a face sporting three days growth of whiskers. "You need to talk. You look like a dog's been chewing on your face," Sam responded as he felt the stubble on his own chin. "Where are we anyway?"

"We're at Sookerating Airbase," Bobby Joe answered.

Then it came to Sam, and he realized why he felt so tired. For the past four days, they had been flying three missions a day, delivering supplies to Merrill's Marauders in Burma and the besieged British troops around Imphal, India. They had no sooner delivered a load from one base when they were ordered somewhere else to pick up and deliver another load. Whenever darkness came, they would sleep near their airplane at whatever base they happened to be. Last night, they landed at Sookerating after dark. Since Sam had never been to this base before, it explained why everything looked so unfamiliar to him.

"I didn't see you yesterday," Sam said to Bobby Joe. "What missions did they have you on?"

"One of the missions was ta deliver chloride a lime ta the Marauders at Nhpum Ga," Bobby Joe answered. "Y'all wouldn't believe the conditions there, partner. The battle ended on the ninth, and the place is just littered with bloated carcasses. They sez there's millions of flies and maggots everywhere. Them Marauders been sprayin' flame throwers everywhere ta kill 'em, and they'll use the chloride a lime ta disinfect everythin' before they start ta bury the bodies. How 'bout y'all? Where did y'all fly yesterday?"

"We flew supplies into dirt strips around Imphal yesterday. Today we're supposed to drop supplies to the surrounded Brits at Kohima. It sounds like another situation like Nhpum Ga," Sam said.

"It's worse than Nhpum Ga, Sam. I was on a drop there the day before yesterday. The drop zone is surrounded by high ridges that are occupied by the Japs. It's like flyin' inta a shootin' gallery. We lost one plane there, and everythin' we dropped fell inta enemy hands."

"That doesn't sound encouraging," Sam responded. "I guess I'll have to keep my head down."

"Y'all gonna need all the luck ya kin git," Bobby Joe said earnestly as he walked toward his waiting plane. "Good luck, partner."

Sam waved to his friend and turned to the task of overseeing the loading of his own cargo plane. When the job was done, he just had time to grab a quick breakfast before they took off to deliver a load of ammunition, food, and water to the British troops at Kohima. Besides Sam, the crew for this flight was made up of personnel from the Seventeenth Troop Carrier Squadron of the Sixty-fourth Troop Carrier Group. The pilot was Captain John Stacey from Ames, Iowa, and the copilot was Lieutenant Calvin Inge of Pueblo, Colorado. Sam had flown with both men back in Sicily, and he knew they were good pilots. The other two men on board were the radio operator, Sergeant Max Tubbs, from Tupelo, Mississippi, and fellow kicker, Corporal Wayne Burns, from Syracuse, New York. Sam didn't know either of these men, but he was comforted when he saw that they were capable airmen.

As they made their way toward Kohima, they were joined by two more C47s from the Seventeenth Squadron. The weather along their route was marginal, and they flew above a layer of clouds so that the ground was not visible. When the planes began to descend through the cloud layer, Sam knew they must be nearing the target area, and as they broke through into clear air at around five thousand feet, he could see that they were flying over an area of steep ridges and narrow valleys. The three cargo planes flew over the ridges for a short time, and then Sergeant Tubbs announced that they had arrived at the drop area as the C47s began to circle. Sam could see a cluster of buildings in a narrow valley below, and as their plane descended, he watched as signs of the battle raging below became more and more evident. Sergeant Tubbs told them they would be third in line to drop supplies, and so they watched from above as the first plane dropped into the narrow valley to deliver its load.

As the first C47 descended into the valley and approached the drop zone, tracer shells from enemy guns erupted from the ridges on both sides of the valley. Sam watched as the tracers probed to reach the first cargo plane. Sam knew that for every tracer, you could see there were ten other shells that weren't visible. He watched as the tracers slowly followed the C47 trying to converged upon the defenseless aircraft. Parachutes appeared as supplies were kicked from the plane, and it looked like the first plane made it through the gauntlet of enemy fire.

Sam's plane continued to circle and descended a little more as they watched the second C47 begin its approach to the drop zone. Once again, enemy tracers reached out from the surrounding ridges and clawed at the approaching plane. This time, the aim of the enemy gunners was more accurate, and the tracers converged upon helpless aircraft. Sam could see flashes appear along the body and wings of the plane as the enemy bullets struck. The C47 appeared to shudder under the impact of the shells, and then a tracer reached the gas tanks and the right wing disappeared in a fiery explosion. The crew of Sam's plane watched in horror as the crippled C47 flipped over and crashed in a ball of fire and smoke. It was their turn next.

Captain Stacey continued to circle as Sam, Sergeant Tubbs, and Corporal Burns prepared their cargo to be dropped. With everything in place, the men waited expectantly for the captain to begin their descent into the drop zone and the hell they knew was coming. They didn't have long to wait as the pilot descended into the narrow valley and began their first pass. Max took the kicker's position on the floor of the plane as Sam and Wayne stood ready to shove additional containers in front of the doorway. From Sam's position near the door, he could see the steep walls of the ridges as the C47 sank below their crests. It seemed as though the plane's wing tip was almost touching the wooded hillside as they descended further into the narrow valley. Finally, the airplane leveled off about three hundred feet above the valley floor, and the captain slowed the aircraft down in preparation for the drop. As they approached the drop zone, all along the ridge Sam could see the winking lights of muzzle flashes as the enemy gunners opened fire on them. He could distinctly see hot tracer rounds as they arched out of the wooded hillside and probed the sky all around the C47. Sam had never seen so much enemy fire, and he knew it was only a matter of time before the gunners zeroed in on their slow moving aircraft.

They hadn't quite reached the drop zone when the first shells struck the plane. Holes appeared in the roof and sides of the C47 as .30-caliber machine gun bullets tore their way through the thin aluminum covering of the plane. The airplane shuddered and seemed to wobble as explosive twenty-millimeter cannon shells slammed into it. The signal to jettison their load never came, so Max shouted for them to stand down as he rose and limped toward the cockpit, a stream of bright red blood stained his right pant leg. When Max reached the cockpit, he found Lieutenant Inge unconscious and Captain Stacey bleeding from multiple shrapnel wounds. The windshield on the copilot's side was shattered, and the compass that normally sat atop the instrument panel was gone. Shrapnel damage from an explosive cannon shell was everywhere. The instrument panel itself was a wreck, and the port engine was sputtering and trailing black smoke. The wounded captain struggled to control the aircraft as he attempted to climb out of the valley.

"Tell the crew to prepare to bail out," ordered the captain. "I'll try to get us some altitude before I give the order."

"Yes, sir," Max responded as he turned and hurried back into the cargo bay.

"The captain has ordered us to get our chutes on and get ready to bail out," the sergeant said to Sam and Wayne. "He'll give us the word when it's time to jump."

The men looked at each other in disbelief and then hurried to their parachutes and began to put them on. In the meantime, Captain Stacey had managed to climb the plane above the ridges, but without the aid of a compass and weakened by his wounds, he didn't realize they had turned east and were flying over Japanese-held territory. By the time they reached a safe altitude, he realized they were headed in the wrong direction, but the right engine was now acting up, and he was losing oil pressure in both engines. Knowing they were about to lose both engines, he informed Sergeant Tubbs of the situation and gave the order for the crew to bail out.

Sergeant Tubbs hurried back to the cargo bay and told Wayne and Sam the captain had given the order to bail out and that they were over enemy territory. He had each man don his web belt with pistol and canteen attached and then their parachutes. He checked their parachute straps for tightness and ordered them to jump. Corporal Burns was the first to go, and he disappeared out the cargo bay door. Sam motioned for the wounded sergeant to go next, but he refused and signaled for Sam to jump. Sam stood in the doorway and looked at the jungle below. He knew he had no choice, so he gripped the rip cord in his right hand and tumbled from the damaged aircraft.

As he exited the plane, the blast of the C47's slipstream hit Sam with surprising force. It was a strange sensation to find himself tumbling in space with nothing around him. After a few seconds, he pulled his rip cord and felt a jolt as the parachute opened and snapped him into an upright position. Looking around, he tried to spot Wayne or Sergeant Tubbs, but neither man was anywhere in sight. The only thing to be seen was the C47 as it receded in the distance with smoke now pouring from both engines. Sam looked at the ground below and saw jungle in every direction as far as he could see. It looked foreboding, and he realized he was about to enter a totally alien world. He knew the jungle was filled with deadly animals, reptiles, and diseases. He knew the enemy was down there, and they would hunt him down and kill him if he were caught. As his parachute steadily lowered him toward the dangers below, he never felt so alone. He looked at his wristwatch and noted that it was 10:00 a.m. He thought of Eleanor and the folks back home and wondered if he would ever see them again.

* * * * *

Half a world away, Eleanor was suddenly overcome with a total feeling of loneliness. She laid the book she was reading on her nightstand and looked at the empty space in the bed beside her. Her loneliness grew more profound as she thought of Sam. The most difficult part of her life was not knowing where he was or what was happening to him. In an effort to understand what he might be experiencing, she avidly read newspaper accounts and listened to radio broadcasts about the war in Burma. Nothing she read or heard had been encouraging. She looked at the clock beside her bed and did the conversion in her head. It was 10:00 a.m. in Burma, and she wondered what Sam was doing.

* * * * *

Sam noticed that the ground appeared to be approaching faster now. There were no open spaces in sight, so he knew he was going to land in the thick jungle growth. He pressed his feet and knees firmly together in preparation for the entry into the canopy of the jungle, and at the last moment, placed his hands in front of his face for protection. As he plummeted into the upper levels of the jungle, branches and leaves slapped against his body and broke beneath his weight. His descent continued unabated until the chute finally caught on a branch above and brought him to an abrupt halt. He hung there for a moment, swinging back and forth, but then the silk material in the chute began to tear, and he found himself plunging downward once again. The parachute continued to snag on branches slowing his progress through the canopy, and he eventually came to a complete stop. He held his breath for a moment to see if the chute was going to hold and then pulled on the shroud lines to test how secure they were. Finally convinced his descent was over, he relaxed and began to access his situation.

Sam was still securely suspended in his parachute harness. The jungle growth surrounding him was so thick nothing could be seen but foliage in any direction. A check of his body revealed that he had survived his first parachute jump in surprisingly good shape. Other than a few minor abrasions, there were no open cuts or broken bones. Knowing he was in enemy's territory, he listened for sounds of approaching danger. Hearing nothing, he turned his attention to the dilemma of reaching the ground. With no idea of how far he was above the ground, he looked about for a tree or limb that would afford a way of climbing down. Finding nothing suitable, he considered cutting the shroud lines and risking a drop of unknown height. However, he discarded the idea when he realized a broken leg or sprained ankle could well be a death sentence in the current situation. There had to be some way to determine how far the ground was below him. Remembering he had some Indian coins in his trouser pocket, he retrieved one and dropped it, hoping to hear it strike the ground. To his surprise, he thought he heard it hit the ground almost immediately. His excitement increased as he retrieved another coin and dropped it. In about one second, he was rewarded by the sound of a metallic clink as the second coin struck the first. Knowing he couldn't be very high, Sam removed the knife from his web belt and began cutting the shroud lines. After severing the last line, he was greatly relieved when he only dropped eighteen inches before striking the ground unharmed.

Using his knife to cut away some of the thick undergrowth, Sam cleared a small area around him and then removed the jungle kit from the bottom of the parachute pack. Upon inventorying the contents of the kit, he discovered it was missing some items; however, it did contain a K-ration dinner unit, a cloth map of Burma and India, a compass, a bottle of halazone tablets, and a packet of sulfa powder. He still had the knife and a canteen of water from his web belt, but his holster was empty. Sometime during the bailout, his .45 pistol must have been jarred loose and was gone. Realizing he did not have much to help him survive in the jungle, Sam tugged vigorously on the shroud lines until he was successful in pulling down a small portion of the parachute's silk canopy. He cut the silk free from the shroud lines and rolled it into a small package. Then he cut the shroud lines into useful lengths and used one of them to tie the silk bundle to his belt. By the time he finished, he was perspiring profusely from the stifling heat and humidity of the jungle.

Sam sat down to determine his next course of action. Taking a swig of water from his canteen, he opened the map of Burma and China. He remembered Sergeant Tubbs telling him they were over enemy's territory before he bailed out, and he knew their drop zone at Kohima was very close to the Burmese border. This information led him to the conclusion that he must be somewhere along the border in the jungles of Nagaland. If that were true, the nearest friendly forces should be somewhere to the northwest. The jungle was too thick for him to be spotted from the air, so he decided to begin walking in the hopes of finding friendly natives or British troops. Using his compass as a guide, he began to cut his way through the jungle in a northwesterly direction. However, the density of the underbrush made it almost impossible to make any headway, so he dropped to his hands and knees and began to crawl through the tangled masses of vegetation. Several times he encountered the webs of large ugly spiders and altered his course around them. Once he was stopped when he saw a large snake in his path. Not knowing if it was poisonous, he waited for it so slither away before continuing his laborious trek. The heat and humidity were almost unbearable, and Sam soon found his clothing was completely soaked from perspiration. To make matters worse, a steady rain began to fall, soaking him even more. With the rain came hordes of mosquitoes and biting flies. The bites from the flies burned like fire, and he was forced to wrap his head and exposed hands in parachute silk.

Hour after hour, Sam crawled through the dense jungle. Finally, he came to a place where the underbrush was not so thick and he was able to stand up. Using his knife to cut away vegetation, he continued on, but progress was still painfully slow. He prayed that he would soon find a trail or stream that would afford easier passage. However, his prayers went unanswered as the hours dragged on. Due to the intense heat, he had to drink frequently from his canteen. Several times he had to stop and fill the canteen with rainwater dripping from the plants. Each time, he was careful to add a halazone tablet to purify the precious liquid. The sun was beginning to set, and Sam could feel his strength waning when he encountered his next challenge in the form of a solid wall of bamboo that stretched across his intended path. Most of the bamboo that confronted him were six inches in diameter, and he was unable to cut through it with his knife. He tried to push his way through but was unable to penetrate the bamboo due to the density of its growth. Realizing it would soon be dark and nearing the end of his endurance, he wearily sat down as the rain began to pour from the heavens in sheets. Cutting a large frond from a nearby plant and placing it over his head to deflect the rain, his strength finally gave out, and he fell into a deep sleep.

Sometime during the night, the rains had stopped, and Sam awoke to the realization that he was still in the jungle. He had slept all night in a sitting position with his back against the thick bamboo, and his legs stretched out before him. When he looked down, he was shocked to see both legs of his pants, and the front of his shirt was soaked with blood. Confusion filled his head as he hastily unbuttoned his shirt. He knew he hadn't been injured the day before. He quickly tore off his shirt and t-shirt and stood in horror at the sight of two bloated leeches attached to his chest. Blood still dripped from the wounds where they clung to his flesh. He hurriedly removed his trousers and found one leech on his left leg and two on his right. Panic gripped him, and he wanted to tear the vile creatures from his skin, but he remembered being told never to do that because the head could stay attached and cause infection. He searched the rest of his body and was relieved to find no more of the disgusting creatures. He knew the leeches would drop off on their own when they became full, but he couldn't stand the thought of the ugly worms gorging on his blood. Remembering stories of removing leeches with the heat from a lit cigarette, he searched his jungle kit and removed the cigarettes and matches that were part of the K-ration unit. After lighting one of the cigarettes, he gently applied the lit end to one of the leeches on his chest. At first there was no reaction from the leech, but after repeated attempts, he was rewarded when the creature released its bite and dropped to the jungle floor. Excited by his success, Sam repeated the process until he had rid his body of the remaining bloodsuckers.

Blood continued to ooze from the wounds caused by the leeches, so Sam applied sulfa powder to the bites and bound them with strips of parachute silk. He donned his clothes and tied the bottom of his pant legs with pieces of shroud line to prevent further incursion by the leeches. Then he fully buttoned his shirt and tucked it tightly into his trousers. When he was satisfied, he had done all he could to protect himself from leeches, Sam turned his attention to the remaining contents of the K-ration. He found a can of cheese, biscuits, malted milk balls, chewing gum, and a packet of powdered orange drink, which he added to the water in his canteen. He ate the cheese and biscuits, washing them down with orange drink, and decided to keep the malted milk balls for later. With his hunger temporarily abated, he turned his attention to the problem of the bamboo forest.

Realizing there was no way he could penetrate the bamboo thicket, Sam decided to follow the edge of the bamboo until it came to an end or he had found a way through. As he stooped to pick up his gear, he noticed several leeches crawling up the outside of his trousers. He brushed them off, checked the rest of his clothing, and found nothing. However, he became aware of hundreds of the vile creatures slowly inching their way along the ground toward him. Revulsion filled him as he grabbed his gear and hurriedly departed.

Keeping the bamboo thicket on his left, Sam proceeded through the thick jungle. His progress was slow, and he only stopped long enough to take a drink and eat a few malted milk balls. Each time he stopped, he was disgusted to discover leeches on his clothing, but he was relieved to find that none of them had been able to get to his flesh. After a few hours, he finally came to the end of the bamboo and was able to resume a northwesterly course. The jungle never relented in its effort to slow him down, and he frequently tripped over exposed roots or became entangled in thorny vines. At one point, when he sat down to rest, he had to quickly evacuate the area when he was attacked by a swarm of red ants. The ants inflicted several painful stings to the back of his hands before he was able to get away. From that point on, he only stopped when he had to and then not for long.

Exhaustion overcame Sam late in the afternoon. Clearing a small space on the jungle floor, he sat down to finish what was left of the malted milk balls. He used the last of the liquid in his canteen to wash down the milk balls and then sat, silently pondering the seriousness of his situation. He had just finished the last of his food and water, and his map was useless since he had no idea of his current location. Loneliness and despair overcame him as he realized how small and insignificant a human being can be. He wept at the thought that he may never see his family again and they might never know what became of him. He closed his eyes as fatigue engulfed his body.

Just as Sam was about to surrender to sleep, he thought he heard a familiar sound. He was instantly awake and fully alert. Holding his breath and listening intently, he heard the sound again. He was sure it was the sound of water running in a stream. His exhaustion gone, he excitedly jumped to his feet and hurried in the direction of the wonderful sound. As he approached, the sound of the bubbling water became more distinct, and he soon arrived at the bank of a small jungle stream. His first order of business was to fill his canteen with the life-giving liquid and add a halazone tablet. Next he splashed cool water on his face and then proceeded to remove the blood-caked parachute dressings from his leech wounds. Relieved to find the bleeding had stopped, he used treated water from his canteen and clean silk padding to carefully wash the dried blood from his skin. After applying fresh sulfa powder, he rebound the wounds and prepared to continue his trek.

The stream was about two feet wide and flowed in a westerly direction. Sam felt it would be easier to wade in the stream rather than fight his way through the tangled jungle underbrush, so he removed his shoes and socks and began to follow the stream. Several times, the slippery rocks in the stream bed caused him to fall, so he donned his footgear and the wading became easier. After several miles, the little stream emptied in to a much larger one. The new stream averaged six to eight feet wide and had occasional stretches of sandy beach that Sam utilized as resting places. During one of his rest stops, he removed his footwear and discovered sand had gotten into his shoes. The sand had irritated the skin on his feet until they were bright red in color. He immediately washed the sand from his shoes and rinsed his stockings as best as he could before putting them back on. He knew he would have to be careful that blisters didn't form and impede his walking ability. Sam continued to follow the big stream and constantly kept on the lookout for a road or trail along the banks. However, his vigilance was not rewarded, and as night fell, he stretched out on a stretch of sandy beach and immediately fell into a fitful sleep.

22

APRIL 13, 1944
NAGALAND, BURMA

SAM AWOKE TO the sound of monkeys chattering in the trees nearby. Hunger gnawed at his stomach, and he searched his jungle kit for something to eat. Nothing remained of the K-ration except for a pack of chewing gum. Figuring there would be at least some nutritional value in the gum, he popped a stick in his mouth while he watched the monkeys across the stream. They appeared to be playing, but then he noticed they were eating something from a small tree along the stream. His hopes rose as he waded across the stream to where the monkeys were feeding. As he approached, they became very agitated, and he could see they were feeding on a small reddish fruit from the tree. Sam's proximity to their feeding place finally unnerved the monkeys, causing them to scurry higher into the jungle growth where they chattered excitedly among themselves.

Upon reaching the tree, Sam saw that it produced its fruit in clusters. Examining one of the clusters, he found the individual fruit were about two inches long and slightly oval in shape. Their leathery reddish skin was covered with soft spines that reminded him of the chestnuts from back home. Removing one of the fruit, Sam cut it open, revealing a central seed surrounded by white flesh that was translucent and slightly gummy to the touch. He tentatively tasted the flesh and found it had a pleasant sweet but slightly sour flavor. Further experimentation revealed that he could easily extract the flesh of the fruit by cutting the rind part way around and prying it open. This technique left the pulpy white flesh in one half of the rind, and he was able to easily pop it out with a slight squeeze. Assuming the monkeys knew what was safe, Sam ate his fill of the fruit and then filled his jungle kit with as much as it would hold.

With his hunger satisfied, Sam turned his attention to the task of escaping from the jungle. Since the stream was flowing in the general direction that he wanted to go, he decided to continue following it in the hope of discovering a trail or native village. The stream also provided an easy source of much-needed water, so he collected his gear and continued his journey.

After several hours, Sam noticed the stream was beginning to widen and get deeper in spots. He knew the natives built their villages near streams, so he stayed close to the shoreline and proceeded cautiously. He had been told that not all the natives were friendly, and some would turn American soldiers over to the Japanese in exchange for money or opium. Being careful not to make much noise, Sam continued to the follow the stream until he came to a point where it emptied into a sizable river that was flowing in a southerly direction. The shoreline of the river consisted of a narrow strip of pebble and sand-covered beach that would allow easy walking. He decided his best option was to follow the river to the north, so he left the stream and began walking along the river's sandy beach.

The river's relatively clear shoreline enabled Sam to make good progress. So far, he had found no trails leading away from the river, and he had seen no signs of habitation. He was approaching a bend in the river and had become a little lax in his vigilance, when he heard the sound of an approaching outboard motor. He jumped into the thick vegetation along the shore just as a boat containing a dozen Japanese soldiers rounded the bend. Sam burrowed deeper into the vegetation, listening for any indication that he had been seen. The sound of the boat's motor remained the same, and he heard no shouts from the men on board, so he lay still and watched as they slowly approached. It was then that he saw his footprints clearly imprinted in the sand of the beach. The boat was very close now, and Sam could distinctly see the Japanese soldiers on board. They were only about twenty feet from the shore, and he knew they would be able to see his footprints from their vantage point.

Sam held his breath and prepared to bolt into the jungle as the boat approached his position. Just before the boat reached a point opposite his hiding place, a Japanese soldier appeared on the opposite side of the river and began shouting and waving to his comrades on the river. The boat was immediately turned toward the opposite shore, and Sam watched in relief as they proceeded across the river and stopped to talk to the gesturing soldier. After a few minutes, the soldier climbed aboard the boat, and it continued its journey down the opposite shoreline. Sam watched until the enemy boat disappeared from sight. He knew that if they returned along his side of the river his footprints would be discovered, so he decided to turn away from the river and proceed through the jungle where it would be harder for the enemy to find him.

His progress through the jungle was slow, but Sam felt safer among the thick undergrowth. He now knew he was definitely behind enemy lines, so he proceeded with great caution. After traveling about a mile directly away from the river, he abruptly came upon a well-used trail. He knew he couldn't continue through the jungle without exhausting all his energy, so he decided to follow the trail in the hope of finding a friendly village. As he followed the trail in a northwesterly direction, every sense and nerve in his body was on the alert for danger.

Travel along the trail was easy, and Sam was able to cover several miles before he came to a large clearing in the jungle. The opening was about sixty yards wide and the trail led directly through it. Sam waited silently in the shadows of the jungle. Other than the normal sounds of the jungle, he heard nothing to indicate the presence of danger, so he decided to cross the clearing as quickly as he could. Cautiously stepping into the open, he was about to dash across the clearing when a Japanese soldier appeared on the other side. Both men were stunned when they saw each other, and there was a second of inaction until more enemy soldiers appeared behind the first one. Without further hesitation, Sam turned and fled in the opposite direction as angry shouts erupted from the enemy patrol.

Sam could hear the Japanese soldiers behind him as he raced along the jungle trail. Suddenly, the pathway didn't seem as wide as it was before, and his progress was slowed as thorns and creepers clawed and tore at his clothing and exposed flesh. The enemy seemed to be closing the gap behind him, and he redoubled his efforts to escape. At one point, he looked back and caught a glimpse of his pursuers and saw the menacing long sword carried by their leader. He could feel his strength waning, and he knew he was approaching the point of total exhaustion. Desperation gripped him as he suddenly remembered his recurring nightmare and realized it was coming true. He tried to run faster but tripped over a jungle vine, and his pursuers gained ground on him. He scrambled to his feet and rounded a turn in the trail where he came face-to-face with a lone Naga warrior. Panic overcame Sam as he realized there was no escape.

The Naga warrior was a good seven inches shorter than Sam, but he didn't hesitate in grabbing the larger man and pushing him forcefully into the thick growth alongside the trail. Caught completely by surprise, Sam rolled into the brush and remained still as the Japanese soldiers rounded the turn. The warrior gestured frantically to them, indicating the American had continued down the trail. The lieutenant leading the patrol was immediately suspicious and ordered half his men to continue the pursuit and the other half to search the brush around the warrior. Sam curled into a ball as the Japanese soldiers probed the bush with the long bayonets on the end of their rifles. Luckily for Sam, he had been pushed into a particularly thick patch of underbrush and could not be easily seen. However, he did have one close call when a soldier thrust his bayonet into the brush just inches from Sam's body.

The Japanese soldiers completed their search of the surrounding area without discovering Sam's hiding place. When the remaining soldiers returned empty handed, the lieutenant turned his wrath upon the Naga warrior. Sam watched the scene as the irate officer interrogated the warrior. Sam could not understand the words, but he knew the lieutenant was demanding to know the whereabouts of the American soldier. Never looking in Sam's direction, the brave Naga warrior simply shook his head, indicating he knew nothing. Finally, the lieutenant came to the end of his patience and issued a harsh command. Immediately the soldiers surrounded the warrior and began to strike him with the butts of their rifles. The helpless Naga fell to the ground covering his face and head as the soldiers viciously kicked and struck him repeatedly.

As Sam watched from his hiding place, he became aware of a burning pain on the calf of his right leg. That pain was soon followed by another, and he knew immediately he had been discovered by a colony of stinging red ants like the ones he encountered yesterday. Now he could feel the insects as they crawled relentlessly up his leg, and it was all he could do to keep from screaming as they bit and stung his flesh. He couldn't make a sound, and he couldn't move without alerting the enemy to his presence. As the vicious ants probed further up his leg, he squeezed his legs tightly together to keep them from reaching his genital area. Clenching his teeth against the mounting pain, it was all he could do to keep from screaming as the persistent insects reached his buttocks. Tears welled in his eyes, and he prayed the torment would stop.

Sam's attention was drawn back to the scene before him when he heard the Japanese lieutenant issue a guttural command. The soldiers immediately stopped their abuse and stepped back as the officer stood over the bleeding warrior. For the first time, Sam could see the condition of the Japanese soldiers. Their uniforms were mildewed and rotting. Many had rags wrapped around their feet in place of shoes, and all of their emaciated bodies were dirty and covered with jungle sores. Without exception, their eyes revealed the malevolence and hatred they felt toward the Naga warrior. Sam also saw nothing but contempt and hatred in the eyes of the lieutenant as he glared down at his prisoner. The officer barked another command, and two soldiers stepped forward, lifting the warrior into a kneeling position and forced his head down. Sam forgot his own pain, and a cold chill ran down his spine as he realized he had been in there in his nightmare many times. He knew what was in store for the brave Naga warrior. The soldiers stepped back, and the officer's eyes gleamed in anticipation of the elimination of another enemy of the Japanese empire. Clasping his sword with both hands, the lieutenant raised the keen blade far above the Naga's exposed neck. Shouts of triumph erupted from the throats of the soldiers. They were about to witness the culmination of a grizzly ritual from their ancient past.

Sam knew he couldn't let this happen. He couldn't let the Naga die to save himself. He was just about to reveal his presence when the warrior raised his head slightly and looked in Sam's direction. With an imperceptible motion of his head, the brave Naga warned Sam to remain still and then the wicket blade made a hissing sound as it plunged downward. Sam closed his eyes as the warriors head toppled from his body, and blood spurted from severed arteries. More cheers erupted from the soldiers as the lieutenant kicked the lifeless head into the underbrush. With the gruesome task completed, the soldiers left the body lying on the trail and continued their search in the direction they believed Sam had gone.

Sam suffered silently in the underbrush until he could no longer hear the departing enemy, and then he stood and frantically slapped at his legs and shook his clothing to rid himself of the vicious ants.

When he was convinced there were no more ants on his body, he cautiously crept from his hiding place and stood beside the lifeless body of the Naga warrior. Tears streamed down Sam's face as he wept for this unknown warrior who had given his life for a total stranger. He gently moved the body to the side of the trail and retrieved the warriors head from the brush; then, with only his knife and bare hands, he began to dig a shallow grave beside the trail. He became totally engrossed in the task at hand and didn't stop until he sensed the presence of other human beings. Looking up from the shallow hole he was excavating, he saw two Naga warriors watching him intently.

The warriors looked much like the man who had given his life for Sam. The only clothing they wore was a loin cloth. Their hair was short and looked as if it had been cut after a bowl was placed over their heads. Each man wore a necklace of bone and beads, and each had a long white feather stuck in a woven grass band around their head. Sam's attention was drawn to the wicked-looking knives the men carried. The wooden handles were about eighteen inches long with a twenty-inch metal blade attached. The blades were four inches wide and square on the end before tapering down to about one inch where they were attached to the wooden hilt. The blades appeared to be extremely sharp and gave the appearance of elongated meat cleavers. A friend of Sam's back at Dinjan had acquired one of these knives as a souvenir and told Sam it was called a *dao*. Sam knew the Nagas were headhunters, and he wasn't at all sure of the intentions of these warriors.

Long anxious moments passed before the Naga warriors finally moved. They came quietly to Sam's side and began to use their daos to help him dig the grave. The daos proved to be very effective digging tools, and the three men soon had an adequate grave prepared. Sam watched as the Nagas gently placed their kinsman into the shallow hole, and then he helped to cover the body with dirt. When the task was done, the warriors motioned for Sam to follow as they proceeded down the trail in the direction of the jungle clearing. Sam had difficulty standing up and realized the ant bites had caused his leg to swell. He experienced considerable pain as he limped along behind the Nagas. They had only walked a short distance when the warriors suddenly stopped; then turning quickly, they grabbed Sam and dragged him into the underbrush. Believing he was about to become the next victim of the headhunters, Sam attempted to fight back, but the Nagas motioned for him to be silent as they pointed frantically toward the trail. When he saw the warriors were not going to harm him, he stopped resisting and crouched silently with them amid the dense underbrush.

They didn't wait long before Sam heard a group of men approaching, and then he watched quietly as another Japanese patrol filed past their hiding place. When the enemy soldiers were gone, Sam attempted to rise but was restrained by the Naga warriors. Confused and not understanding why they continued to hide, he waited until he saw a lone Japanese soldier trailing the main group. Sam was amazed at the ability of the Nagas to detect the presence of others in the dense jungle. When the soldier stopped directly in front of the hiding men and cautiously looked around, Sam was sure their presence had been detected, and he prepared to flee further into the jungle. The soldier took another look around and then turning his back on the silent watchers undid the front of his trousers. Sam could hear the sound of liquid splashing on the leaves as the soldier urinated into the brush. With the soldier's attention averted, the warrior closest to the trail stepped silently onto the pathway, and in one quick movement, decapitated the unsuspecting soldier with his dao. The Naga warriors moved quickly, and in total silence, they dragged the body into the brush and removed the ears from the severed head before tossing it away. At first, Sam was horrified by the actions of the Nagas, but when he remembered hearing that the British would pay in silver or opium for the ears of the enemy, he understood the motives of the warriors.

The Naga warriors made sure the body of the Japanese soldier would be difficult to find and then led Sam for a short distance onward. They departed from the main trail and onto a side trail that was difficult to see. The new trail was narrow and arduous to traverse, as it wound its way up the side of a steep ridge. The pain in Sam's legs continued to increase, and he found it difficult to keep up with his native guides. He had to stop often, and each time the warriors waited stoically until he was able to continue. They crossed several more ridges until finally arriving at a Naga village nestled along a stream at the foot of the last ridge.

Sam could see the village was built for protection. It was surrounded by a thick fence of thorn-covered shrubs and stinging nettles. Access to the village was through sunken pathways that led to sturdy wooden doors. Sam could see that the fortifications would deter animals and primitively armed men, but they would offer little resistance to soldiers with modern weapons. His Naga guides led him into the village where they were met by a throng of villagers and several yapping dogs. The villagers ranged in age from toddlers to adults of various ages. Like the Nagas who guided him here, the men and young boys wore only a loin cloth and a headband. Some of the headbands had one, two, or three feathers, and others had none. Sam figured the number of feathers must indicate status among the tribe. The females all wore garments that appeared to be woven from a course fiber and were decorated with red and black designs. The maidens had their bodies completely covered, while most of the older women left their bosoms uncovered. Sam assumed the married women were the ones with uncovered breasts.

The villagers crowded around Sam, jabbering in a language he could not understand. Their talk ended abruptly, and the throng parted at the approach of a wizened old man who was dressed like the other men, with the exception of a necklace made of boars' tusks and a human skull. The old man also carried a dao with a hilt that appeared to be adorned with human hair. This was obviously the village headman, and Sam stood motionless as he approached. The old man conversed with the men who had brought Sam until he appeared satisfied with their story. He then spoke a few unintelligible words to Sam before motioning him to follow. The old man led Sam toward the largest of the houses in the village.

As he followed the headman, Sam had a chance to study the Naga structures. The houses appeared to be randomly placed within the surrounding fence. Each house was built above the ground on wooden poles. The thatched roofs were very steep to facilitate the runoff of rain, and the walls were made of narrow bamboo poles lashed together with vines. The spaces under the houses were occupied by a mixture of chickens, goats, and pigs. Sam followed the old man up a bamboo ladder and into the big house. The house had several rooms with bamboo floors, and in the middle of the largest room was a crude firebox. The firebox consisted of a log crib filled with dirt and placed in the middle of the floor. A small fire was burning in the firebox, and the smoke drifted upward, filtering through the thatch roof. The old man took a seat on a thatched mat and motioned for Sam to sit on a similar mat. Sam's swollen right leg made it difficult for him to sit, and he grimaced in pain as he lowered himself to the mat.

The headman barked an order, and two of the women in the house immediately came forward and began tugging at Sam's trousers. He motioned them away, but they persisted in unbuckling his belt and proceeded to pull his trousers from his body. The pain caused by the scraping of the cloth over the ant stings was excruciating. When his trousers were finally removed, Sam was shocked by the sight of his leg. It was swollen to nearly twice its normal size and covered with large red welts. The women left the room and returned shortly with a wooden bowl containing water and an assortment of dried leaves and roots. They crushed the leaves and roots into the water and then soaked larger leaves in the mixture. When the large leaves had soaked for a few minutes, they were removed from the bowl and gently applied to the welts on Sam's leg and buttocks. The cool leaves immediately provided some relief, and in a matter of minutes, Sam was surprised to find his pain subsiding. The women kept the leaf compresses moist with water from the bowl, and within half an hour, Sam found himself completely pain free.

Seeing that his guest was comfortable, the headman issued another order, and the women began preparing a meal. Sam watched with interest as the women added wood to the firebox and placed a large pot filled with water over the hot coals. More wood was added to the fire around the pot, and when the water began to boil, handfuls of rice, bamboo shoots, and small red peppers were added. After the women were satisfied the mixture had cooked long enough, they brought forth a small covered basket and poured some of the contents into an elongated wooden bowl. Sam was aghast to see the bowl contained the dried bodies of some type of brown beetle. Using a stone pestle, the women proceeded to grind the beetles into small pieces before adding them to the rice mixture. When the concoction was cooked to the women's satisfaction, they ladled some into a small bowl and presented it to the headman. The old man tasted the brew and, nodding his head in approval, handed the bowl to Sam. The Nagas waited expectantly for their guest to begin to eat. Torn between two dilemmas, Sam had to either eat the bug-laced mixture or take the risk of insulting his host. He decided that eating the bugs would be better than losing his head, so he tentatively tasted the brew and found it wasn't at all bad. Smiling his approval, the headman ate heartily from a second bowl the women provided for him. After a few more bites, Sam decided the meal was quite palatable, although he did learn to avoid eating the red peppers which were fiery hot.

After the meal of rice and bugs, the women brought in small bamboo cups filled with a fermented mixture. The head man downed his with gusto and waited for Sam to do the same. Once again, not wanting to insult his host, Sam downed his cup in one gulp and gasped at the potency of the drink. He was glad he couldn't speak the Naga language, because he was unable to speak for several moments.

Nodding his approval, the old man signaled for their cups to be refilled before repeating the process. Sam followed the old man's example, and before long, they had consumed several cups of the potent brew. The last thing Sam remembered seeing before he passed out was the smiling face of his host as he downed yet another cup.

The next morning, Sam was shaken awake by one of the warriors that had accompanied him to the village the day before. Sam's reactions were slow, and his head throbbed from the effects of the previous night's drinking. The warrior shook him again and motioned frantically for him to follow. The urgency in the warrior's demeanor brought Sam to full alert, and he followed the Naga outside where they were met by several more warriors. Motioning feverishly for Sam to follow, the warriors led him to a small exit at the rear of the village. They pushed him through the exit and into the jungle where they led him up the slope of the steep ridge above the village. There was no distinguishable trail, but the Nagas seemed to know where they were going. They prodded Sam along while constantly looking back to be sure they weren't being followed. Finally, the lead Naga stopped at a spot overlooking the village and pushed aside some underbrush to reveal the entrance to a small cave. Sam marveled at how well the entrance was concealed.

They pushed him into the cave where he was joined by two of the warriors. At first, everything was totally black inside, but soon his eyes began to adjust to the darkness, and he was able to distinguish details. The cave was about four feet wide at the entrance and widened to around ten feet at the back. The entire length of the cave was about twenty feet and afforded ample space for the three men. Several sleeping mats were placed along the walls in addition to a half dozen covered baskets. Sam assumed the baskets contained rice and other edible items and wondered if one of them was filled with brown beetles. It was obvious the Nagas used the cave for refuge in time of danger. Sam's inspection of the cave was interrupted by the sound of distant shouting. The Naga warriors motioned for Sam to follow as they crept to the mouth of the cave. After he joined them, they carefully parted the foliage in front of the entrance so they could see the village below.

The scene in the village was one of total chaos. Villagers were scurrying to escape the village while Japanese soldiers ran from house to house as if they were searching for someone. Sam recognized the lieutenant that had led the patrol that chased him through the jungle and knew they were probably looking for him. Several soldiers were holding a group of villagers at gunpoint, and soon the headman was dragged from his house and brought before the lieutenant. Sam watched tensely as the officer began to interrogate the old man through one of his soldiers who acted as an interpreter. The silent men in the cave watched as the headman shook his head no in response to each question. They could see the lieutenant becoming more and more agitated as the questioning wore on. Finally, the officer drew his pistol and threatened the old man. When his threat drew no response, the irate lieutenant struck his helpless victim across the face with the pistol. The old man fell to the ground, and Sam could feel the bodies of the warriors next to him become tense.

The lieutenant stepped forward and raised his hand to strike the headman again when he was stopped by a shout from one of his soldiers. The soldier could be seen running through the village shouting and carrying something in his hand. Sam was shocked when he realized the item in the soldier's hand was a U.S. Army jungle kit. His shock turned to horror when he realized he had left his jungle kit behind in his haste to leave the village.

Two soldiers hauled the headman to his feet as the lieutenant stood before him holding the jungle kit. The officer placed the barrel of his pistol against the old man's forehead and barked another question. When he received no answer, he pulled the trigger, sending a crimson spray of blood and brains into the air. Another order from the lieutenant sent the soldiers scurrying about, killing every animal in sight, and as they departed from the village, they set fire to all the houses. From their vantage point in the cave, Sam and the two Naga warriors watched as the village soon became a raging inferno. Sam had wondered why the Nagas were willing to give up their lives for a stranger, and now he understood. The treatment they received at the hands of the Japanese had filled their hearts with resentment and hate.

The tinder-dry materials in the houses burned quickly, and the village was soon completely destroyed. Nothing remained but smoldering ashes and the bodies of dead animals and the old man. The villagers who were spared shuffled through the ruins, and wails of grief could be heard by the men in the cave above. The two warriors with Sam motioned for him to stay put, and they departed from the cave. He observed the scene below and, after a little while, saw the warriors enter the ruined village and collect the body of the old man. He watched with tears in his eyes as the man he had dined and drank with the night before was laid to rest.

Sam spent the remainder of the day alone in the cave as the people of the village started the process of cleaning up what remained of their homes. By the end of the day, the construction of new houses had begun, and the two warriors returned to the cave where they built a smokeless fire and cooked rice for their evening meal. After darkness fell, Sam curled up on a sleeping mat and fell into a restless sleep.

Sometime during the night, Sam became delirious, and his body was wracked by a fever. The next morning, he remained unconscious and his fever began to climb. The warriors brought women from the village to tend to Sam, and knowing there was nothing more they could do, the men left to help rebuild their homes. The women bathed Sam's body with cooling water and prepared herbal drinks to alleviate his fever. They did the best they could to make him comfortable and settled back for the long wait to see if he would survive.

23

APRIL 18, 1944
MOSHANNON VALLEY, PENNSYLVANIA

LIFE HAD TURNED into one monotonous day after another for Eleanor. Working the midnight shift at the sewing factory and being five months pregnant was beginning to take its toll on her, and lately, she had begun to feel tired all the time. The one bright spot in her life was the fact that May lived across the street and was able to take care of Billy while she worked and slept. She missed Sam and constantly worried about him, and she missed being able to spend quality time with Billy. Normally, she would go straight to bed after her shift at the factory, but this morning, as she rode home with her sister-in-law Lynette, she decided to visit her son and May before going to bed.

She said goodbye to Lynette and checked to see if the mail had arrived. Finding nothing in the mailbox, she slowly walked across the street to May's house. When she entered the front door, she received a cheerful greeting from Paul.

"Well, how's my favorite sister-in-law this morning?" Paul asked from the sofa.

"I've had better days," she responded. "How's your recovery from the accident going?"

"Each day is better than the last, and I should be able to go back to work in another four weeks," he said.

"That's wonderful," Eleanor said. "Where's May and Billy?"

"May is in the kitchen having coffee with our neighbor, Nan Herring. I imagine Billy is having a glass of milk with them."

"Coffee sounds good. I think I'll join them. Can I get you anything?" Eleanor inquired.

"I'm fine, dear. Go and enjoy some coffee with the women," Paul answered.

Eleanor entered the kitchen and was warmly greeted by the women and by Billy who ran over and gave his mother a big hug. She poured herself a cup of coffee and went to join the others. As she took a seat at the table, the indirect glances May and Nan exchanged gave Eleanor the unmistakable impression that she had interrupted a sensitive conversation.

"Did I come at an inopportune time?" she asked.

"No, dear. It's just… Well, Nan was telling me about the latest talk around town," May responded.

"Oh, is it something you don't want me to know about?" Eleanor continued.

"We don't want to upset you. We know how worried you are about Sam," Nan said.

"Nothing will stop me from worrying about Sam," Eleanor replied. "So what's the latest talk going around?"

"Well, Mr. Stein, the manager of the A&P, and his wife were just notified that their eldest son, John, was killed in the fighting in the South Pacific," May said while watching for Eleanor's reaction.

"I'm sorry to hear that," Eleanor responded with a slight quiver in her voice. "I went to school with John. He was always a nice young man. They have another son in the army too, don't they?"

"Yes, their second son is stationed in England. Are you all right, Eleanor?" Nan asked. "Have you heard from Sam lately?"

"I'm okay, Nan. The last letter I got from Sam was dated April 4. He said things were heating up, and he was flying a lot of missions. The censors won't allow them to write any details, so I don't know exactly what he is doing."

"I'm sure everything is okay, Eleanor," Nan said, "Keep your chin up and don't lose faith."

"I'll try," Eleanor said halfheartedly as she rose from the table. "Well, I guess I had better get some sleep. I'll pick Billy up around two o'clock."

"He'll be all ready for you," May responded.

Eleanor gave Billy a hug and walked to the front door followed by May and Nan. She was just about to open the door when she saw Ed Fleagle, the mailman, coming down the street. She watched as he approached her house across the street, but instead of putting her mail in the mail box, he stepped up onto the porch and knocked on the door. Eleanor's heart froze when she saw he had a Western Union telegram envelope in his hand.

May noticed Eleanor's body stiffen. "What's wrong, Eleanor?"

"The mailman has a telegram. Oh, May, something has happened to Sam," Eleanor said as a lump formed in her throat.

"Now don't jump to conclusions. We'll see what this is all about," May cautioned as she opened her door and called to the postman. "Eleanor is over here, Ed."

They watched as Ed crossed the street and stepped up onto May's porch. There was a look of sorrow on his face as he approached the door and handed the envelope to Eleanor.

"I hope this isn't bad news, Mrs. Huber," Ed said solemnly. "I can't tell you how much I hate delivering these things."

Eleanor's hands shook as she took the envelope from the postman. She watched as Ed sadly turned and continued down the street, and then she broke down and began sobbing uncontrollably. May led her to a chair and made her sit down.

"You should open the telegram and see what it's all about," May said as she tried to control her own emotions.

"I can't," Eleanor said as tears streamed down her face, and she handed the envelope to May. "I'm afraid of what it might say."

"Maybe you should open it, May," Nan said.

May hesitated and looked at the envelope in Eleanor's shaking hands. "I don't want to be the first one to know if something bad has happened," she said as she choked back her own tears.

Billy entered the room and saw the two most important women in his life weeping. He too began to cry and ran to his mother. "What wrong, Mama? What wrong?" he sobbed.

Eleanor picked her young son up and cradled him in her lap. She was unable to speak as thoughts of raising him without a father raced through her head.

"I'll open it," Paul finally said as he took the envelope, extracted the telegram, and read the message it contained. "It's not good news, but it's not the worst either," he said as he handed the telegram to Eleanor.

Paul's words gave Eleanor a slight glimmer of hope as she read the contents of the telegram.

Dated <u>WASHINGTON DC 4/17/44</u>
To <u>MRS HUBER</u>
<u>300 PRUNER ST OSCEOLA MILLS PA</u>

<u>THE SECRETARY OF WAR DESIRES ME TO EXPRESS HIS DEEP REGRET</u>
<u>THAT YOUR HUSBAND PVT. SAMUEL D HUBER HAS BEEN REPORTED</u>
<u>MISSING IN ACTION SINCE 11 APRIL IN BURMA IF FURTHER</u>
<u>DETAILS OR OTHER INFORMATION ARE RECEIVED YOU WILL BE</u>
<u>PROMPTLY NOTIFIED CONFORMATION LETTER TO FOLLOW</u>

<u>JULIO THE ADJUTANT GENERAL</u>

"How can this be? How can he be missing? How do we know he isn't dead?" Eleanor sobbed.

"Now don't get yourself all worked up," Paul cautioned. "The telegram just says he's missing. It doesn't say he's dead and downed airmen are rescued all the time."

"Paul's right, Eleanor," May added. "We can't give up hope, and you're not alone. I think it would be best if you stayed here with us until we know more."

"I suppose your right. I don't think I could be alone right now," Eleanor said despondently. "I'll go home and get some things and be right back."

Eleanor crossed the street to her home. As she entered the front door, she was overcame with memories of the times she and Sam spent there. This had been their home for most of their marriage. This is where they lived and loved and where their unborn child had been conceived. This had been a place of happiness, but now it seemed lifeless and lonely. As she packed a few articles of clothing, she was glad to be leaving, glad to be able to be with family.

APRIL 18, 1944
NAGALAND, BURMA

Sam struggled to open his eyes. His head throbbed, and his body felt so weak that he didn't feel he could move his arms or legs. Slowly, he opened his eyes to a world that seemed strangely out of focus, and then everything turned dark again as he slipped back into unconsciousness. The Naga woman who was watching over him noted the change in his condition and slipped from the cave to bring a special visitor.

Sam opened his eyes again. This time, his head didn't hurt as much, and his vision cleared so that he could see his surroundings. At first, he was confused by the stone walls that surrounded him, but then he remembered the cave and the scenes he had witnessed of the destruction of the Naga village. He slowly rolled onto his side and came face-to-face with a grinning Naga warrior.

"Hi, Joe, you okay?" asked the warrior.

Sam nodded but his weakness caused him to lie back down as the warrior continued. "I speak pretty good English, Joe?"

Sam nodded once again.

"Good, Joe, you okay now. I go get help," said the warrior who departed before Sam could respond.

The warrior was replaced by two married Naga women who proceeded to dab his forehead with cool water from a jar. Somewhat disconcerted by the women's bare breasts, Sam was still thankful for the relief the water brought to his weakened body. When they were finished dabbing his forehead, the women fed him some hot stew from a pot on the fire. The stew contained rice and vegetables along with what Sam thought were pieces of black mushrooms. All in all, the stew was hot and nourishing, and he could feel his strength returning with each spoonful. When he was finished eating, the women ate some of the stew and then set about refilling the pot. Sam watched idly as they added more rice and vegetables, but his attention was brought to a heightened state when they produced a bowl of water filled with live black tadpoles and poured them into the pot. Sam decided right then and there that he would no longer watch as the Nagas prepared food.

APRIL 20, 1944
MOSHANNON VALLEY, PENNSYLVANIA

After receiving the telegram notifying her of Sam's missing-in-action status, Eleanor decided it would be best to continue working in order to keep her mind occupied. However, taking into account that she was pregnant and under considerable stress, her boss had placed her on day shift. Since she depended on her sister-in-law for transportation, the boss was also kind enough to put Lynette on day shift. Work kept Eleanor busy during the day, and Paul and May kept her occupied in the evening. However, her bedtime hours were still filled with loneliness and fear of the news the next day might bring.

Lynette had just dropped her off at May's house, and Eleanor automatically looked across the street to see if there was mail in her mailbox. It had been two days since she received the telegram from the adjutant general, and she desperately wanted more information about Sam. Her spirits dropped when she saw the box was empty. She stood staring at her empty home and wondered if it would ever see her family together again.

May saw Eleanor standing on the porch and rushed to open the front door. "Eleanor, Ed Fleagle knew you were staying here, so he delivered this to me today," May said as she held an unopened envelope out to Eleanor. "It's from the War Department."

Eleanor rushed into the house and took the letter from May. With trembling hands, she opened the envelope and read the letter within.

Dear Mrs. Huber:

This letter is to confirm my recent telegram in which you were regretfully informed that your husband, Pvt. Samuel D. Huber, U.S. Army Air Force, has been reported missing in action since 11 April 1944 in Burma.

I know that added distress is caused by failure to receive more information or details. Therefore, I wish to assure you that at any time additional information is received it will be transmitted to you without delay, and, if in the meantime no additional information is received, I will again communicate with you at the expiration of three months.

The term "missing in action" is used only to indicate that the whereabouts or status of an individual is not immediately known. It is not intended to convey the impression that the case is closed. I wish to emphasize that every effort is exerted continuously to clear up the status of our personnel. Under war conditions this is a difficult task as you must readily realize. Experience has shown that many persons reported missing in action are subsequently reported as prisoners of war, but as this information is furnished by countries with which we are at war, the War Department is helpless to expedite such reports. However, in order to relieve financial worry, Congress has enacted legislation which continues in force the pay, allowances and allotments to dependents of personnel being carried in a missing status.

Permit me to extend to you my heartfelt sympathy during this period of uncertainty.

Sincerely yours,
T.J. Julio
Major General
The Adjutant General.

After Eleanor finished reading the letter, she handed it to May and went to the sofa and sat down. The army apparently had little information about Sam. They had no idea if he was dead or alive, and if he's alive, there's a good chance he's a prisoner of war. The only positive news was that she would continue to receive her allotment check, but money was a poor substitute for someone you love.

May finished reading the letter and sat down beside Eleanor. There were a few minutes of silence before she spoke. "The general says they will expend every effort to find out what happened to Sam, and there's a good chance he's alive."

"They don't really know if he is alive, May, and if he is, he may be a prisoner of war. We've heard how the Japanese have tortured and brutalized some of our men. They beheaded some of the airmen they captured from the Doolittle raid. I can't bear the thought of that happening to Sam."

"I don't have any answers for you, Eleanor, but I do know you have one precious child and another one on the way. You have to find it within yourself to go on for them, and you know Paul and I are here for you."

"Thank you, May. I think I'll go lie down for a while. I know you have supper ready, but I'm not very hungry right now."

"Paul and Billy are upstairs playing. Would you send them down for supper? I'll keep things warm in case you get hungry later," May said sadly.

APRIL 20, 1944
NAGALAND, BURMA

It had been two days since Sam's fever broke, and his strength increased with each passing day. The Nagas would not let him leave the cave, so he spent the days watching from the cave as they gathered materials and began to rebuild their village. He wished there was someone who could understand him. He wanted to convey his desire to be led to friendly forces, and he wondered if he had just hallucinated or there really was an English-speaking Naga in the cave when he came to. In any event, he felt he was strong enough to begin the walk to safety if the Nagas would guide him. He decided that the next time a warrior came to the cave, he would try to use sign language to communicate his wishes.

"Hey, Joe, you there?" came a voice from outside the cave.

Fearing the Japanese had found his hiding place, Sam remained silent. However, his Naga attendants immediately began jabbering to the person outside in their native language. Presently, a Naga warrior entered the cave, and Sam recognized him as the one who had spoken English to him a few days ago.

"Hi, Joe, you come. Go home," said the warrior as he motioned for Sam to follow him.

"You understand English?" Sam asked excitedly.

"Yes yes, speak English. Come, come go home," answered the Naga.

"Where are we going?" Sam inquired.

"To fly bird. Take home," the Naga said with a smile.

"How far to fly bird?" Sam asked.

"Not far, two hours. Come, come," replied the warrior.

"What's your name?" Sam inquired.

"You call me Fred," responded the Naga proudly.

Sam was amazed that rescue was so close at hand, and he followed Fred from the cave where they were met by several other Naga warriors. The group motioned for Sam to follow as they wound their way down the steep ridge and into the thick jungle below. The Nagas knew the jungle well, and they led Sam along a maze of paths and animal trails. Their progress went quickly until the lead warrior stopped and signaled for everyone to take cover. Sam watched as the warriors ahead of him melted silently into the foliage along the trail, and then he followed Fred into the dense underbrush.

They remained concealed for a good five minutes before Sam whispered to Fred, "Why are we hiding?"

"Yellow soldiers on trail," Fred whispered back.

Sam remained still and waited for what seemed like an eternity. Finally, he heard the sound of men approaching. He watched as a Japanese patrol filed past their hiding place, and he wondered how the Nagas knew they were coming so far ahead of time. He realized the Nagas were primitive by western standards, but they were ideally suited to their environment. Their skills were seeing him safely through enemy territory, and their knowledge of jungle medicine had probably saved his life. He wondered if he would ever find a way to repay these brave people.

When the warriors were satisfied the danger had passed, they continued to lead Sam through the jungle until they came to a wide river with broad sandy beaches along the shore.

"What river is this?" Sam asked.

"It called Chindwin," Fred answered.

"How do we get across?" Sam inquired.

"No cross. Wait here fly bird come," Fred responded.

Sam looked around in confusion. There was nothing in sight but thick jungle and the river. He couldn't understand how he was going to be rescued by an airplane when there was no place to land one. He expressed his concerns to Fred.

"Where is the fly bird going to land?" he asked.

"Here," Fred insisted. "Fly bird come soon. You go home."

Sam had seen enough of the abilities of the Nagas, and he wasn't about to question them now, so he settled down in the shade along the river bank to await the arrival of the "fly bird." It wasn't long before the heat of the afternoon sun and the rigors of his jungle trek took their toll, and he was soon sound asleep.

He was dreaming of insects buzzing around his head when he realized the sound was not coming from insects but from a small engine overhead. Sam awoke instantly to see a small aircraft circling above. The airplane looked just like the yellow Piper Cubs he remembered at the local airport back home, except this one was painted olive drab and had U.S. Army markings painted on the wings and fuselage. The plane circled lower, and Sam stood up and waved his arms frantically. The pilot wagged the wings of the plane in acknowledgment and then flew down the river a short distance before turning back. Sam watched as the aircraft descended until its wheels were only a few feet above the beach. The pilot flew slowly past as he searched for a place to land, and Sam could see the side doors of the plane had been removed. The pilot was plainly visible inside, and he waved as he passed and then flew back down the river before turning back in their direction for a second time. This time, Sam could see that the pilot intended to land on the sandy beach.

He held his breath as the airplane approached at a shallow angle. He heard the pilot cut the engine and watched as the plane descended toward the beach. The pilot slowed the little aircraft down and held it off the ground until it gently settled onto the sand. Sam saw the wheels begin to sink into the soft sand, but the pilot added just enough power to keep the airplane moving until he came to a stop in front of Sam and the awestruck Nagas.

The pilot kept the engine running and motioned for Sam to come closer. Sam ran to the plane where the pilot handed him a small ball about a quarter inch in diameter of some black substance.

"This is opium," shouted the pilot. "Give it to the Nagas as payment for your rescue."

Sam ran back to the waiting Nagas and gave the opium to Fred. "Thank you, Fred, and tell the rest of your people I will never forget what they did for me."

"You okay, Joe. Now go home," Fred responded.

Sam ran to the waiting aircraft and turned to wave to his Naga friends. They raised their hands in farewell, and Sam knew he would never see any of them again.

"Get in," yelled the pilot over the noise of the engine. "The Japs probably heard the plane and are on their way here right now."

As Sam climbed into the empty seat in the front of the plane, he noted with interest that the pilot wore the stripes of a staff sergeant. Up to now, he thought all pilots were officers, but he didn't give it a second thought as he buckled up in preparation for takeoff. The sergeant didn't hesitate in applying power to the engine, but the little plane didn't move. He applied more power and still the plane would not budge. Sam looked out and saw that the tires had sunk deeply into the soft sand.

"Get out and push against the wind strut, while I try to wiggle us free. When we start moving, jump back in," instructed the pilot.

Sam got out and began pushing against the wing strut as the pilot worked the rudder back and forth while applying bursts of power to the engine. At first, the little plane remained mired in the sand, but gradually the movement of the rudder, combined with Sam's efforts on the wing strut, unlocked the grip of the sand, and the plane began to slowly move forward. Sam climbed aboard as the pilot continued to nurse the aircraft forward. There was not enough space ahead of them to allow for a takeoff, so the pilot turned the plane around and applied full throttle. The tiny plane seemed to wallow at first, but under the masterful technique of the sergeant, it began to pick up speed. Soon the tail wheel lifted free of the sand as the plane continued to bounce along the sandy beach, but it still was not able to gain enough speed for takeoff. From Sam's vantage point in the front seat, he could see the end of the beach approaching quickly. He thought for sure the pilot would abort the takeoff and try again, but the airplane kept forging ahead. The last of the beach was just ahead of them now, and Sam braced himself for the impact of slamming into the river. Just before they reached the edge of the water, Sam felt the plane lift free of the clutching sand, and he breathed a sigh of relief as they slowly climbed into the Burmese sky. For the first time in nine days, he was safe, and his thoughts turned to the selfless Naga people who gave up their lives and their homes to make this moment possible. He could never repay them, and he would never forget them.

24

APRIL 20, 1944
THE SKIES OVER NAGALAND, BURMA

AFTER THEIR HARROWING takeoff from the beach, the sergeant took up a westerly heading and flew the little plane very low over the jungle. Now that they were safely off the ground, Sam had a chance to take a look at the aircraft. There were two tandem seats in the plane, and the interior was barely wide enough to accommodate Sam's broad shoulders. The pilot sat in the rear seat, and Sam sat in the front seat where he had a good view of the instrument panel. After seeing the cluttered instrument panel in C47s, he was surprised to see only an altimeter, engine tachometer, airspeed indicator, compass, and combined oil pressure/temperature gauge. Flying in the small plane was also much different from a C47 in that he felt more like he was flying. The light weight of the plane caused it to react more to heated air over the jungle and produced a somewhat bumpy but not uncomfortable ride. The wings of the plane were placed on top of the fuselage, so there was nothing to obstruct Sam's view of the earth through the windshield and side windows. All in all, Sam liked flying in the tiny airplane and especially so, since it was taking him back to civilization.

"Glad to be out of the jungle?" the pilot inquired.

"It was an experience I don't want to repeat," answered Sam.

"Welcome aboard. My name's Walt Grimes. Just call me Walt," continued the pilot.

"I'm Sam. Sam Huber," Sam said glancing over his shoulder at the sergeant.

"Where are you from, Sam?" asked Walt.

"I'm from a little town in Pennsylvania called Osceola Mills," Sam answered.

"Well, can you imagine that?" Walt responded. "I've flown into the airport at Osceola many times. I'm from Lock Haven."

"No kidding, Lock Haven is only about fifty miles away," Sam said. "What were you doing at the Osceola airport?"

"I worked as a test pilot and flight instructor for the Piper Aircraft Corporation. I took students on cross-country flights to Osceola and other airports in the area," the sergeant answered. "Is Joe's Malt Shop still open in Osceola? I remember having some great burgers and shakes there."

"It's still there," Sam responded. "I took my wife there when we were dating. Does your wife live back in Lock Haven?"

"Not married, but my parents live in Lock Haven," Walt answered.

"How did you end up here?" Sam asked.

"I gave up my life as a civilian flight instructor and volunteered for the army after Pearl Harbor. I gave primary flight instruction to military cadets for a while, and eventually the army sent me here as a 'maytag pilot.'"

"What's a maytag pilot?" Sam inquired.

"The foot soldiers think these small planes sound like washing machines, so they call us maytag pilots. This plane is a Piper J-3 Cub built in Lock Haven. The army officially calls it an L4, but because of the way we hop in and out of the jungle, the troops call it a 'grasshopper,'" Walt said.

"Besides rescuing downed airmen, what else do you guys do?" Sam asked.

"I'm with the 165th Liaison Squadron of the First Air Commando Group," Walt answered. "We carry mail and supplies, evacuate wounded, rescue airmen, fly reconnaissance missions, spot for artillery, and just about anything else the brass can think for us to do. Oh, we also do our own aircraft maintenance, since there are no mechanics assigned to us."

"Sounds just like the army," Sam responded. "Where are we headed?"

"I'm stationed at Jorhat, but I have orders to take you to your base at Dinjan. Sit back and enjoy the ride. This little grasshopper can't get high enough to fly over some of these mountains, so we'll have to fly through a pass or two. I may have to ask you to pick up your feet at times."

Sam thought the sergeant was kidding until they approached the first gap in the mountains. Clouds shrouded the tops of the mountains on either side of the pass, and as the little L4 climbed to stay above the rising floor of the pass, the cloud deck above grew closer and closer. Soon they were skimming along just below the clouds and yet the ground continued to rise under them. Sam could see that they would soon have to either enter the clouds and risk crashing into the mountains or turn around and fly out of the pass. He knew the small plane couldn't carry much fuel, and he wondered if he was about to become a downed airman again.

Walt kept the plane so close to the bottom of the clouds that they occasionally entered into the mist for a second or two. Sam watched as the earth rose steadily beneath them until it was just a few feet below the landing gear. The visual effect of the speeding earth below and the racing clouds above began to make Sam feel nauseous. The space between the clouds and the ground narrowed even more and then suddenly widened as the earth dropped sharply beneath them. Sam breathed a sigh of relief as they descended on the other side of the pass.

"Well, we're through, Sam. I wasn't sure we were going to make it, but the gods were with us today," Walt said. "Sorry to put you through that, but the sides of the pass got so close we didn't have room to turn around."

Sam's throat was so dry he couldn't respond, so he simply nodded his head in acknowledgment. The remainder of the flight to Dinjan was uneventful, and they landed and taxied to a stop among the towering C47s. Sam's commanding officer, Captain George Cummings, was there to meet them.

"Welcome back, Private Huber," the captain said in greeting.

"Thank you, sir. It's good to be back," Sam responded.

"I'm going to send you over to the hospital to be checked out and get some rest," the captain continued, "but first I want you to know that the C47 you bailed out of made a successful crash landing in Burma, and the pilot, copilot, and radio operator were rescued. Unfortunately, the other crewman, Corporal Burns, has not been heard from since he bailed out with you. My driver will take you to the hospital. When you're released, report to me for a debriefing on your experiences. I'll contact the War Department to notify your family that you're all right."

As he rode to the hospital, Sam thought of all the things that happened to him in the jungle. He hoped Corporal Burns would be as lucky, but he knew his chances for survival were slim.

APRIL 22, 1944
MOSHANNON VALLEY, PENNSYLVANIA

Eleanor sat at her sewing machine and tried to concentrate on the task before her. She was aware of the furtive glances coming from some of her fellow workers. It had been this way ever since it became known her husband was missing in action. People on the street and at the factory avoided making eye contact and hardly anyone initiated a conversation with her. A few people did express genuine sympathy, but on the whole, she felt ostracized. When time for her break came, she went outside and stood alone reading the letter she received from Sam yesterday. It was dated the day before he went missing in action.

April 10, 1944

Dearest Eleanor,

Thought I would take a few minutes to write and let you know I am all right. We have been flying 3 and 4 missions a day supplying the troops in the jungle. The missions have been rough but not as rough as those poor devils on the ground have it.

I did get a break from the war and went on a tiger hunt. It was very exciting and my friend Bobby Joe actually got a shot at the tiger. Our host Mr. McGregor finally killed the animal.

I finally got to fly over the hump. The Himalayan Mountains are really something to see. We had some Chinese soldiers as passengers. Boy, they are sure different from our troops.

I hope to get a three-day pass soon. I want to pick up some souvenirs for you and the rest of the family. Well, I have to go. Another mission awaits. Tell everyone I love them and I enjoy their letters.

Love always,
Sam

Eleanor folded the letter and returned it to her purse, wondering if these were the last words she would have from her husband. She went back to her sewing machine and worked steadily until the buzzer ending her shift sounded; then she hurried to the parking lot and joined Lynette who was waiting in the car.

"How was your day, dear?" Lynette asked.

"Terrible," Eleanor responded. "I feel like a pariah. Hardly anyone will talk to me and those who look at me have such pity in their eyes. It constantly reminds me about Sam."

"It's difficult for people to talk to someone in your situation Eleanor," Lynette explained. "Most of them have loved ones in the military, and deep down, they may feel guilty at feeling relief that it wasn't them who received the telegram. I'm sure it's hard for them to find words that won't remind you of the possibilities and make you feel worse."

"What possibilities are you talking about?" Eleanor asked.

"Well, Eleanor, you have to face the fact that Sam's situation can end in one of four ways. He may never be found. He may be dead. He may be a prisoner of war, and chances of surviving a Japanese prison unharmed are poor, or he may be found alive. There's only a 25 percent chance of a good outcome. Sam's my brother, and I love him dearly, but we have to face reality and be here for each other."

Eleanor knew her sister-in-law was right. They had to face the possibility that Sam may never come back, and she knew if he didn't come back, she had to go on for her children. However, knowing these things didn't ease her anxiety or fear. It seemed like every day someone in town was receiving bad news from the War Department.

During the remainder of the drive to May's home, both women remained silent and immersed in their own thoughts. When Lynette stopped in front of the house, May was waiting on the porch with a telegram envelope in her hand. Eleanor's heart raced as she and Lynette hurried from the car.

"This came a few hours ago," May announced as she handed the envelope to Eleanor. "Are you going to be able to open it?"

"Yes, I pray its good news and ends the uncertainty we've been going through," Eleanor said as she opened the envelope and read the telegram.

Dated <u>WASHINGTON DC 4/21/44</u>
To <u>MRS HUBER</u>
<u>300 PRUNER ST OSCEOLA MILLS PA</u>

<u>I AM PLEASED TO INFORM YOU REPORT JUST RECEIVED STATES YOUR</u>
<u>HUSBAND PVT. SAMUEL D HUBER WHO WAS PREVIOUSLY REPORTED</u>
<u>MISSING IN ACTION WAS RESCUED AND RETURNED TO HIS DUTY</u>
<u>STATION UNHARMED ON 20 APRIL 44</u>

<u>TJ JULIO THE ADJUTANT GENERAL</u>

May and Lynette waited nervously as Eleanor read the telegram. "Is it good news?" May asked.

"Yes, thank God they found him, and he's alive and safe," Eleanor answered as she handed the telegram to May and threw her arms around Lynette.

When the sisters had all read the telegram, they sat down together on May's sofa, and tears of joy and relief streamed down their cheeks.

25

APRIL 25, 1944
DINJAN AIRBASE, INDIA

AFTER FOUR DAYS in the base hospital, Sam was more than ready to get back to his duties. The doctors at the hospital were amazed that he had come through his jungle ordeal in such good shape. Four days of rest and relatively good food had rebuilt his strength, and he was pronounced fit for duty. While Sam was hospitalized, he noticed a great deal of activity at the airbase. From dawn to well past sundown, air traffic in and out of Dinjan had been heavy, and he speculated the demand for supplies by the troops in the field must still be great. As he sat in the headquarters building, waiting to see his commanding officer, he hoped the captain would bring him up to date on the fighting in Burma as well as Imphal and Kohima.

The door to Captain Cumming's office finally opened, and Corporal Finney, the company clerk, approached. "The captain will see you now," he said as he went to his desk and began sorting papers.

Sam entered the office and stood at attention before his

commanding officer. "Private Huber, Samuel D. reporting for duty, sir," Sam announced as he saluted the captain.

"At ease, Private, have a seat," Captain Cummings said, returning the salute. "You're looking fit. Did they treat you well at the hospital?"

"Yes sir, I feel fine, and I'm ready to go back to work."

"That's good to hear. The Nagas must have treated you pretty well," the captain continued.

"Yes, sir, they are an amazing people. I wouldn't be alive today if it hadn't been for them. Some of them even gave up their lives to save me."

"I wouldn't doubt that one bit. The Nagas have been helping the Brits around Imphal, and the Japs haven't taken kindly to it. We've had numerous reports of Japanese atrocities against the natives in that area," said the captain.

"I know, sir, I witnessed some of the things that are being done," Sam responded.

"When you get a chance, I would like a written report of the things you saw," the captain said, "but first, I'm afraid I have to put you back on the job. After what you've been through, I would normally give you a pass to Calcutta, but the Japs are still a serious threat. The Brits finally have them stopped around Imphal, but plenty of supplies are still needed to finish the job. I promise you a three-day pass to Calcutta as soon as I can, but in the meantime, check with Corporal Finney for an assignment."

"Thank you, sir," Sam said as he stood, saluted his CO, and left the room.

"The captain says you have an assignment for me," Sam said to Corporal Finney.

"Yeah, Sam, Wimpy Hutton is on the flight line right now, loading supplies for the Imphal area. Go down and give him a hand and then join the crew. Oh, and see if you can keep Wimpy from eating everything before it gets to the Brits," Finney responded.

"That will be a tough job," Sam said. "Who is the pilot on this mission?"

"Lieutenant Thomas is the pilot," Finney answered, "I think you've flown with him before."

"Yeah, I've flown with LT many times. He's a good pilot," Sam said as he left the office.

Sam walked to the flight line and began looking for Corporal Hutton. From a distance, he spotted him standing beside a C47 with a truck backed up to the cargo door. As he approached, he wasn't surprised to see Wimpy eating a candy bar while supervising the loading of the plane. Sam was surprised to see the cargo consisted of bamboo cages filled with live chickens.

"Hey, Wimpy, what's with all the chickens?" Sam asked.

"Can you believe it, Sam? A whole plane load of drumsticks on the hoof, and it's all going to the Brits at Imphal," Wimpy answered. "There must be a thousand breasts and drumsticks on that plane. What I couldn't do with just one crate of those tasty critters? I'd have fried chicken and roast chicken and eggs. Oh, fresh eggs—what I wouldn't give for some fresh eggs? If I could only get my hands on at least one of those crates."

"I don't want to know about it if you do," Sam said, shaking his head in amazement. "It looks like it's going to be difficult securing all of these crates."

"We'll have to tie them down as best as we can because there are monsoon storms predicted for this flight," Wimpy answered as he finished his candy bar and pulled another one from his pocket. "Care for a candy bar? I've got more in my pocket."

"No, thanks, Wimpy. I think we better get busy securing these crates," Sam said.

The two kickers climbed aboard the plane and were immediately accosted by the smell of hundreds of chickens and the din created by their cackling and crowing. The sun was beginning to heat the interior of the plane, making the smell even worse, and LT informed them he had to get the plane off the ground before the heat killed the chickens. In addition to the smell, noise, and heat, the fragile construction of the bamboo cages complicated the task of securing the load, but Sam and Wimpy soon had the job done and closed the cargo doors.

The engines were started and the plane began to taxi, but due to the closed doors, the heat inside the cargo bay continued to rise. Soon it became evident the chickens were beginning to feel the effects of the heat. Both men were sweating profusely by the time the C47 finally took off and climbed into cooler air aloft.

"I hope these chickens survive," Wimpy said as he reached into his pocket for a candy bar. "I sure wouldn't want to see all that good meat go to waste."

"It starting to cool off now," Sam said, "I think everything will be okay."

"Aw damn!" Wimpy exclaimed.

"What's wrong?" Sam inquired.

"My candy bars melted," Wimpy responded as he held out a fist full of melted chocolate. "What am I going to eat now?" he moaned as he licked the chocolate from his fingers.

Wimpy didn't have time to contemplate his epicurean predicament, because the plane suddenly entered a monsoon thunderstorm. At first the turbulence was mild, but it soon intensified until the aircraft was being thrown wildly about the sky. They were caught in an updraft that lifted the C47 upward several thousand feet, and then just as quickly, they were plummeted downward. Neither Sam nor Wimpy could remain standing, and they grabbed for whatever handhold they could find. The plane continued its wild roller-coaster ride, and they could see the bamboo cages were not going to withstand the punishment much longer.

The first indication of trouble came when a sharp cracking sound erupted from somewhere within the mass of cages. Soon there were more ominous cracks, and as the turbulence continued unabated, the cages began to come apart. Sam and Wimpy could only watch in dismay as the entire load disintegrated in a pandemonium of squawking chickens, feathers, and smashed bamboo.

The terrified chickens, freed from their bamboo prisons, scattered throughout the pitching aircraft. Before anyone could react, several of the frightened birds found their way into the cockpit. The radio operator tried to close the cockpit door, but debris from the shattered cages jammed it open. Soon, several dozen more birds had entered the cockpit area. The pilot's view through the windshield was blocked as the birds flew into it in their frenzied attempts to escape from the airplane. Visibility within the cockpit was further limited by feathers and chickens flying everywhere. The problem was further complicated when the frightened birds began to defecate everywhere. Before long, many of the instruments on the instrument panel were covered with chicken droppings, and to the total dismay of the harried pilots, they too became the targets of the birds bombardments.

The radio operator finally managed to close cockpit door and stop any further chickens from entering the cockpit area. LT and the copilot slid the side windows of the cockpit open and proceeded to toss the offending fowl into the open air outside. In the meantime, the C47 exited the thunderstorm and arrived a few hundred feet above the airstrip at Imphal. British and Indian soldiers at the airstrip were amazed to witness the aircraft as it flew by with a plume of feathers trailing behind. They were further amazed when dead chickens dropped out of the sky and landed at their feet.

"I say, the Yanks seem to have come up with a novel way of delivering supplies," said an observing British Major.

"Quite so, and they've saved us the trouble of killing and plucking the buggers," responded a fellow officer.

With all of the chickens cleared from the cockpit, LT was able to regain control and maneuver the plane onto final approach for a landing. Since most of the instruments were unreadable due to their covering of bird droppings, he had to fly the plane without reference to his airspeed and altitude. Even so, LT's vast experience enabled him to bring the plane in for a near-perfect wheel landing, and he gave a great sigh of relief as their speed diminished and the tail wheel settled onto the dirt runway. However, his euphoria was short-lived, for at that moment, a chicken that had become lodged under the control panel suddenly freed itself and flew into his face. Startled by the errant fowl, LT's foot jammed down on the right rudder pedal, causing the C47 to swerve to the right in a ground loop. The violent maneuver caused the right tire to blow out and the contents of the cargo bay were further jumbled and piled against the right side of the plane.

When the C47 finally came to a rest, personnel on the ground rushed forward to assist the crew of the crippled plane. As they approached the aircraft, the cargo doors suddenly opened, spilling a profusion of dead and living chickens, feathers, and bamboo pieces onto the ground. The would-be rescuers stood in amazement as the crew of the plane—their uniforms plastered with splotches of bird droppings and feathers—piled from the reeking aircraft.

As the dazed crew was led away, Wimpy turned to the British major and said, "I'll take any of those chickens you can't use, sir."

They were taken to a place where they could clean up, and then to Wimpy's delight, they were each given British ration consisting of a can of bully beef and a hard tack biscuit. Wimpy attacked his ration with gusto, but the rest of the crew found the beef unappetizing and biscuits much too hard to chew.

"Aren't you guys going to eat your rations?" Wimpy asked when he noticed everyone had set theirs aside. "If you don't want them, I'll take them," he added hopefully.

Without exception, the remainder of the crew donated their rations to Wimpy and then sat around watching as he proceeded to consume his windfall with utter delight.

"You men stay here and watch the human garbage disposal while I find out how we can get out of here," LT said as he strode off in the direction of some C47s being unloaded. A short while later, he returned to find most of his crew napping and Wimpy still munching on his British rations.

"Wimpy and Sam, I found you men a ride back to Dinjan on a plane from the Seventeenth Troop Carrier Squadron. Sam, I think you know the crew from your time in Sicily," LT announced. "The rest of us are staying here until we get a new tire for our C47, and then we'll be taking a load of wounded back to Chabua."

"What's the number of the plane we're to be on LT?" Sam asked.

"Number 224, Captain Hank Straham is the pilot," LT answered.

"I've flown with Captain Straham before. He's a good pilot," Sam said.

"I've heard he's one of the best," LT continued. "You men better hurry up and get aboard. They're almost ready to leave."

Sam and Wimpy hurried back to the flight line and quickly located Captain Straham's airplane. They were just finishing the loading of a group of wounded Sikh soldiers when Sam and Wimpy arrived.

"Private Huber, it's good to see you again. How are things going? I heard you had quite an interesting flight coming down here," Captain Straham said.

"Yes, sir, I guess you could say it was for the birds," Sam responded, eliciting a chuckle from the captain. "This is my crewmate Corporal Hutton, sir."

"Welcome aboard, Corporal," the captain said as he noticed Wimpy's pockets bulging with tins of bully beef and hard tack.

Seeing the puzzled look on Captain Straham's face, Sam hurriedly explained, "Corporal Hutton likes to eat, sir."

"Yes, sir, I do like to eat a lot," Wimpy added.

"Well, climb on board, gentlemen," the captain continued. "The weather is clearing up, so the flight to Dinjan should be pretty smooth."

Sam and Wimpy boarded the aircraft and found the cargo bay

floor completely covered with wounded soldiers. Some of the soldiers were only slightly wounded, but others had severe wounds that made their chances of survival bleak. Wimpy found a place to sit next to the cargo doors after they were closed, and Sam found a small place at the entrance to the cockpit. Captain Straham soon had both engines running, and it wasn't long before he had the plane off the ground and headed for Dinjan at about five thousand feet.

Sam was looking out the window on his right when he saw another C47 from the Seventeenth Troop Carrier Squadron slide into formation beside them. They were only about ten minutes into the flight when the radio operator announced he was picking up a transmission indicating there were enemy fighters in the area. At the same time, Sam saw what he thought were lights flashing along the fuselage and wings of the C47 flying beside them. He was confused by the lights until a Japanese fighter plane flashed past their formation. At that point, he realized it was not lights he was seeing on the other C47 but flashes from explosive shells as they struck the helpless aircraft. More flashes appeared on the right wing of the C47 as another enemy plane sped by. Sam watched as the damaged plane seemed to shudder under the impact of enemy fire, and the right wing disintegrated before his eyes. The crippled plane went into a steep diving spiral, and Sam knew immediately no one would survive the crash.

Everything had happened so quickly that Captain Straham didn't have time to react, but now he put his plane into a steep dive to get closer to the ground where his plane couldn't be attacked from below. Sam hurriedly climbed up into the astrodome where he had a 360-degree view of the sky around them. When he reached the astrodome, his heart froze at the sight of two Japanese Oscars bearing down on them from behind.

"Two Oscars approaching from seven o'clock," Sam yelled.

Captain Straham immediately pulled out of his dive and started a left-hand turn. "Tell me what they're doing, Sam," he shouted.

"They're still coming. It looks like they're setting up for a deflection shot from the left," Sam answered.

The captain pressed hard on the left rudder pedal, putting the plane into a skidding left turn. "Tell me when they start firing," he commanded.

As the first Japanese pilot lined up for his deflection shot, he aimed his gun sight in front of the C47 so that when he fired his target would fly into the bullets. However, Captain Straham's skidding turn made the C47 appear to be turning faster than it really was, causing the enemy to overcompensate.

"He's firing," Sam shouted when he saw flashes of light from the Oscar's guns.

Captain Straham immediately put his plane into a right-hand turn as the Oscar's tracers passed harmlessly in front of the C47. The enemy pilot did not have time to compensate and went into a climbing left turn in preparation for another pass. The second Oscar saw the American plane turning right and set up for a deflection shot from the right.

"What's the other Oscar doing, Sam?" Straham asked.

"He's coming in for a shot from the right," Sam answered

Captain Straham applied the same strategy and put his plane into a skidding right turn. Once again, the enemy was fooled, and his bullets missed the C47.

"Tell me what they're doing, Sam," the captain commanded as he continued the right turn.

"The second Oscar is turning for another pass, and the first one is coming in from above and to our right," Sam answered.

"Tell me as soon as he starts firing," ordered the captain.

Hoping to fool the enemy pilot a second time, Captain Straham once again put the plane into a skidding turn and waited for Sam to tell him when the Oscar began to fire. The Japanese pilot realized he had been tricked on his first pass and was determined not to let it happen again. As he dove upon the unarmed American plane, he held his fire and waited until he got close enough that he couldn't miss.

"What's happening, Sam, is he firing yet?" Captain Straham shouted nervously.

"No, sir, he's coming in quickly, but he isn't firing. He's really coming at us. Oh my god… ," Sam said.

Before Sam could finish his sentence, the C47 shook violently and immediately went into a precipitous turn to the left. Sam was knocked out of the astrodome as the plane plummeted toward the ground below.

"He rammed us," Sam shouted as he struggled to get up.

Both pilots fought to regain control of the aircraft. With both pilots applying full right rudder pedal and turning the control wheel fully to the right, they managed to stop the left hand turn and level the plane out. They regained control of the airplane, but with the controls completely deflected to the right, they found they were unable to make right turns. Luckily, left turns could be made simply by easing off a little on the controls.

"Get back up in the astrodome and see if you can tell how much damage we have," Captain Straham said to Sam.

Sam climbed into the astrodome and looked aft. He was shocked at what he saw. "There's hardly anything left of the vertical stabilizer and rudder," he said. "There must be at least seven feet of the tail section missing."

"Do you see the Oscars anywhere?" the pilot asked.

"I only see one, sir, and he's making a pass at us right now," Sam responded.

Captain Straham knew he would be unable to take evasive action and sat waiting for the enemy plane to strike. Sam watched as the Oscar approached and saw tracer bullets arching out from its guns. This time, the enemy pilots aim was true, and his bullets struck the rear of the crippled C47. Captain Straham held his breath as he felt the impact of the bullets and saw the Japanese fighter zoom by to the left. Luckily, no further damage was done to the C47, and Straham continued to maintain control of the plane.

"Where's that Oscar now?" the captain asked Sam.

"He seems to be hightailing it out of here," Sam answered, "and there is no sign of the other one."

Sam continued to search the skies through the astrodome, but he was unable to see any more enemy planes. Everyone was still on edge when Wimpy appeared in the cockpit munching a hard tack biscuit.

"Congratulations on the kill, sir," Wimpy said to the pilot.

"What kill, what the hell are you talking about, Corporal?" the captain said.

"That Oscar that rammed us, I saw it crash into a mountain and explode," Wimpy continued. "You'll get credit for a kill, sir."

Captain Straham just looked at Wimpy in amazement as the news sunk in. He had a verified kill and would be able to paint a small Japanese flag on the side of his plane. However, his wonder didn't last long when he realized they had lost track of where they were in the confusion of the attack. Making left turns only, they steered the plane west toward friendly territory. Flying was difficult, since it took the efforts of both pilots to control the plane. After about an hour of flight, they spotted an airport and prepared to land. The pilots found that once the C47 was slowed down, it only took one pilot to control it, and Captain Straham was able to bring his crippled aircraft in for a successful landing.

Once they were safely on the ground, the crew found out they had landed at the British airfield at Shamshernagar. The wounded Sikh troops were unloaded, and after inspecting their damaged plane, Captain Straham and his crew went to the mess hall for a cup of much needed coffee. They found coffee was not available, but tea was in abundance. As they sat around reliving the day's events over a cup of tea, they were approached by a British major.

"You blokes had a stroke of luck today, I dare say," said the major.

"I wouldn't call having most of the tail section of my plane torn away and begin shot up by Jap fighters luck," Captain Straham responded.

"On the contrary, old boy, you were quite lucky indeed," continued the major. "There were seven C47s in the Imphal area today. The whole lot of you were jumped by twenty Japanese fighters. Five C47s were shot down and destroyed with a total loss of crew and passengers. One was damaged and crash-landed with three dead and seventeen wounded. Your plane was the only one that landed safely with no loss of life."

Captain Straham and his crew were stunned by the news. Their elation at having been responsible for the downing of an enemy plane was replaced by the grief of learning they had lost numerous friends and comrades. Their teacups sat untouched as the major turned and slowly walked away.

26

MAY 14, 1944
DUM DUM AIRPORT, CALCUTTA, INDIA

I CAN'T BELIEVE I finally got a two-day pass," Sam said as the C47 came to a stop in front of the operations building at Dum Dum Airport. For the past two weeks, he had been flying three missions a day, delivering supplies to the embattled troops at Imphal and Kohima. The demand was so urgent that he and the rest of his crewmates slept under the wings of their planes in order to be ready to go at first light. The long hours and stress from exposure to enemy fire had taken its toll on everyone involved.

"Y'all been through a lot in the last two weeks," Bobby Joe responded, "but now ya kin relax and enjoy a couple a days in Calcutta."

"I'll have to depend on you for guidance," Sam said. "This is my first pass in Calcutta."

"Y'all jus relax and foller me," Bobby Joe said as he climbed out of the aircraft.

Sam followed his friend and was soon standing on the tarmac looking at the roof of the operations building. The word *Calcutta* was painted across the roof in large letters to identify the location of the airport. Underneath *Calcutta*, on the left side of the roof, an arrow was painted with the words, New York 11,085 mi. On the right side was another arrow with the words, San Francisco 10,924 mi.

"We sure are a long way from home," Sam commented as he gazed at the roof.

"Y'all kin say that agin partner," Bobby Joe said, "and it seems like it gits further every day."

"I have to admit, I really need this time off," Sam continued. "The stress of being under fire every mission is starting to get to me. I think it would be easier if I could shoot back."

"Y'all ain't the first ta feel that way," Bobby Joe answered. "Some kickers shoot back with their pistols. They ain't got a chance a hittin' anythin', but it makes 'em feel good. Did y'all know some C47s used ta have .50-caliber machine guns mounted in 'em?"

"Wow, that would be great. Why did they take them out?" Sam asked.

"Well, they weren't too effective, and they took up space and weight needed for supplies," Bobby Joe said.

"I wish they'd bring them back," Sam said. "I'm getting tired of being a sitting duck every mission."

"Y'all been trained ta provide the boys on the ground with the supplies ta shoot back. They're the ones that's trained ta do the fightin'." Bobby Joe said. "Now let's git us a taxi and head fer the Grand Hotel."

Bobby Joe led Sam through the operations building to a group of taxis waiting on the other side. The cab they chose was a 1929 open-coach Buick driven by a turbaned Sikh. They threw their overnight bags inside, told the driver where they wanted to go, and sat down to enjoy the ride into Calcutta. The view from their taxi was astonishing. The streets were teeming with people and a variety of vehicles. The women were dressed in saris, and the men were dressed either in suits or robes with what looked like diapers wrapped around their waists. The vehicles varied from overcrowded charcoal-burning buses to horse-drawn carts, man-powered rickshaws, and bicycles. Mixed in with the crowds of people and traffic were numerous cows that roamed about freely. Beggars lined the streets, providing evidence of extreme poverty amid beautiful two- and three-story homes, office buildings, and parks with tropical gardens.

The thing that struck Sam the most was the sickening smell that seemed to pervade the city.

"God, Bobby Joe, where is this terrible smell coming from?" Sam asked.

"Well, partner, look around," Bobby Joe responded, "There's thousands a people sweatin' in the streets and piles a garbage rottin' in the sun. The outdoor markets are sellin' vegetables, fruit, and fish that ain't too fresh, and most a the buildings y'all see dump sewage directly inta the streets. An if that ain't enough, the beggars and cows crap in the streets too. It's a wonder it don't smell worse."

"I don't see how it could possibly smell worse," Sam said. "How do these people get used to it?"

"It's jus normal for them," Bobby Joe answered. "Try breathin' through yer mouth, and it won't seem so bad."

Sam took Bobby Joe's advice, and by the time they arrived at the Grand Hotel, the smells were not bothering him any longer. The Grand Hotel was a four-story building situated on Chowringhee Road. There was a fine dining room on the first floor, and many of the rooms had balconies overlooking the street. Bobby Joe spoke to the clerk at the front desk and was told they could share a room for the night with two other soldiers for six rupees or about two dollars. They accepted the terms and were soon on their way to the second floor where their room was located.

Upon reaching the second floor, they noticed a shared bath and toilet at the end of the hallway. They located their room, and Bobby Joe unlocked the door. Entering the room, they found four cots neatly made up with clean sheets, a desk, and small table with four chairs.

A gentle breeze drifted lazily through French doors that opened onto a balcony. The other two occupants were not present, but their overnight bags were sitting on two of the beds.

"Well, I guess these two beds is ours," Bobby Joe said as he tossed his overnight bag on one of the beds.

Sam placed his bag on the other unclaimed bed and walked to the open French doors. He stepped out onto the balcony and took in the scene before him. The view that met his eyes was a paradox of prosperous food vendors and starving beggars intermingling on the street below. Both groups seemed to be ignoring one another despite their close proximity.

"We still got lots a time 'til dinner," Bobby Joe said. "Y'all want ta do some sightseein' before dinner?"

"Sounds good to me," Sam responded eagerly, "Where do you want to go?"

"Let's go see the Jain Temple. It's jus up the street a bit," Bobby Joe said, "Don't leave anythin' valuable in the room, and keep yer money in yer front pockets."

Sam switched his wallet to his front pocket, and Bobby Joe led him back to the lobby and out onto street. Once outside, they turned north on Chowringhee Road and began to walk through the teeming crowds that seemed to be everywhere. They quickly encountered street vendors hawking a myriad of products and beggars lying in the street with their hands outstretched for alms. They hadn't gone half a block before they were surrounded by deformed children crying, "Baksheesh sahib, baksheesh."

"What do they want?" Sam asked Bobby Joe.

"They's askin' fer money, but don't give 'em any," Bobby Joe said. "Their parents deform 'em at birth so they kin do better at beggin'. If ya give 'em money, it jus encourages the parents ta deform the next kid."

"You mean the parents intentionally deformed these kids?" Sam asked.

"Yup, they break their arms and legs and even cut off hands and feet," Bobby Joe responded.

Sam's stomach churned as he looked at the mutilated children around him. He thought of his own son, Billy, and wondered how self-preservation could lead parents to do such unspeakable acts. The two men continued walking while Sam struggled to ignore the pitiful pleading of the children that followed them. Sam soon learned that it wasn't just children who suffered in India. He saw men who were suffering from elephantiasis, their arms, legs, or testicles swollen to huge proportions. Another common sight on the street was lepers with flesh rotting from their faces and limbs. The sights of human misery were everywhere, and Sam soon wished he had stayed in the hotel.

They walked two more blocks when Sam's attention was drawn to an old hag sitting along a side street. She had a large pile of cow dung before her, and she was shaping the dung into patties and pasting them to a wall beside her.

"What's the poop from the troop?" the old hag asked when she saw Sam watching. She followed her question with a high-pitched cackle.

"That, there's Patty Cake Annie," Bobby Joe explained. "She makes fuel cakes out a dung and sells them ta people."

"I'm amazed she speaks English," Sam said.

"GIs like ta teach these folks ta say all kind a things," Bobby Joe responded. "She more than likely cain't understand a lick a English."

Hearing Bobby Joe's words, the old woman cackled once again and quipped, "You full of shit, GI. I speak plenty good American. You want to buy a cow patty?"

Bobby Joe's mouth dropped open at the hag's putdown. It was the first time Sam had seen his friend speechless, and they both laughed as they continued on their way to the Jain Temple.

As they approached the next intersection, Sam was surprised to see a traffic cop like none he had ever seen before. The policeman stood on a platform in the center of the intersection. He was dressed in a spotless-white uniform with knee-length black boots. He had signs strapped to his chest and back with the word *stop* printed on them in large print. When the traffic cop wanted traffic to stop on a given cross street, he would simply turn facing that street and display the stop signs on his chest and back. When the traffic stopped, he would then motion traffic from the other direction to proceed.

Sam and Bobby Joe watched the policeman for a few minutes and were amazed at how efficiently the system seemed to work. They then continued to the Jain Temple, which was only a block away. As they entered the temple area, they encountered a courtyard with a reflecting pool and beautiful statues. Sam was amazed at the elaborate decorations of colored glass and mirrors adorning the outsides of the temple buildings. There were four different temples in the complex, and the insides of the temples were also decorated with colorful designs made of colored glass and gemstones. Idols made of emeralds, rubies, and other precious stones were distributed throughout the temples. As they exited from one of the temples, Sam noticed several Jain priests who were wearing gauze masks on their faces.

"Why are those priests wearing masks?" Sam asked.

"Them folks believe in nonviolence," Bobby Joe explained. "They don't believe in killin' any livin' thing. They wear them masks ta avoid breathin' in any insects. Sometimes they carry brooms ta sweep the path in front a them ta avoid steppin' on any critter."

"Well, if they don't believe in killing anything, how can they eat anything?" Sam asked.

"They're strict vegetarians," Bobby Joe answered. "They only eat things that don't kill the plant or animal that it comes from, like milk, fruits, and nuts. They don't eat root vegetables 'cause it would kill the plant ta uproot it."

"Wow, that sure limits what a person can eat," Sam observed. "Speaking of eating, I'm getting hungry."

"I could use some vittles myself. Let's git on back ta the hotel and grab us some supper," Bobby Joe responded.

"Sounds good to me," Sam said. "I saw some shops on the way here. Do you mind if we stop on the way back and buy some souvenirs?"

"I don't recommend buyin' this time a day," Bobby Joe answered. "It's best ta buy stuff when the shops first open in the mornin'."

"Oh, why is that?" Sam asked.

"Well, the shop owners is superstitious bout makin' the first sale a the day, and they'll do just 'bout anythin' ta make that first sale," Bobby Joe explained. "Y'all kin git some mighty good prices if yer their first customer."

"Okay, we'll wait till morning then," Sam said, "but let's get a taxi back to the hotel. I don't want to encounter all those beggars on the way back."

The ride back to the Grand Hotel took very little time, and Sam and Bobby Joe soon found themselves seated at a table for two in the main dining room of the Grand Hotel. They were no sooner seated when a waiter approached. He was dressed in a neat brown uniform with a red sash around his waist and a turban on his head. Sam noticed all the waiters were dressed the same and would have been impressed by their appearance except for the fact that they were all barefoot.

The waiter handed the soldiers each a menu and stood by while they made their choices. Sam was surprised to see such an extensive menu. There were thirty-two items listed, and for the price of three rupees or about ninety-eight cents, they could order as many items as they wanted. Sam ordered consommé soup, a salad, roasted duck, coffee, and strawberry ice cream for dessert. Bobby Joe mumbled about not eating rabbit food and ordered soup, two steaks with roasted potatoes, and vanilla ice cream. He also ordered a local beer to go with his meal.

Both men were very hungry, so when their food arrived, they dug in and spoke very little until the meal was over. Bobby Joe did grumble about the beer tasting like dishwater, but Sam felt the coffee was very good. They did agree that the meal was better than what they got in the mess hall, and after dessert, they went to their room to retire for the night.

When they got to their room, their two roommates where already there. They introduced themselves, and Sam was delighted to learn they were with the 758th Railroad Battalion. When the new men learned Sam was a railroader in civilian life, they spent long hours talking about their mutual railroad experiences. Bobby Joe soon tired of the railroad talk and fell asleep early in the evening, but Sam and his new friends talked until one o'clock in the morning before retiring to their respective cots.

Sam awoke early the next morning eager to be the first customer in one of the nearby shops. Bobby Joe was already up and standing on the balcony, watching the streets below. Sam joined his friend and took in the scene before them. As the first rays of light crept through the streets, Sam could see the forms of hundreds of people lying on the sidewalks below.

"What's going on down there? Was there a riot?" Sam asked.

"Nah, they're jus homeless people sleepin' in the streets," Bobby Joe answered.

There appeared to be no activity on the streets until two scruffy looking men, one on each side of the street, appeared in the distance on Chowringhee Road. The men seemed to be engaged in a very unusual activity, for when they encountered a sleeping figure on the street, they would kick the individual and rouse him from his slumber. Most of the awakened men shied away from their tormentors, but a few raised fists in anger as the two men walked away.

"Do you see those guys?" Sam said. "What are they, some kind of sleep police?"

"Nah, they ain't no kind a police. Watch and y'all see what they're up ta," Bobby Joe responded.

Sam watched as the two men approached, kicking everybody

on their path and eliciting the same response each time. Sam was beginning to think this was some kind of twisted game until one of the men kicked a body and it didn't move. Immediately, both men descended on the body, turning it over and rifling through its ragged clothing. They removed a few small items from the body and then left it lying in the street as they continued on their way.

"Is that guy dead? Did those men just rob a dead body?" Sam asked.

"They sure did," Bobby Joe answered. "That's life in Calcutta. Hundreds a these street people die every day from starvation or disease and nobody cares. Them thieves y'all jus saw was doin' what they have ta do ta survive. Sometimes they git somethin' they kin sell, and sometimes they git a small bit a food they kin eat. Dyin' don't mean nothin' ta these folks."

"What happens to the dead bodies?" Sam asked.

"They got special crews that patrol the city and pick up the dead, but y'all see another way it happens in a minute," Bobby Joe responded, pointing up the street.

Sam looked in the direction his friend was pointing and saw a horse-drawn wagon and a crew of three men approaching. They were collecting garbage from the street and throwing it on the wagon. As they neared the dead body, they had to chase away a snarling dog that had appeared from nowhere and was beginning to feed on the corpse. When the dog was gone, the men picked up the corpse, threw in on the wagon with the rest of the garbage, and continued on their way.

"They're not going to throw that body away with the garbage, are they?" Sam asked.

"Nah, they'll take it ta a crematorium. I'll take y'all ta see one after we git some breakfast," Bobby Joe responded.

Leaving the grizzly scene from the balcony behind, Sam and Bobby Joe dressed and went down to the dining room, leaving their two roommates from the 758th asleep in their cots. Fresh eggs were available for breakfast, but after the scenes he had just witnessed,

Sam was not hungry and only ordered coffee. Bobby Joe seemed unaffected by the morning's events and ordered scrambled eggs, toast with jam, sausages, and coffee. After breakfast, they sat enjoying their coffee and contemplating their last day in Calcutta.

"What's on the agenda for today?" Sam asked.

"Well, y'all wanted ta do some shoppin', and then I'll take ya ta see the burnin' ghats."

"What's a burning ghat?"

"A ghat is a ceremonial place with steps leadin' down ta some water, like a river. A burnin' ghat is a place where they burn dead bodies and then dump the ashes in the river. I think y'all find it interestin'."

"Well, let's get the day started then. We have to be at Dum Dum to catch our flight back to Dinjan at four o'clock."

They finished their coffee, and Bobby Joe led the way out onto Chowringhee Road. This time, they turned south and began walking in the direction of the burning ghats. The shops were just beginning to open, and Sam kept an eye open for a likely place to buy souvenirs. Most of the homeless people were now awake and begging for *baksheesh*; however, a few of them still appeared to be sleeping on the sidewalk. As they passed the prone figures, Sam couldn't help wondering if they were asleep or dead. They continued a few blocks before they came to a souvenir shop that looked promising.

"This looks like a good place ta get some souvenirs," Bobby Joe said. "Don't forgit ta haggle fer a good price."

They entered the shop and were immediately attended by the shop owner, who seemed more than eager to show them what he had. Bobby Joe was not interested in buying anything, but Sam looked around until he found some embroidered silk pillows. He chose three pillows with the Taj Mahal embroidered in the center and the word "India" across the top. Two of the pillows had "sister" embroidered across the bottom and one had the word "wife."

"Y'alls womenfolk will sure like them pillers," Bobby Joe observed.

"Yeah, I'm happy with them," Sam said. "Now I need to find something for my son and our next child."

"Well, how 'bout these. They'd be good fer a boy or a gal," Bobby Joe said, holding up two small bracelets made from coins.

Sam took the bracelets from Bobby Joe and inspected them. He could tell they were hand crafted with small denomination coins from India and Burma. The coins varied in shape and made quite an attractive bracelet.

"Those are really different and unique. Thanks for spotting them. I think I'll get two," Sam said.

"I kind a like 'em myself," Bobby Joe observed, "I think I'll git one for my ma. How old is your son, Sam?"

"My son is a little over two years old, and my wife is due with our second child in August," Sam replied.

"I'm shur glad I ain't married. It must be hard for y'all ta be away from yer family," Bobby Joe said.

"I think about them every day, and sometimes I wonder if I'll ever see them again," Sam lamented.

"They ain't no guarantees in war, Sam. Jus keep the good Lord on yer side and hope he sees ya through this mess. Let's see what we kin bargain fer this stuff and be on our way."

They were the only patrons in the store, and they approached the store owner and asked what he wanted for the pillows and bracelets. The owner did not quote a price but began to expound at length on the fine quality of the materials and workmanship in the pillows and bracelets. Sam and Bobby Joe listened for a few minutes, and finally, Bobby Joe became impatient.

"Gall dang it, mister, the war will be over afore yer done runnin' at the mouth. Jus tell us how much ya want," Bobby Joe said.

The shop keeper quoted a price of forty-five rupees for a pillow and thirty rupees for a bracelet.

"That's about fifteen dollars for a pillow and ten dollars for a bracelet. What do you think, Bobby Joe?" Sam whispered.

"I think he's tryin' ta skin us, partner. Let's git down ta some serious haggling."

Bobby Joe offered ten rupees for a pillow and six for a bracelet. A look of shock came over the merchant's face, and he clutched his chest as if in pain.

"Ah, you wound me, sahib. I could not possibly let such fine merchandise go for so small an amount," the merchant said.

"Okay, we'll jus go next door and see what yer neighbor has ta offer," Bobby Joe said as he turned toward the door.

"Wait, wait, sahib. I will lose money, but I can sell you one of these exquisite pillows for thirty rupees and a bracelet for twenty," the merchant said.

"Well, I don't think we kin go more than twelve fer a piller and seven fer a bracelet," Bobby Joe countered.

"Sahib, you want my wife and children to go hungry, but you are guests here defending my country, so I will sell you a pillow for twenty rupees and a bracelet for fifteen."

"Dagnabit, mister, at those prices I don't think it's worth defendin' yer gall dern country. Come on, Sam, lets git outta here," Bobby Joe said as he turned toward the door again.

"Okay, sahib. I will have to send my children into the streets to beg, but since you are buying three of each item, I will sell the pillows for fifteen rupees and the bracelets for ten."

"What do ya think, Sam? That'd be 'bout five dollars fer a piller and three dollars fer a bracelet."

"Sound good to me," Sam responded.

"Okay, ya got yerself a deal," Bobby Joe said to the merchant. "Wrap 'em up, and we'll git on out a here."

The store owner wrapped the items up and accepted the agreed-upon amount from each soldier. He saw them to the door of his shop and wished them a prosperous day as they proceeded on their way toward the burning ghats.

"Do you think we got a good deal?" Sam asked his friend.

"Yer darn tootin' we did. We wuz his first customers. He won't sell them pillers fer less than eight dollars or the bracelets fer less than five the rest a the day."

The two friends continued down Chowringhee as pedestrians and traffic began to increase. In the distance in front of them, Sam could see black smoke rising from behind a complex of high gray stone walls.

"Looks like we're in luck. They're crematin' someone taday," Bobby Joe said as they neared the complex. "Are y'all sure ya want ta see this?"

"Let's go," Sam responded as they entered an open doorway leading into the walled complex.

Once inside, they found themselves in a large dirt courtyard that was being used as a crematorium. On the far-right side of the courtyard, a funeral pyre was already burning. Members of the deceased family sat watching the pyre. Sam was struck by the fact that no one was crying or appeared to be sad.

"Why aren't those people upset about losing a loved one?" Sam asked.

"The Hindus believe in reincarnation, that life is endless. They ain't afraid a death," Bobby Joe said as he pointed toward some men who were preparing for another cremation.

Sam looked in the direction his friend was pointing and saw the men placing a layer of timbers across a trench that was about eight feet long, two feet wide, and eighteen inches deep. When they had completed the first layer of timbers, they placed a second layer at right angles to the first. The clothed body of a corpse was then laid on the pyre, and a priest placed a ball of rice in its mouth and another handful of rice over the navel. More wood was then placed over the body until only the head remained exposed. When the pyre was complete, the priest walked around the body three times and then took a long bundle of dry reeds and broke it in half. He gave one half of the reeds to a male relative of the deceased and then ignited the end of each bundle. The priest and relative stood at opposite ends of the funeral pyre and placed the burning reeds in the trench under the pyre. Soon the pyre was fully ignited, and relatives took their places to watch.

"What do they do with the ashes after these people are cremated?" Sam asked.

"The priest gathers 'em up and puts 'em in a clay pot. Then he gits the family tagether and says a prayer and throws the pot agin the wall and then the kin folk leave," Bobby Joe explained.

"Then what happens?" Sam asked. "I don't see ashes and pieces of pot scattered along the walls."

"I'll show y'all," Bobby Joe responded as he led Sam to another doorway on the other side of the courtyard.

The doorway led to a broad set of steps that led down to a river. As Sam watched, a worker carrying a shovelful of ashes appeared through the doorway of an adjacent courtyard. The man went down the steps and threw the shovelful of ashes into the river. Sam watched as the ashes mingled with the waters of the river and slowly drifted away. His gaze followed the ashes until he saw another set of steps just downstream. The steps were lined with people who were waiting while others, already in the water, scooped up handfuls of ash-laden water and poured them over their heads and bodies. Bobby Joe could see the consternation on Sam's face.

"That there's a ceremonial ghat. Them folks is anointin' themselves," Bobby Joe explained.

"That doesn't seem very sanitary to me," Sam said, but his sentence was cut short when he saw a body floating past in the river. "There's a dead body in the river," he exclaimed.

"That's what they do with them street people," Bobby Joe said.

"They don't have any kin folk and can't afford ta be cremated, so they jus throw 'em in the water and let the river take care of 'em."

Sam watched the body as it floated slowly down the river. He noticed that none of the people at the ceremonial ghat paid any attention to the body as it drifted past.

"Them folks is use ta death. They're surrounded by it every day. Kinda sad, ain't it?" Bobby Joe said.

Sam just nodded his head and then turned to his friend. "I've seen enough. Let's get back to the airport and away from this city."

27

MAY 17, 1944
MYITKYINA (MITCH-IN-AW), BURMA

AFTER THE BATTLE for Nhpum Ga, the troops of Merrill's
Marauders were physically exhausted. They had spent nearly
eighty days marching and fighting through five hundred miles of
extremely difficult jungle terrain and lost nearly 25 percent of their
men killed, wounded, or sick. Nearly all of the remaining men
suffered from ulcerous sores caused by the leeches as well as dysentery
and fevers. They lived almost entirely on airdropped K-rations and
desperately needed time to rest and recuperate, but the limits of their
endurance were to be tested even further. Fifty miles to the south lay
the principal Japanese base at Myitkyina, the center for support of
all Japanese operations in Northern Burma. In addition, Japanese
aircraft based at Myitkyina harassed American transport planes
carrying supplies to Allied troops in Burma and China. Myitkyina
was also strategically important to the Allies, because it was situated
along the proposed path of the Ledo Road, which was to eventually
join with the Burma Road and provide a land link between India
and China. The importance of this pivotal site in Burma led General

Stillwell to order the Marauders to undertake a surprise thrust deeper into Japanese territory to capture Myitkyina.

Because of the weakened state of the Marauders, General Stillwell reinforced their ranks with Kachin and Chinese troops and brought their total strength up to seven thousand troops, which he designated the Myitkyina Task Force. The Task Force was further divided into commands, which were named the H, K, and M forces. In forming these units, Stillwell was careful not to place Kachin soldiers alongside Chinese troops, for the Kachins and Chinese had been enemies for generations.

The operation to capture Myitkyina commenced amid monsoon rains on the twenty-eighth of April when the task force began moving over the treacherous Kumon mountain range. Rain fell every day, and the heat and humidity was oppressive. The trails they followed were steep and the rains soon made them slippery with mud. The normally sure-footed pack mules slipped on the trails and many plummeted to their deaths in the valleys below. The men, in their mud soaked uniforms, slipped from tree to tree while trying to maintain their balance and dig footholds for the pack animals. Progress was agonizingly slow as they inched their way toward Myitkyina.

Thirteen days into their trek, H and K forces were still about thirty-five miles northwest of their target. On May 11, H force began a devious course toward Myitkyina in an effort not to be seen by the Japanese or native Burmese. Their objective was to spring a surprise assault on the Myitkyina airstrip. At the same time, the K force began a series of diversionary attacks to draw the enemy's attention away from the H force.

H force's stealthy approach to the Myitkyina airfield depended on the knowledge of one man, a Kachin scout who lived in the area. However, less than ten miles from their objective, the scout was bitten by a poisonous snake and became too sick to move. A doctor with the unit said the scout would risk death if he continued on. The mission of the H force was in deep trouble, because no one else knew the way through the maze of jungle paths to the airfield. Finally, it was decided to lance the snakebite and suck the poison out. After two hours, the scout, in great pain, was placed astride a horse where he continued to lead H force to its objective. On the morning of May 17, Colonel Hunter, the commander of H force, had his men concealed and ready for an attack on the airstrip. The attack was to begin at ten, but because of problems transmitting vital messages, the attack was scheduled for ten thirty. Among Colonel Hunter's men were Sergeants Bill Wesley and Roy Matamoto who fought with the Second Battalion at Nhpum Ga. Both men were suffering from dysentery and high fevers. They were tired to the point of exhaustion, but they silently checked their weapons and readied themselves for the coming attack.

"Hey, Bill, do you want something to eat?" Sergeant Matamoto whispered as he offered a biscuit to his friend.

"No, I'm sick of K-rations," Bill replied. "I'll tell you what I could eat though. I could eat some more of that fried chicken and apple turnovers they dropped to us at Nhpum Ga."

"Well, that's long gone," Roy said, looking at his watch, "and we couldn't eat it if we had it. We're going to attack in about one minute."

✳ ✳ ✳ ✳ ✳

Corporal Kenji Yoshizawa, a truck driver in the Japanese army, was happy with his job at Myitkyina. Since Myitkyina was located at the northernmost point on the railroad from Rangoon and at the head of navigable waters on the Irrawaddy River, it was the central point for incoming supplies for the Japanese Army in Northern Burma. Additionally, the airfield offered another alternative for the shipment of military material. Kenji's job was to transport supplies arriving by boat, train, or airplane to the main supply depot in the town of Myitkyina. He liked his job because it gave him the opportunity to pilfer various items from his truck—items which he would then sell on the local black market. He had already amassed quite a nest egg and hoped to live in comfort after the war. Another reason Kenji liked his job was because it enabled him to get away from his supervisor, Sergeant Jukodo. The sergeant felt Kenji was lazy and constantly assigned extra duties for him to perform. Sergeant Jukodo made Kenji's life difficult, and the Corporal was always happy to escape the watchful eyes of his sergeant.

Kenji had two reasons to be especially happy today. It was May 17, his birthday, and he was assigned to transport a load of special food from the airfield to the officer's mess. He knew the officers ate well, and he was looking forward to finding some delicacies he could appropriate for his birthday dinner. As his truck was being loaded, he made note of several promising-looking boxes, which he intended to investigate once he was out of sight of the airport. He knew of a secluded spot on the two-mile drive into Myitkyina that would offer him ample opportunity to complete his nefarious deeds.

Once his truck was loaded, Kenji secured the tailgate and entered the driver's compartment with great anticipation. He ground the transmission as he jammed it into low gear and quickly pulled away from the transport plane. Checking his wristwatch, he saw that it was almost ten thirty. If he hurried, he would have ample time to rifle through his cargo before he was scheduled to deliver it to the officer's mess hall. However, his euphoria was soon dashed. He had only driven a few hundred yards when the first shells began to explode all around him. One shell detonated directly in front of his truck, and as he swerved, a second shell exploded near the rear wheels, lifting the truck off the ground and turning it upside down. Kenji watched through the windshield as the world in front of him spun crazily, and then everything turned black.

* * * * *

Their weapons ready for the attack, Bill Wesley and Roy Matamoto watched from concealed positions at the edge of the airstrip. Directly in front of them, a group of Japanese soldiers were passing supplies from a transport plane to a nearby truck.

"What do you suppose is on that plane?" Roy asked.

"I don't know, but it's soon going to be filled with lead," Bill answered as he released the safety on his Thompson submachine gun.

Their job was to secure the main runway of the airstrip, so they knew the first order of business would be to destroy the enemy cargo plane and all the Japanese soldiers in the area. They observed the enemy soldiers complete the loading of the truck and watched as it began to drive away. At that moment, the attack began as the first rounds of artillery and mortar shells started to fall on the airfield. Bill thought how unlucky the driver of the truck was as he watched him drive directly into the path of a series of mortar shells. He saw the truck overturn and then ordered his men to attack.

The men of H force burst from the jungle and caught the Japanese completely by surprise. Bill and his unit gunned down all the enemy soldiers in the vicinity of the cargo plane and then destroyed the aircraft with hand grenades. They spread out along the edge of the runway and continued fighting until there was no further resistance. The attack was such a total surprise that the airfield was captured in less than one and a half hours. Sergeant Wesley and Roy took up a position in a shell crater not far from the overturned Japanese supply truck. They ordered their men to dig in a long runway. Around three thirty in the afternoon, hundreds of Allied transport planes began to arrive as the fighting continued to eliminate pockets of enemy resistance at the edges of the airport. Planes towing gliders full of reinforcements also began to arrive. However, the situation at Myitkyina was by no means safe, as Allied aircraft were greeted by enemy artillery and sniper fire as they approached and landed at the airfield.

MAY 17, 1944
Chabua Airbase, India

Sam was extremely tired. Since his return from Calcutta, he had picked up right where he had left off, sleeping and eating on the flight line and flying up to three missions a day. He and his crew, led by LT Thomas, had already flown two missions today, and now they were awaiting orders to fly a load of antiaircraft guns to the airfield at Myitkyina. They had been briefed on the assault on Myitkyina and knew the airstrip must have fallen because a plane had arrived from there, carrying wounded from the battlefield. Among those wounded was a Kachin scout that had been bitten by a poisonous snake.

As the afternoon wore on, other planes began to arrive from Myitkyina, and their crews told stories of the battle still going on around the airport. They said both ends of the runway were still controlled by the Japanese, and aircraft had to fly a gauntlet of enemy fire to takeoff or land. Even on the ground, they were subjected to Japanese mortar and sniper fire.

Finally, late in the afternoon, LT announced they had received their orders to proceed to Myitkyina, a distance of about two hundred miles. All the way to their destination their minds were filled with the tales of the crews that preceded them. They arrived at Myitkyina about two hours before sundown and joined a queue of five other planes circling to land. From their vantage point above the airfield, they could see puffs of smoke on the ground as the enemy continued to shell the airstrip. As they watched a C47 touching down, it was hit by mortar fire and skidded off the runway and exploded in a ball of fire. Tensions mounted as they circled lower and lower until it came their turn to land.

LT stayed as high as he could on his final approach and then quickly lowered the plane toward the runway at the last moment. The distinct sound of bullets striking the aluminum skin of the aircraft could be heard by the entire crew. One of the bullets must have struck the left engine and smoke began to pour from it as they landed. LT deftly guided the crippled plane to a stop just off the runway.

"Everybody get out of here before the fuel in that wing explodes," he commanded.

Sam flung the door of the C47 open, and the crew jumped to the ground and scattered, taking cover wherever they could find it. Sam ran toward a nearby overturned truck and jumped into a shell crater occupied by two soldiers in torn and muddy uniforms. Startled by Sam's sudden appearance, one of the occupants of the crater turned in his direction. Sam's heart stopped when he realized the man was Japanese, and he frantically fumbled to reach the pistol strapped to his waist.

"Hold on there, flyboy. I'm on your side," the soldier said holding up his hand.

When the soldier spoke perfect English, Sam stopped his attempts to reach for his pistol. The fact that the soldier had a submachine gun pointed at his stomach reinforced his decision.

"I told you them slanted eyes was going to get you in trouble someday, Roy," the other soldier said as he turned to inspect Sam.

"Aw, shut up, Bill. These slanted eyes have saved your bacon plenty of times," Roy responded.

Sam could see now that both men were wearing U.S. Army uniforms, but they were torn and muddied almost beyond recognition. He noted tattered sergeant's stripes on their shoulders, but the thing that struck him the most was the men's emaciated appearance. Their faces were pale and sallow, and their sunken eyes gave them the appearance of skeletons. Neither man appeared capable of fighting a battle.

"You flyboys got any chow on that plane?" Bill said, motioning toward the disabled C47.

"No, I'm sorry it's loaded with antiaircraft guns, but there is a K-ration on board I can get for you," Sam said as he rose to go back to the plane. His efforts were stopped by the ping of a sniper's bullet that ricocheted off a nearby rock.

"You better get down before that sniper gets lucky," Roy cautioned as Sam quickly ducked back into the crater and lowered his head.

"Too bad you don't have any fried chicken on that plane like them flyboys dropped to us back at Nhpum Ga," Bill lamented.

"Yeah, but the apple turnovers were the best," Roy added.

"Were you guys with the Marauders at Nhpum Ga?" Sam asked incredulously. "I was on the mission that dropped the chicken and turnovers."

The two sergeants looked at Sam in disbelief and then extended their hands in friendship.

"I never thought I would get the chance to thank someone personally for that drop," Bill said sincerely, "but thank you."

"Amen," Roy added.

It made Sam feel good to realize his efforts had done some good and were appreciated by these men. He only regretted that he did not have some substantial food to give them now.

"Well, we better get ready. It'll be dark soon, and the Japs like to counterattack at night," Bill said as he rolled over onto his stomach and peered cautiously over the edge of the crater. Sam was astonished to see that the seat of the sergeant's pants was completely gone, exposing his bare rump.

Roy must have seen the look on Sam's face. "When you get a bad case of the jungle trots, you don't always have time to pull your pants down," he said as he rolled over, exposing his own bare bottom.

Sam wondered at the strength and fortitude of these jungle fighters. As the last glimmer of daylight faded, he realized how tired he was, and he rested his head against the walls of the crater and closed his eyes.

∗ ∗ ∗ ∗ ∗

The darkness that surrounded Kenji's consciousness slowly began to disappear. The last thing he remembered before his world turned upside down and everything went black was the realization that the air base was under attack. As his senses became more acute, he slowly opened his eyes and was surprised to see the seat of a truck hanging directly over his head. After a moment of confusion, he remembered shells exploding all around him and his truck turning upside down. He looked around and saw he was lying on his back on the ceiling of the cab of his overturned truck. Fearful that he might be injured, he slowly moved his arms and legs and found that nothing seemed to be broken. All the parts of his body were intact, and except for a headache, he could feel no other pain. He raised his hand to his forehead, felt a large bump there, and surmised that he must have hit his head on something when the truck rolled over. Relieved that he was not seriously injured, he relaxed and listened to the sounds of the battle that was still raging around him. He could hear the rattle of machine guns and the crack of rifle fire in the distance. The occasional thump of artillery and mortar fire shook the earth beneath his body. He could also hear the sound of aircraft as they landed nearby. Not knowing if he was still in danger, he lay still and listened intently. Soon, the sound of human voices reached his ears.

The voices were muffled but didn't seem to be too far away. They appeared to be coming from outside the window behind him. He couldn't tilt his head back far enough to see through the window, so he slowly and silently rolled over. The open window of the driver's door was directly before him now, but debris was blocking his view. He slowly inched forward and carefully raised his head until he could just peer over the debris. He was startled to see American transport planes landing on the runway next to his overturned truck. He searched for the source of the voices and finally spotted two soldiers huddled down in a shell crater about fifty feet from his position. He strained his ears to hear what they were saying, but their voices were too low. Not wanting to reveal his hiding place, he quickly ducked his head so the men couldn't see him.

Kenji realized the desperation of his situation. He was trapped behind enemy lines, but he knew from the sounds of battle that his comrades were not far away. He searched for the rifle he carried in his truck but was unable to find it. He checked for the jungle knife he kept in a sheath on his belt and found that it was still there. Satisfied that he had some form of weapon, he began to think of ways to get back to his own lines. He hadn't thought long before he was distracted by the sound of aircraft engines approaching.

Kenji raised his head cautiously until he could see what was happening outside. He observed an American twin-engine transport plane swerve off the runway and come to a stop not far from his hiding place. Smoke was pouring from one of the engines. The door of the aircraft opened abruptly, and four crewmen from the plane quickly jumped to the ground as an artillery shell exploded nearby. The four airmen scattered in all directions trying to find protection from the incoming artillery. One of the airmen ran to the nearby crater occupied by the two soldiers and jumped in. One of the soldiers turned to face the airman, and Kenji's heart leapt with hope when he saw the soldier was Japanese. However, his hopes were dashed when the soldier spoke to the newcomer in perfect English. He listened and watched as the men conversed in their foreign language, and then a strange thing happened. The airman suddenly stood up as if to leave the protection of the crater but ducked back down when a bullet from a sniper's rifle struck a rock nearby. Kenji shook his head at the poor marksmanship of his countryman and wished he could find his own rifle. The three Americans were easy targets from his hidden position under the truck. He thought of the glory that would be his if he killed three of the enemy, and then maybe even Sergeant Jukodo would treat him with some respect. He searched once again for the rifle but was unable to find it. Frustrated with his unsuccessful attempts to find the rifle, Kenji relaxed and pulled his jungle knife from its sheath. He felt the keen edge that he always kept on the knife and another plan entered his mind. After night had fallen, he would crawl up behind the men in the crater, and then with the element of surprise on his side, he would cut the throat of the nearest man and escape under the cover of darkness.

Kenji waited until his wristwatch told him it was midnight. The battle that raged throughout the day had quieted, and no sound had come from the Americans in the crater for several hours. He looked toward the crater and could barely see it in the faint glow coming from the burning wreckage of a distant aircraft. Detecting no movement in the crater, he was convinced the Americans were asleep. Stealthily he slithered out from under his truck and began to creep toward the crater. His movements were slow and deliberate, and it took him nearly an hour to crawl the fifty feet to the crater. From his prone position at the edge of the crater, he could not see the men inside, but he quietly waited as he listened. The sounds of their breathing were deep and regular, and Kenji was convinced the enemy soldiers were asleep. After ten minutes, he silently drew his knife from its sheath and peered cautiously into the crater.

Kenji could see two soldiers on the opposite side of the crater. He watched carefully for any sign of movement. One of the soldiers was lying on his side in a fetal position. The other soldier was lying on his back, facing Kenji with one hand in plain sight and the other hand hidden by his shirt. Kenji watched this soldier carefully but relaxed when he heard him emit a low-snoring sound. He edged closer to the crater and rose up slightly until he could see the American airman directly below him. The airman was lying on the side of the crater with his head resting upon his left shoulder. The man's neck and jugular vein were perfectly exposed.

Kenji's excitement grew at the anticipation of an easy kill. He had only to extend his knife a short distance, slash the American's throat, and disappear into the darkness. Things were going so well he thought about cutting off one of the airman's ears as a souvenir. Sergeant

Jukodo would be proud of him then. He slowly lowered his knife into the crater, stopping long enough to watch for any movement from the two soldiers. Silently, he moved the knife to within an inch of the man's neck. His muscles tensed as he prepared for the final thrust.

✶ ✶ ✶ ✶ ✶

Sam was suddenly awakened by the crashing sound of a gunshot. Simultaneously he felt the splash of something warm against the side of this face and was jolted by something dropping onto his lap. He was surprised to see the object in his lap was a knife and then he saw Bill with a smoking pistol pointed in his direction.

"I was wondering how long you were going to wait before you pulled the trigger," Roy said nonchalantly.

"I heard him coming half an hour ago, and I've been watching him ever since he poked his head over the edge," Bill replied.

"That snore was a nice touch," Roy observed.

"Yeah, I kind a liked that myself," Bill said.

"What the hell are you guys talking about, and where did this knife come from?" Sam asked in complete bewilderment.

"We had a visitor that was just about to cut your throat," Bill answered, pointing with his pistol behind Sam.

Sam turned and was shocked to see a Japanese soldier at the edge of the crater with a bullet hole in his forehead. He touched the sticky substance on the side of his face and realized it was the soldier's blood. "My god, you saved my life," he said. "How can I ever repay you?"

"No need for repayment," Bill answered. "I figure we're even for the fried chicken and apple turnovers now."

28

JULY 4, 1944
MOSHANNON VALLEY, PENNSYLVANIA

IN THE TINY community of Osceola Mills, the week of the Fourth of July meant one thing: it was time for the annual firemen's celebration. The firemen's carnival had come into town two days ago and set up directly in front of Eleanor's house on Pruner Street. The proximity of the carnival was a source of great excitement for two-and-half-year-old Billy. He spent hours watching the carnival crews during the day, and in the evening, he delighted in riding on the kiddy rides. For Eleanor, the carnival was a mixed blessing. She had only to step out of her front door to see many people she had not seen in a long time, but she had difficulty getting Billy away from the rides. Most of the time she would wait until he fell asleep on one of the rides, and then take him home and put him to bed.

Today was the crowning event of the weeklong celebration, the firemen's parade. Billy was beside himself with excitement as he walked with his mother, May, and Paul to Curtin Street, where they would watch the passing Parade.

"Let's find a spot near the judges stand to watch the parade," Eleanor said.

"That's a good idea," Paul responded. "The bands always perform their best as they pass the judges."

They found a good spot near the judge's stand, and Paul hoisted Billy up onto his shoulders so he would have a better view. It wasn't long before the first elements of the parade appeared. Leading the parade were three members of the Armed Forces carrying American flags. As they approached, the people along the street saluted the flags and then cheered as the military men passed.

Eleanor's mind flashed back to the parade in 1939. It was the first time she saw Sam. So much had happened in the past five years and she desperately wished he could be with her now.

"Are you all right, Eleanor?" May asked, noticing a tear in Eleanor's eye.

"I just wish Sam could be here," Eleanor said as she touched her swollen stomach. "He sounds tired in his latest letters, and I'm afraid something will happen to him."

"We all worry about him," May said. "The only things we can do are pray and go on with our lives."

Eleanor touched her stomach again. The baby was due in another month, and she wondered if it would ever see its father.

July 4, 1944
Shingbwiyang (Shim-boo-yang), Burma

Sam was weary as he climbed down from the C47 and helped Bobby Joe limp to the waiting ambulance. They just completed their third mission of the day, and it did not go well. They had been dropping rice to Chinese soldiers near Myitkyina, and on their first approach to the drop zone, the soldiers opened fire on their aircraft. Bobby Joe was slightly wounded in the leg, and the drop had to be aborted until the pilot contacted commanders on the ground to get the firing stopped. The thing that bothered Sam was that this wasn't the first time Chinese soldiers had fired upon American planes.

"Your wound is just superficial, Bobby Joe," Sam said. "You should be back in the saddle again in a day or two. It amazes me that, after all the times the Chinese troops had been supplied from the air, they still don't seem to recognize friendly aircraft."

"I'm beginnin' ta suspect it's a case a sport shootin'," Bobby Joe replied, "but it's a hell of a way ta git a purple heart, ain't it?"

Sam watched the ambulance pull away, and he thought about what his friend had just said. Was it a case of sport shooting or was it something else? He thought of another thing that occurred during the mission that was leading him to believe it may be something else. The incident happened during their second pass over the drop zone. They were flying at 150 miles per hour at an altitude of four hundred feet and were free-dropping sacks of rice without parachutes. Sam had just tossed a fifty-pound sack out of the aircraft and watched as a Chinese soldier rushed into the drop zone and tried to catch it in his arms. The soldier was killed instantly. Sam was becoming convinced that the lack of education and primitive nature of the Chinese soldiers led them to do things without realizing the consequences of their actions.

As Sam turned away from the flight line and began walking toward the mess hall, he remembered it was the Fourth of July and looked at his watch. It was 5:00 a.m. back home in Pennsylvania, and the firemen's parade would be starting in another six hours. He yearned to be back there with his family, watching the parade and enjoying the holiday festivities. After the parade, he knew May would have the family over to her house. She would serve a picnic lunch with meat loaf and potato salad. Sam always felt May's potato salad was the best in the world, and when he thought of the powdered potatoes and greasy spam that awaited him in the mess hall, he decided to skip supper altogether.

As he walked slowly in the direction of his basha, he thought about the direction the war was taking and wondered how long the fighting would go on. The Japanese had finally been defeated at Imphal, and the remaining enemy forces in India were being routed. Things had improved so much in the Imphal-Kohima area that Sam's old unit, the Sixty-fourth Troop Carrier Group, returned to Sicily in mid-June. The airstrip at Myitkyina was captured back in May, but fighting still raged to take the town. When the airstrip was first attacked, there were only four or five hundred Japanese troops in the area, but enemy reinforcements quickly flooded in from surrounding areas, swelling their numbers to between four and five thousand. Things were not looking good for the Japanese in Burma and India, but the offensive they began back in April to capture American air bases in China was going well. At this point in time, the war didn't look as if it would end anytime soon.

Sam's personal world had also changed recently. His unit had been moved from Dinjan Airbase in India to Shingbwiyang Airbase in northern Burma in order to bring them closer to the action. Where Dinjan was surrounded by tea plantations and jungle, Shingbwiyang was completely surrounded by jungle. The Burmese jungle differed from the Indian jungle in that the trees were taller and the undergrowth a little thicker. The oppressive heat and humidity was ever present as well as leeches and poisonous snakes.

Since moving to Shingbwiyang, Sam's new basha was a tent that he shared with Bobby Joe and four other soldiers. The tent provided some protection from the elements and the sides were rolled up to allow for ventilation. However, sleeping at this new base was complicated by the presence of swarms of buffalo flies. The flies were small enough to penetrate their sleeping nets, and they bit any exposed flesh and fed off the blood. The only way Sam found to avoid their irritating bites was to roll up in a blanket so that no skin was exposed. However, that made sleeping difficult due to the stifling heat. He was not looking forward to another tormented night.

"Hey, Sam, are you up for a beer flight tomorrow?"

Sam turned to see his friend Sergeant Walt Grimes, the man who rescued him from the Burmese jungle back in April and who had also recently been moved to Shingbwiyang.

"I can't, Walt. I'm scheduled for a couple of missions tomorrow," Sam answered disappointedly.

Walt had devised a process where he wrapped a couple of cans of beer in a wet sock and attached them to the landing gear of his L4. He then flew up to five thousand feet, and by the time he landed, the evaporation of the water in the sock provided a refreshingly cool can of beer.

"Too bad, I'll drink one for you," Walt said. "Hey, how about coming along on a reconnaissance flight soon? It would be a good opportunity to give you another flight lesson."

"I'd like that," Sam said as he continued toward his basha. "I'm not scheduled for any missions the day after tomorrow. Maybe we can get together then."

"I'll get back to you on that," Walt said, waving goodbye.

Since his rescue from the jungle, Sam had become close friends with Walt and had flown in the L4 with him on several mail runs. During those flights, Walt started to teach Sam how to fly the small plane, and he was proving to be a good student. He could now maneuver the plane in the air and had even made a couple of takeoffs under Walt's watchful eye. Sam liked flying the small aircraft so much he was considering getting a pilot's license after the war.

JULY 6, 1944
SHINGBWIYANG, BURMA

Sam met Walt on the flight line in eager anticipation of the reconnaissance mission they were about to fly and a possible flight lesson. Sam looked forward to flying in the L4. He got more of a sensation of flying in the small plane than he did in the large C47s. What he enjoyed the most was actually being in control of the airplane.

"I have the plane all ready and waiting," Walt said as he led Sam across the tarmac. "We'll be flying a reconnaissance mission around Myitkyina today and the weather is looking good."

"Great," Sam responded, "Will we be able to get in a flying lesson?"

"You can count on it," Walt said. "With you flying the plane, I get a chance to relax and enjoy the scenery."

When they reached the plane, Sam was surprised to see a different airplane than the one Walt usually flew. "Aren't we flying in the L4 today?" he asked.

"No, today we're using an L5. It's the military version of the Stinson Sentinel. It'll be good for you to get some experience in a different airplane. Go ahead and get in the rear seat," Walt said.

Sam entered the aircraft, and the first thing he noticed was the outside visibility. There were Plexiglas windows all around, and he could see why the plane was well suited for reconnaissance missions. The next thing he noticed was the structural metal tubing that was everywhere. He was completely surrounded by the tubing, and it gave him the impression of being in a cage. Everything about the L5 gave him the impression of begin ruggedly constructed right down to the control stick which had a big, beefy appearance.

Sam had just finished buckling himself in when Walt tossed a heavy bag and a Thompson submachine gun onto his lap. Sam looked into the bag and saw it was filled with hand grenades.

"What's this stuff for?" Sam asked.

"That's in case we get the chance to do a little more than just reconnaissance," Walt replied with a grin.

Sam stowed the munitions while Walt climbed aboard and started the engine. In a matter of minutes, they were airborne and heading south toward Myitkyina. When they reached an altitude of six thousand feet, Walt let Sam take control of the airplane and instructed him on how to maintain his altitude and heading in the bumpy air over the Burmese jungle. As they approached their reconnaissance area, Sam continued to fly the plane while Walt used the radio to contact the commander on the ground.

"I'll take control now, Sam. They want us to find some camouflaged enemy artillery pieces on the ridge to our left," Walt said as he took over the controls. "Keep a sharp eye out for those guns."

Walt turned the plane and flew along the ridge at an altitude about two thousand feet above the crest. "I didn't see anything. How about you, Sam?" he asked after he completed their first pass over the ridge.

"I didn't see anything either," Sam responded. "Those guns must be very well concealed."

"We'll have to get a closer look," Walt said as he descended and turned to make another pass one thousand feet above the ridge. Both men scanned the ridge carefully. They had almost completed the second pass when Sam saw something.

"I think I just saw sunlight reflecting off something about halfway down the ridge," Sam said.

Walt immediately put the little plane into a tight right-hand turn and descended until they were only five hundred feet above the tree tops. Sam directed him toward the area where he saw the reflection. From their new vantage point, they were able to see glimpses of a trail under the jungle canopy.

"That trail could be used to bring in supplies for the artillery," Walt said as he followed the course of the trail along the side of the ridge. As they approached the area where Sam saw the reflection, Walt slowed the airplane down.

"There they are," Sam shouted. "Just off the right-wing tip."

Walt looked in the direction Sam indicated and saw three Japanese artillery pieces cleverly hidden under camouflaged netting. Walt noted their location on his map and immediately turned away from the ridge. He climbed back up to five thousand feet and radioed their findings to American artillery units on the ground.

"They want us to spot for an artillery barrage," Walt explained. "It will begin in two minutes."

Walt positioned the plane, so they had a good view of the ridge. It wasn't long before they saw the first shells explode about a hundred yards above and to the left of the enemy guns. He reported the results to the gunners on the ground and waited for the next barrage. Meanwhile, Sam observed Japanese soldiers stripping the camouflage nets from their artillery.

"Those guys are going to start shooting back," Sam said as the second round of American shells struck twenty yards to the right of the enemy emplacements.

Walt radioed more corrections to the American gunners as the Japanese gun crews started to return fire. "The next barrage should be right on target," he said.

Sam watched as the third salvo from the American artillery arrived, and Walt was correct in his assessment. The U.S. gun crews had found their target. He saw two of enemy cannons receive direct hits and explode in tangled masses of fire and steel. However, the third gun was untouched and continued to fire back at the Americans. The artillery battle continued for five more minutes, and although there were some near misses, the enemy cannon remained unscathed.

Walt radioed the American gunners and then turned to Sam. "I asked them to cease fire," he said. "Get that bag of grenades ready. We're going to try to knock that gun out ourselves, and get the Thompson submachine gun ready too."

Sam looked at Walt in disbelief, but he opened the bag of hand grenades and removed two of them as Walt descended toward the remaining enemy cannon. He also checked the submachine gun and assured it was ready to fire.

"Open your side windows, and get ready for some action," Walt instructed as he maneuvered the little plane into position. They were now flying just a couple of hundred feet above the treetops and quickly approaching the enemy position.

"Pull the pins on two of those grenades and drop them out the window when I tell you," Walt said.

Sam had handled grenades in basic training, so he knew the procedure. He pulled the pins on two grenades and held them out the right window. On Walt's command, he dropped the grenades and looked back to see them explode just short of the enemy gun. He also saw enemy soldiers firing at them with their rifles.

"Looks like I called that one a bit prematurely," Walt said. "Get the Thompson ready. We'll make a strafing pass to try to subdue some of that rifle fire."

Sam held the Thompson submachine gun out his left window as Walt turned the aircraft for another pass. On Walt's command, Sam began spraying the side of the ridge with machine gun fire. The sound inside the little plane was deafening, but he continued firing until Walt turned the plane for another pass.

"Okay, get two more grenades ready," Walt instructed as he once again headed for the enemy gun emplacement. "Let 'em go," he shouted.

Sam dropped the grenades precisely on command and looked back once again. This time, he was rewarded to witness a spectacular explosion as the grenades detonated a stack of artillery shells and sent the enemy cannon tumbling down the side of the ridge. The impact from the explosion reached their plane almost immediately, and the L5 was thrown wildly about the sky. They were in a nearly inverted position when the plane went into a vertical spin. Sam watched in horror as they plummeted toward the jungle below. The world spun crazily before his eyes, and the centrifugal force of the spinning plane pinned him to the side of the fuselage as the ground drew nearer. Walt fought to regain control of the L5 and finally managed to stop the spin and pull out of the dive just a few feet above the trees.

"I think that's enough excitement for one day," Walt exclaimed. "Let's get the hell out of here."

They climbed back up to an altitude of five thousand feet before Sam was able to speak. "I thought we were goners back there, Walt. How were you able to get us out of that crazy mess?"

"It was a simple spin-recovery maneuver that every pilot has to learn," Walt explained. "We were lucky that we had enough altitude for the recovery. If we would have been twenty feet lower when the spin started, we wouldn't have made it. I want you to take the controls for a while now."

Sam was reluctant to fly the airplane after what he had just gone through, but he did as Walt asked and took control of the L5.

"Are you telling me if I want to get a pilot's license, I will have to purposely put an airplane into a spin like that and then recover from it?" Sam asked.

"That's part of basic flight training," Walt answered. "It's really not all that difficult to learn."

Sam began to realize there was more to flying an airplane than he had experienced so far. They were fifteen minutes into their flight back to Shingbwiyang when Walt received a radio message.

"I have the plane," Walt said as he plunged the L5 down to the treetops.

"What's going on?" Sam asked with concern.

"Apparently, we raised some hackles back there. Enemy fighters are reported in the area," Walt answered. "It's safer for us down here where we're not silhouetted against the sky and we blend in with the jungle. Keep a sharp lookout for any signs of aircraft."

Sam scanned the skies the remainder of the way to Shingbwiyang and was relieved to arrive safely back at the airfield. As they circled the field to land, Walt turned the controls over to Sam and instructed him in proper approach and landing procedures. Sam had never landed a plane before and was extremely nervous. However, Walt stayed on the controls and aided him in a successful landing. When they taxied to a stop, Sam climbed out of the airplane and realized his shirt was soaking wet with sweat.

"You look like a drowned rat," Walt said.

"I feel like one too," Sam responded.

"Well, it isn't everyone who can claim he destroyed a cannon and landed an airplane for the first time in the same day," Walt said. "Let's go to the mess hall and celebrate with a cup of coffee."

"Sounds good to me," Sam answered as they walked toward the mess hall.

The two men talked about the day's events over several cups of coffee, and Sam began to relax.

"You're a good flight student, Sam," Walt said. "If we can continue to fly together, I think I can have you ready to get your pilot's license before you go back to the States."

"I know I have a lot more to learn," Sam said. "I think I would like to get a license, but right now, I think I would like to get a shower."

The two friends parted company, and Sam headed for his basha and the prospects of a refreshing shower. The path to his company area led along the edge of the jungle, and he was near to his destination when his attention was drawn to the sound of something crashing through the jungle undergrowth. Wary that some dangerous animal might be approaching, Sam listened tensely as the sounds drew nearer. He reached for his sidearm before realizing he did not have it with him and prepared to run for his life.

The crashing sound grew louder and nearer. Sam could see the underbrush giving way to something large. Whatever was approaching was moving swiftly, and Sam turned to flee. He hadn't taken two steps when something came out of the jungle and collided with him from behind. Sam rolled over quickly and came to his feet, facing his attacker. He was prepared to see a tiger or some other large animal. Instead, he saw a soldier lying facedown in the dirt pathway.

"What the hell is..." Sam's words stopped short as the soldier scurried to his feet and turned to face him. "Kerby! Is that you?" he continued.

"Sam! Oh Lord, I never expected to see someone from home here," Kerby said as he rushed forward and embraced his old friend.

"What are you doing here, Kerby?" Sam asked.

"After basic training, they sent me to cook's school," Kerby answered. "When I got out of school, I was assigned to Fort Dix in New Jersey."

"How did you get from New Jersey to here?" Sam inquired.

"Well, somehow some of the base commander's private stock of booze disappeared, and they thought I had something to do with it," Kerby said. "It really wasn't all my doing, Sam. Anyway, instead of court-martialing me, he said he was going to send me as far away as he possibly could. I guess this is as far as he could send me. I've been here since January."

"I just got here five days ago," Sam said, "I had no idea you were here. What were you doing charging through the jungle?"

"Oh, that," Kerby said hesitantly. "I was just taking a walk in the jungle when I thought I saw a tiger and felt I'd better get out of there."

Sam was about to question Kerby further when a soldier stepped out of the jungle about fifteen yards in front of them. As the soldier approached, Sam could see he was wearing a military police armband.

"I've been chasing a soldier suspected of making moonshine back in the jungle," the soldier said as he eyed Sam and Kerby's sweat-soaked fatigues. "Did you soldiers see anyone come out of the jungle just now?"

Kerby turned pale, and Sam could tell from the look on his face that he was the culprit.

"No, we've just been doing a little jogging, and no one has come past us," Sam said.

"Yeah, just jogging," Kerby repeated.

The MP looked suspiciously at Kerby and then at Sam. "Well, if you do hear anything about a still in the jungle, report it to your CO at once," the soldier said as he turned and reentered the jungle.

When the MP was gone, Sam turned to his old friend. "What's going on here, Kerby?" Sam asked.

"Well, I sort of met a guy in the motor pool from South Carolina. His last name is Kline, the same as mine." Kerby said. "Anyway, he made moonshine back home and wanted to know if I would like to help him make some here. You know, since I have access to canned fruit and other stuff that can be distilled."

"And of course, you couldn't resist," Sam said.

"It ain't really hurting anyone," Kerby answered, "and we get a good price for our shine from the engineering battalions building the Ledo Road. Would you like to come in on it with us, Sam?"

"Kerby, you know if they catch you, you'll be court-martialed and put in prison," Sam responded.

"They won't catch us, Sam. We move the still every few days so it's not easy to find. Think about it, Sam. I have to go now. I'm on duty in the chow hall in twenty minutes," Kerby said as he hurried off.

Sam watched his friend disappear in the direction of the mess hall and shook his head. It was good to see a face from back home, but it appeared Kerby was never going to change. In any event, he was looking forward to seeing him again.

29

AUGUST 10, 1944
MOSHANNON VALLEY, PENNSYLVANIA

E LEANOR AND BILLY had just finished eating lunch when May came hurrying into the house with a newspaper in her hand. Eleanor could see it was a copy of the *Osceola Leader*, the local newspaper.

"Eleanor, there's an article about Sam on the front page of today's paper," May said excitedly.

"About Sam, oh let me see it," Eleanor said.

"It tells about medals he's been awarded and the kinds of things he's been doing in Burma," May explained as she handed the paper to Eleanor.

Eleanor took the paper from May and found the article in the middle of the front page. May picked up Billy and watched as Eleanor read the article.

**PFC. SAMUEL D. HUBER AWARDED 2
DECORATIONS FOR ACTION IN BURMA**

Pvt. Samuel D. Huber of 300 Pruner St. Osceola

Mills, who on July 31, 1944, completed 148 combat flying missions, has been awarded the Distinguished Flying Cross and an Oak Leaf Cluster to the Air Medal for extraordinary achievement in aerial flights over Burma.

He is a member of a unit which successfully provided food, clothing, mail, medical supplies, and other war materiel—through means of parachute dropping—to forward elements of American, Indian, British, and Chinese troops fighting in the mountains of Upper Burma during tropical and monsoon weather.

The citations, which cover the period from April 2, 1944 to July 31, 1944, were released through the Office of the Division Engineer, Middle Atlantic Division, Baltimore, Md.

During the missions, exposure to enemy ground and aerial fire was probable and expected. The citations conclude: "All individuals have with courage and fortitude accomplished their assignment and have brought much credit upon themselves and the military service of the U.S."

Eleanor finished reading the article and slowly sat down. Her complexion had turned a pale white.

"Oh, my Eleanor, you don't look well. Has the article upset you? I thought you would be proud of Sam's medals," May said.

"I am proud of him, May, but Sam's letters never said anything about being under fire. This article says enemy fire was probable and expected during his missions. He must be in more danger than we ever thought. He might be under fire this very moment," Eleanor said.

"He wouldn't be under fire now, dear, its midnight over there,"

May said, trying to calm Eleanor down. However, she could see her words were having little effect.

"Why do we have this stupid war, May? Why is the world so crazy and violent? It doesn't make sense for us to be killing each other all across the globe," Eleanor sobbed.

"The world is full of evil, Eleanor. It's always been that way, and I suppose it always will be," May responded.

"I'm worried about Sam, and if this craziness doesn't stop, I'm worried Billy may someday have to go to war. I'm not sure I want to bring another baby into this world," Eleanor said as tears streamed down her cheeks.

May didn't know how to respond to Eleanor's worries. She sat silently holding Billy and praying Eleanor's fears would not come true. She was about to suggest they have a cup of tea when Eleanor gasped and clutched her stomach.

"Are you all right, Eleanor?" May asked.

"My water just broke," Eleanor explained as the first labor pain struck. "I think it's time to go to the hospital."

May hurried to the phone and called her husband, Paul, at the machine shop. Paul left his job immediately and arrived at Eleanor's house in less than ten minutes. When he entered the front door, May had Eleanor ready to go.

"You take Eleanor to the hospital, and I'll stay here and care for Billy. I'll call the hospital and let them know you're coming," May said.

Without further delay, Paul got Eleanor into his car and drove away. Eleanor's labor pains were coming closer together and strengthening as they headed for the hospital. The Philipsburg Hospital was only five miles away, but Paul began to fear they wouldn't make it in time. As Eleanor's labor intensified, he worried about the baby coming before they got there. He drove as fast as traffic would allow and was relieved when they finally arrived at the emergency entrance. A nurse met them at the door and whisked Eleanor away to the labor room.

Paul was directed to the maternity waiting room where he nervously awaited the arrival of the family's newest member.

The time between Eleanor's labor pains had dropped to three minutes when her doctor, Dr. Steven Funk, came to assess the situation. Eleanor liked Dr. Funk. He was young and personable with an excellent bedside manner. Eleanor really would have liked Sam's uncle, Dr. Flynn, deliver the baby, but he retired completely after he delivered Billy. Eleanor thought it ironic that May had been the first baby Dr. Flynn delivered and Billy was the last.

Eleanor's musings were cut short when Dr. Funk told the nurses to take her into the delivery room. Her pains were almost continuous now, and Eleanor had to concentrate to follow the doctor's instructions. It seemed like an eternity to Eleanor, but in reality, the birth took less than five minutes. The pain and the pressure were finally gone, and she heard the cries of her newborn child. Dr. Funk appeared at her side, carrying a small bundle wrapped in a blanket.

"Congratulations, Eleanor, you have a beautiful baby boy," he said as he placed the bundle in her arms.

Eleanor looked upon her new son for the first time and was very pleased. He had a full head of wavy black hair, and even though his features were still swollen, she could see he bore a striking resemblance to his father. She completely removed the blanket and checked his tiny hands and feet for deformities.

"He's all there, Eleanor," Dr. Funk said reassuringly, "and he seems very healthy. What are you going to name him?"

"My husband is in the Army Air Corps, and they use the term 'roger' in their radio communications to indicate a transmission has been received and acknowledged," Eleanor said. "So we decided, if it's a boy, to name him Roger."

"Well, he certainly has been completely received and acknowledged, so Roger it will be," Dr. Funk said with a smile.

As they wheeled Eleanor from the delivery room, she wondered how long it would be before Sam got to see his new son. She tried not to think of the possibility that he may never see him.

AUGUST 14, 1944
THE SKIES OVER NORTHERN BURMA

It was never easy dropping supplies to the Chinese soldiers in Burma, and today was no exception. In addition to ground fire from the enemy, Sam's plane had once again received friendly fire from the very Chinese troops they were supplying. Sam was angry enough about being shot at by friendly forces, but his crewmate, "Wimpy" Hutton, was simply livid. During their last pass over the target area, a well-placed Chinese bullet struck a bag of sandwiches Wimpy had stashed away and flung its contents all over the cargo bay.

"Look at that, Sam," Wimpy lamented. "All them good sandwiches just wasted. I'm telling you Sam, the next time I drop rice to them heathens I'm sticking a live hand grenade in it."

"Don't you think that's a bit of an overreaction?" Sam said with a chuckle. "We should be back at base in time for evening chow."

"It ain't funny, Sam. I had to pay that cook, Kerby Kline, good money for them sandwiches. If I didn't have another bag stashed, I'd really be mad," Wimpy said as he retrieved a second bag of sandwiches and immediately began munching on one of them. "You want a sandwich Sam?" he asked.

"No, thanks, Wimpy, but how do you know Kerby?" Sam asked

"I know he's the worst cook in the army, and he overcharges me for sandwiches," Wimpy replied. "He does have access to some of the best moonshine I ever tasted though. Some of the guys say he's got a still hidden somewhere in the jungle."

"I don't know about a still, but I have to agree his cooking leaves something to be desired," Sam said. "Enjoy your sandwiches. I'm going to check with the pilots on our estimated time of arrival back at Shingbwiyang."

"Hey, tell LT to take it easy on them bumps," Wimpy said. "A man can hardly eat with the plane bouncing around like this."

Sam shook his head as he entered the cockpit where his friend Lt. L. T. Thomas was at the controls. "Any idea when we'll get back to the base?" Sam asked the pilot.

"We'll be landing in about thirty-five minutes," LT answered, "but we just received some bad news over the radio for you, Sam."

Sam immediately became concerned as thoughts of a tragedy back home raced through his mind. "What bad news, LT?" he asked.

"I know you pride yourself on being one of the most accurate kickers in the army," LT said, "but some little lady back in the States just did you one better."

"What are you talking about, LT?" Sam responded. "There aren't any women kickers in the army."

"Well, this one dropped a load dead center on target," LT said as he handed Sam a transcription of the radio message.

Sam took the paper from LT's hand and quickly scanned the message written upon it.

To: Pfc. Samuel D. Huber
5331st Air Supply Dropping Platoon
APO 487

The American Red Cross is pleased to inform
you of the birth of your son on Aug. 10, 1944.
Mother and baby are doing fine.

"Congratulations, Daddy," LT said as he extended his hand to Sam. "What are you going to name him?"

"Roger," Sam answered.

"I know you understand the question," LT continued, "but what are you going to name the baby?"

"Roger," Sam said perplexed. "We're naming the baby Roger."

"Well, roger that," LT responded. "I guess you're getting the boy ready to be a pilot right from the start."

Everyone had a good laugh over the misunderstanding as Sam read and reread the message. His heart ached to be home with his family, and it saddened him to know he was probably not going to see his new son for a long time.

They arrived back at Shingbwiyang airfield at the time LT predicted. Sam and Wimpy were about to disembark when LT called from the cockpit. "I just got a call over the radio. The CO wants to see you in his office right away, Sam," he said.

"Well, I guess I'd better get over to HQ right away," Sam said to Wimpy.

"Yeah, good luck, Sam. I'm heading for the chow hall so I can be first in line for Kerby's slop. I'm so hungry my stomach thinks my throat's been cut," Wimpy responded.

Sam watched as Wimpy hurried toward the mess hall. It amazed him how one individual could eat so much and stay so slim. As he walked to the headquarters building, Sam thought about roller-coaster ride this day had been. He had been shot at by friendly troops, received news of the birth of his new son, and was now headed for who-knows-what in the commander's office. There was one thing he was sure about though. He was in no hurry to face another of Kerby's concoctions of watery instant potatoes and greasy Spam that the hapless cook so proudly called Spam-in-a-Cloud.

Sam arrived at the HQ Building and was told by Corporal Finney to go right into the CO's office.

"Private Huber reporting as ordered, sir," Sam announced as he stood at attention before his CO.

"You can dispense with the formalities, Sam," the captain said as he rose and extended his hand. "Congratulations on the birth of your son."

"Thank you, sir. It's a relief to know the little guy if finally here," Sam said.

"I'll bet it is," continued the captain. "I called you here for two reasons, Sam. First I wanted to inform you that you've earned another oak leaf for your Air Medal, and due to the dangerous nature of the missions you've been flying, I'm recommending you for a second Distinguished Flying Cross."

"Thank you, sir. I'm honored by your recommendation," Sam said.

"You've earned it, Sam," the captain said. "The second thing I wanted to do is give you a two-day pass to Calcutta. I know you have been under a lot of stress lately, and I feel you could use a break."

"Thank you again, sir. It will be nice to get away from things for a couple of days," Sam responded.

"It's done then," Captain Cummings said as he handed Sam the pass. "There's a plane leaving for Calcutta first thing in the morning."

Sam shook hands with the commander once again and then departed to pack an overnight bag for his upcoming liberty in Calcutta.

30

AUGUST 15, 1944
SHINGBWIYANG, BURMA

S AM ARRIVED ON the flight line fifteen minutes before his plane
was scheduled to depart for Calcutta. When he climbed aboard
the C47, three other soldiers were already on board. The men were in
the process of introducing themselves when they were distracted by
the sounds of voices shouting and jeering outside the plane.

"Hey, guys, looks like our lucky day. Maybe we'll get some decent
chow now," one man shouted.

"Yeah, wherever you're goin', cookie, I sure hope you stay there,"
another man jeered.

Sam turned toward the doorway just in time to see Kerby scramble
aboard the plane. Kerby stood in the doorway and shouted back to
the hecklers.

"You mugs wouldn't know good food if you saw it, but enjoy your
Spam while I'm gone. I'll think of you while I'm eating a big steak in
Calcutta," he said as he dodged to avoid a screwdriver thrown in his
direction.

"I should have known it was you, Kerby," Sam said on his way to close the cargo door.

"Sam! I didn't know you were going to Calcutta. This is great. We can celebrate the birth of your new baby," Kerby said enthusiastically. "I already have a room at the Grand Hotel booked, and you can bunk with me."

"Oh, I wouldn't want to get in your way," Sam answered.

"You better take that offer," one of the other soldiers said. "I heard the Grand is completely booked."

"Then it's a done deal. You'll share my room, Sam. Now anyone interested in a game of poker," Kerby said as he pulled a deck of cards from his pocket.

Sam groaned at the thought, but realizing there was no place to hide aboard an airplane, he joined the game to try to keep Kerby out of trouble. It was beginning to look like he would have his hands full for the next two days.

The flight to Calcutta was uneventful, and as far as Sam could tell, Kerby did not cheat at cards. In fact, his friend bet extravagantly and lost money during the games. The losses didn't seem to bother Kerby at all, since he appeared to have an unlimited supply of money. After they landed at Dum Dum Airfield, Sam and Kerby parted company with the other soldiers and caught a taxi into Calcutta. Over Sam's objections, Kerby insisted on paying for the taxi when they arrived at the Grand Hotel. It was too early to check into their room, so they left their overnight bags with the desk clerk and went outside to see the sights.

As they walked along Chowringhee Road, Sam was not surprised to see that little had changed in the bustling city. The streets still teemed with all manner of humanity and the smells were just as offensive as ever. What did surprise Sam was how well Kerby seemed to know his way around.

"You seem to know your way around Calcutta very well," Sam said to his friend.

"Yeah, I come here as often as I can," Kerby answered. "It gives me a chance to get away from the base and all the griping about the food back there. At least here, a man can get a decent meal."

Sam knew they had limited supplies back at Shingbwiyang, but he refrained from commenting on the food because he knew Kerby had a poor reputation as a cook. When he thought about some of the concoctions Kerby prepared, he had to agree the reputation was not totally underserved.

"This looks like an interesting shop," Sam said. "Let's go inside and check it out."

"You go ahead, Sam," Kerby responded. "I want to see what some of these street vendors have to offer. I'll meet you right here in fifteen minutes."

Sam entered the store and began looking at some jewelry that was displayed in the glass cases. His attention was drawn to a beautiful necklace. The chain seemed to be made of fine links of gold, and the pendant appeared to be at least a three-carat ruby surrounded by gold filigree.

"You have an eye for fine jewelry," said a voice in perfect English.

Sam turned to see an Indian man dressed in a fine western style suit. "I was admiring this necklace," he said.

"Yes, I noticed," the man said. "It is the finest piece I have in my shop. It is a splendid three-and-a-half-carat Burmese ruby with twenty-four-karat gold chain and filigree."

"You speak excellent English," Sam said. "Did you study in the United States?"

"Yes, I graduated from the University of Southern California, and I am a certified gemologist," the merchant said. "I can guarantee all of my pieces are created with genuine gemstones."

"How much is this piece?" Sam asked, pointing to the ruby necklace.

"The ruby necklace is priced at one thousand rupees. That would be about three hundred American dollars," the merchant said. "It is a rare ruby. Notice how deep the color is."

"Yes, it certainly is a beautiful stone," Sam said, "but it's a little too expensive for me."

"I understand," the merchant answered. "Continue looking and let me know if I can be of help. I am Mr. Dutta, the proprietor."

Sam thanked the store owner and continued looking around. Fifteen minutes later, he was waiting outside, and Kerby was nowhere in sight. He waited another ten minutes and was about to return to the hotel when he saw his friend hurrying toward him.

"Sorry I'm late, Sam," Kerby said. "I was dickering with a street vendor for some rubies."

"You didn't buy rubies from a man on the street, did you?" Sam asked unbelievably.

"Yeah, I really took him for a ride. Look at these beauties," Kerby said as he handed Sam four glistening red stones. "I got all four for only fifty bucks. The guy told me they should bring at least a hundred bucks apiece back in the States."

Sam looked at the stones and saw they were indeed nicely cut and faceted. However, their color was nowhere as deep and rich as the ruby he just saw inside the store, and he began to suspect they were not real rubies.

"I was just looking at rubies in this store," Sam said. "The owner's a gemologist. Let's take these inside and have him appraise them."

"Good idea. They may be worth more than a hundred bucks apiece," Kerby responded excitedly. "You may be looking at a rich man, Sam."

Kerby eagerly followed Sam back into the store where they approached the proprietor.

"Ah, you have decided to buy a fine piece of my jewelry?" Mr. Dutta said to Sam.

"Not at the moment, sir," Sam responded, "but my friend just bought these stones on the street. Would you be willing to appraise them for him?"

"It would be my pleasure," Mr. Dutta said as he took the stones from Sam.

Kerby watched excitedly as the store owner held each stone up to the light and then looked at them through his jeweler's loupe. Satisfied with what he saw, he returned the stones to Kerby.

"These are fine examples of the exceptional workmanship of our local craftsmen," Mr. Dutta said.

"See, I told you, Sam. I'm a rich man," Kerby said exuberantly.

"I wouldn't go so far as to say that," Mr. Dutta interrupted. "They are fine pieces of cut glass and worth no more than two dollars as costume jewelry."

The expression on Kerby's face turned from excitement to bewilderment and finally to anger. "That lousy thief," he said. "I'm going back there and wring his neck until he gives my fifty bucks back."

"Oh, dear, you have indeed been swindled," Mr. Dutta said, "but it will do you no good to try to find the man. He will have long since departed from the area. Unfortunately, this type of swindle is a common thing in Calcutta. You should only buy gemstones from an accredited jeweler like me."

Kerby looked despondently at the glass stones and then at Mr. Dutta and finally at Sam. "I guess I learned an expensive lesson today," he said. "Oh well, it's just money. Let's go have a good dinner at Firpo's, Sam."

They thanked Mr. Dutta and headed down Chowringhee Road toward Firpo's restaurant. Sam had never been to Firpo's, but he knew it had a fine reputation for excellent food. As they approached the restaurant, Sam could see it had a second-story veranda overlooking the street that was crowded with patrons having drinks before dinner. They entered the building and saw the dining room was completely full.

"We'll be forever getting a table here," Sam said. "Let's find another place to eat."

"Just follow me," Kerby said as he approached the maitre d'.

"It is a pleasure to see you again, Mr. Kline," the maitre d' said. "Would you like your usual table, sir?"

"Yes, that would be fine," Kerby responded as he winked at Sam and motioned for him to follow.

They followed the maitre d' across the dining room to a small windowed alcove that contained a table set for two. The table was covered with a white linen tablecloth and was set with bone china dinner ware, polished silver utensils, and starched linen napkins. There was also a silver vase in the center of the table containing colorful tropical flowers. The maitre d' snapped his fingers, and two waiters appeared to help the soldiers into their seats. The waiters were dressed in red turbans and starched white uniforms. They had brass identification numbers pinned to their chests and, just like at the Grand Hotel, were not wearing shoes.

Once Sam and Kerby were seated, one of the waiters handed each of them a menu and waited to take their order. The other waiter filled their water goblets with ice water and then stood by to refill them when needed. Sam looked at the menu and saw all the dinners were five courses and all were priced at four rupees or about $1.20. Kerby ordered chicken shorba soup, a chef's salad, and a T-bone steak with baked potato. Sam ordered curry soup, a chef's salad, and pheasant under glass. As they waited for the meals to arrive, a stringed orchestra began to play soft classical music.

The atmosphere and service at the restaurant was excellent and so was the food. Both men ate heartily and finished their meals with chocolate éclairs and rich dark coffee. After dinner, Kerby insisted on paying the bill over Sam's objections, and then they proceeded to the Grand Hotel. The desk clerk at the Grand recognized Kerby immediately and, handing him a room key, informed them their bags had already been delivered to the room. Sam, totally baffled by the treatment Kerby was receiving, followed his diminutive friend to their room.

When they arrived at the room, Sam was shocked to discover it was not a room, but a luxurious suite. There were two bedrooms, a sitting room, and a private bath. The suite was lavishly decorated, complete with fresh flowers, a box of chocolates, and a bottle of champagne in a bucket of ice.

"Well, this is home sweet home for tonight, Sam," Kerby announced. "I hope you like it."

"What's not to like," Sam said, "but I can't afford a room like this Kerby."

"Don't worry about it, Sam. Everything's on me," Kerby said.

"But, Kerby, you're a private like me. How can you afford it? You've been throwing money around all day," Sam said.

"I can afford it," Kerby answered. "My enterprises back at Shingbwiyang are paying off in a big way. I got plenty of money."

"What enterprises are you talking about?" Sam asked with a growing feeling of anxiety.

"You know about the still," Kerby said. "We're getting a good price for our moonshine."

"You said enterprises, Kerby. What else are you involved in?" Sam asked.

"Well, I can't tell you, because I don't want to get my partners in trouble," Kerby said, "but I wouldn't recommend playing any bingo back at the base."

Sam realized he didn't want to know anything more about Kerby's enterprises and decided to take a hot bath.

AUGUST 16, 1944
DUM DUM AIRPORT, CALCUTTA

After a glorious night's sleep, Sam and Kerby arrived at Dum Dum Airport with plenty of time to catch their plane back to Burma. However, they were told the flight would be delayed until food supplies for Shingbwiyang arrived and were loaded aboard.

"I'm going to walk down the tarmac and see if there are any crewmen I know," Sam said.

"Okay, Sam. I think I'll stay here and be sure our supplies get on board okay," Kerby answered.

Sam felt sure Kerby couldn't get into any trouble on the flight line and ambled off in search of anyone he might know. Kerby lingered in the shade under the wing of their plane until he saw a supply truck approaching. The truck stopped a short distance from the plane, and the driver got out with a puzzled look on his face. Kerby started to walk toward the truck when a second supply truck stopped alongside the first one. By this time, Kerby was close enough to hear the conversation between the two drivers.

"Hey, Mac," the first driver said. "This is my first time delivering to the airport. I got a load of food for Shingbwiyang. Got any idea what I should do with it?"

"Yeah, I got a load of goodies for the Brits up in New Delhi," the second driver answered. "Just leave your manifest on the seat of the truck, and an aircrew will take care of everything."

"Thanks, Mac," said the first driver. "I'm sure glad I don't have to eat the crap they're sending to those poor louses at Shingbwiyang."

"I know what you mean," said the second driver. "The Brits eat a lot better than our guys. You should see the stuff I got on my truck."

"How about I buy you a cup of Joe and you can tell me all about it?" the first driver said.

Kerby watched as the two drivers walked toward the terminal

building. When they were out of sight, he opened the door of the first truck and found the manifest. The top sheet of the manifest listed Shingbwiyang as the destination for the load and the number of the aircraft that was to deliver it. Kerby noted the aircraft number was the same as the plane he was to fly on. He then browsed through the remainder of the manifest. What he saw filled him with despair. The items on the list were the same things they had been eating at Shingbwiyang since he arrived there—powdered potatoes, powdered eggs, powdered coffee, and canned Spam. The men back at the base blamed him for the poor quality of their food, and he dreaded the thought of not having something different to cook. He remembered the second driver's comments about having a load of goodies for the Brits, and although he knew he shouldn't do it, he went to the second truck and retrieved the manifest.

Kerby couldn't believe his eyes when he saw what was destined for New Delhi. The list showed cases of canned fruit, cheese, canned bacon, vegetable stew, and fresh eggs. His heart began to race as he went down through the manifest, and it nearly stopped when he saw what was listed last. There were three cases of Haig and Haig Scotch, two cases of old Beefeater Gin, and a fifty-five-gallon drum of rum. There was no doubt in Kerby's mind what he had to do. Looking around to be sure no one was watching, he switched the destination sheets of the manifests, placed them back in their respective trucks, and returned to his plane to wait.

It wasn't long before a group of soldiers arrived to unload the trucks. The sergeant in charge took the manifest from the second truck and read the top page. Looking around, he spotted the number on Kerby's plane and walked over.

"Are you on this plane?" asked the sergeant.

"Sure am. What can I do for you, Sarge?" Kerby answered.

"Is this plane going to Shingbwiyang?" the sergeant continued.

"Sure is," Kerby said.

The sergeant turned to his waiting crew and ordered them

to begin loading the contents of the second truck onto the plane. Kerby watched nervously as the supplies meant for New Delhi were loaded onto his plane. When the process was completed, the sergeant approached Kerby.

"Sure seems like an unusual load to be headed for Shingbwiyang," the sergeant said as he looked over the manifest.

"Why do you say that, Sarge?" Kerby asked nervously.

"This is the kind of stuff we normally ship to the Brits," the sergeant said.

"Oh well, we recently had a battalion of British troops moved into Shingbwiyang," Kerby said.

"Funny I don't remember hearing anything about that," the sergeant said.

"I heard it has something to do with a secret mission," Kerby said hopefully.

"Well, I just do what the manifest says. Give this to the pilot and have a good flight, Mac," continued the sergeant as he handed Kerby the manifest.

Kerby watched as the sergeant departed with his men. Apparently, another crew would be along shortly to unload the truck with supplies for Shingbwiyang. Kerby hurried over to the truck and quickly switched the destination sheets back to their original manifests. He then hid the New Delhi manifest under the seat of the empty truck and scampered back to his plane. Climbing aboard, he began looking for something to cover the British supplies. There was nothing in sight except a flight jacket with lieutenants bars on it. Finding nothing else, he decided to rearrange the cases so the contents could not be read. He had only managed to turn the cases of whiskey and gin when a second crew arrived to load the supplies for Shingbwiyang. Thinking quickly, Kerby donned the lieutenant's jacket and met the crew's sergeant at the door.

"We're here to load the supplies for Shingbwiyang, sir," said the sergeant.

"Well, get your men moving, Sergeant. I've got to get this plane in the air," Kerby responded. "Get a couple of men on board, and I'll show them where to put the stuff."

The sergeant ordered his men to start loading the aircraft and Kerby directed the placement of the cases so that the British supplies were soon covered and out of sight. When the job was done, the sergeant and his crew departed and Kerby stood admiring his handiwork. He was so enthralled with his achievement that he didn't hear Sam approach.

"Kerby, what are you doing wearing an officer's jacket?" Sam asked nervously.

Startled by Sam's sudden appearance, Kerby responded, "I got a sudden chill and needed to put something on."

"It's got to be a hundred degrees in here," Sam said skeptically.

"I think I'm coming down with some kind of tropical fever," Kerby answered.

"Well, get that jacket off and put this on before you get charged with impersonating an officer," Sam said as he handed him his shirt.

"Thanks, Sam," Kerby said sheepishly.

Sam was about to question Kerby more when they were interrupted by the arrival of the flight crew. Kerby was relieved by the distraction and even more relieved after they had taken off and were headed back to Shingbwiyang. He knew Sam suspected something and pretended to sleep all the way back to Burma. After they landed at Shingbwiyang, Kerby hung around the C47 after everyone disembarked.

"Aren't you going back to your tent?" Sam asked.

"No, I'm going to hang around and be sure these supplies get safely to the mess hall," Kerby answered.

Sam was still somewhat suspicious of Kerby's motives but decided he didn't want to know if his friend was up to something. "Okay, I'll see you later," he said.

Kerby watched Sam walk away and then climbed back aboard

the airplane. He located a case of the Beefeaters Gin and removed several bottles before settling down to wait for the unloading crew to arrive. By the time the crew got there, he had consumed about half a bottle of gin and was teetering in the aircraft doorway. Kerby was pleased to see the sergeant in charge of the crew was one of the men who helped him run the crooked bingo games. He motioned for the sergeant to board the plane and showed him a bottle of gin. The sergeant immediately ordered his men to wait outside while Kerby filled him in on what was going on.

It didn't take the sergeant long to realize the value of the cargo on board, and for the price of a case of scotch, he agreed to help Kerby. The sergeant shouted outside for one of his men to bring him a tarp from the truck. When the tarp arrived, he covered the liquor and ordered his men to unload the remainder of the cargo. Once the plane was unloaded, he told the crew to deliver the supplies to the mess hall and then return with the empty truck. When the truck finally returned, the sergeant dismissed his men. He and Kerby then loaded the truck with their treasure of liquor and drove to the quartermaster warehouse where they hid it for future fun and profit.

AUGUST 30, 1944
SHINGBWIYANG, BURMA

The past two weeks had seen a marked improvement in Kerby's reputation. The quality of his cooking hadn't improved, but the fresh eggs, bacon, and other items from the British supplies were a big hit with the men who ate in his mess hall. They no longer jeered at him and called him names. Kerby's status was further enhanced when he let it be known he had a supply of quality booze for sale under the table.

Kerby was serving a special concoction of vegetable stew laced with rum when he was approached by a sergeant he had never seen before.

"Are you Private Kline?" the sergeant asked.

"Sure am, Sarge. Would you like some stew?" Kerby said.

"Smells good. I think I will have some," replied the sergeant, "and after I finish it, I have orders to escort you to the base commander's office."

Kerby nearly dropped his ladle into the pot of stew but managed to fill a bowl for the sergeant. He watched nervously as the NCO sat down at a table nearby. All kinds of thoughts raced through Kerby's mind as he watched the sergeant eat, but he had a feeling his visit with the base commander was not going to be a good one. The sergeant finished his stew and walked back to the serving counter.

"You fellows sure eat well here," the sergeant said to Kerby.

"Would you like some more stew?" Kerby asked, hoping to forestall the inevitable.

"I'd like to, but I have to get you over to Colonel Burke's office," replied the sergeant.

"Maybe I should put on some clean clothes," Kerby said.

"No, the colonel wants to see you right away," the sergeant answered. "Let's go, soldier."

Neither man said a word as they walked to the base's headquarters building. Kerby became more and more nervous with every step, and when they finally arrived, he was sweating profusely. The sergeant led him to a door labeled Colonel Burke, knocked, and opened the door. Kerby could see the colonel sitting at his desk. He was a big man with thinning white hair and a ruddy complexion. His eyebrows were bushy white, and his nose looked like it had been broken in several places. Kerby's could not force his legs to move until the sergeant gave him a shove into the room.

Kerby stood before the colonel, shaking. "P-Pr-Private Kline reporting ah as ordered, sir," he said as he stood at attention and saluted.

"At ease, Private," the colonel responded as he looked Kerby over with a keen eye. He picked up a paper from his desk and continued.

"You were on a flight carrying supplies from Calcutta to here on August the sixteenth, were you not?"

"Yes, sir," Kerby answered.

"This report indicates a load of British supplies disappeared that same day," the colonel said, "and it seems similar supplies are showing up in your mess hall. Do you know anything about that?"

"I… uh… know we received some unusual supplies on that flight, sir, but I thought the army meant them for us," Kerby said.

"And you don't know how those supplies mistakenly got on your plane?" the colonel asked.

"Oh no, sir. The plane was already loaded when I got there," Kerby answered.

"The report says a lieutenant directed the loading of the plane. Did you see a lieutenant around when you got there, private," the colonel said looking directly at Kerby.

"No, sir, there was no one on board when I got there," Kerby responded nervously.

"I see," said the colonel. "I know we're at the end of the supply chain here, and I know the British receive much better food than we do. I guess I couldn't blame some enterprising soldier for taking advantage of a mix up."

"I suppose you're right, sir," Kerby said hopefully.

"The Brits are upset about the missing food, but they're really in a tizzy about the loss of some scotch, gin, and rum," the colonel continued.

Kerby didn't answer but stood shaking before the colonel.

"Well, I think I can report that this base knows nothing about the missing supplies," said the colonel, "but it sure would be nice if some good liquor mysteriously appears at our officer's club."

"Yes, sir. I'm sure that would be nice," Kerby answered.

"Very well, Private, you're dismissed," the colonel said with a knowing smile.

31

NOVEMBER 15, 1944
SHINGBWIYANG, BURMA

For the first time in several weeks Sam was not scheduled for a mission. He decided to spend the day relaxing and catching up on his letter writing. His friend Bobby Joe also had the day off and was dozing in his cot. Sam had tried to start a letter to Eleanor several times, but Bobby Joe's snoring kept breaking his concentration. Finally, he arose from his bunk and went outside. Finding a secluded spot under a towering teak tree, he sat down and began to write.

Pvt. Samuel Huber 33761617
5331st Air Supply Dropping Platoon
APO 487 %PM NY NY

Hello Eleanor,
I'm sorry I haven't written in a while, but they have been keeping us pretty busy delivering supplies to the troops in the jungle and in China. As you have probably seen in the newspapers, the war in Burma is going well. We finally drove the Japs out of Myitkyina and this has

allowed our cargo flights to China to use a less dangerous route around the Hump rather than over it. It's still a hazardous flight because of the bad weather around here. I'm sure you also heard the war in China is not going so well. The Japs have captured our airbases at Lingling and Kweilin and are threatening to take Kunming. That would not be good because we fly a lot of supplies there. I'm sure the censors will delete the names in this paragraph, but you will get the drift of what I'm saying.

I am doing ok. I am constantly tired from working all the time and the food we're getting is the worst since I got here. It doesn't help that our friend Kerby is the cook. He tries hard, but he seems to have a knack for turning anything into slop. I've lost about 15 pounds over the past two months. I'd give anything for one of May's roast beef dinners.

I hope you and the boys are doing well. The pictures you sent of them really cheered me up. I have them pinned to the wall above my bed, and I go to sleep every night wishing I could be there with all of you. It was exactly a year ago today that I left you, and it seems like an eternity. At times I think this war is never going to end.

Well, it's almost time for lunch. I was thinking about skipping it, but maybe I'll go just to see what kind of mess Kerby has whipped up today. Write soon.

Love
Sam

Sam folded his letter and walked back to his basha where he found Bobby Joe still sleeping and snoring like a buzz saw. He walked over to his friend's bed and shook him awake.

"Hey, whata y'all doin' shakin' a man like that?" Bobby Joe complained.

"I had to," Sam responded. "You were snoring so loud the guys in the next tent were threatening to lynch you."

"Aw, Sam, now y'all know ah don't snore. Least ah never heard myself snorin'," Bobby Joe said.

"Believe me, you snore," Sam said.

"Well, it cain't be that bad," Bobby Joe said as he pulled his boots on.

"It's bad enough," Sam said. "The Chinese soldiers won't even come near this place. They think a demon lives here."

"Now, Sam, y'alls just exaggeratin'. Is it time for lunch yet?" Bobby Joe asked.

"Yeah, I thought I'd go see what kind of surprise Kerby has for us today," Sam said. "Are you coming?"

"Ah, guess so," Bobby Joe answered. "Y'all know we wouldn't even let that feller fix slop fer the hogs in Texas."

"You Texans are smarter than I thought," Sam said. "Come on, we have to eat sometime."

The men picked up their mess kits and walked slowly to the chow hall. On the way, they talked about their recent missions and how they thought the war was going. Both men agreed things in Burma seemed to be improving, but they also noted they were still receiving plenty of enemy fire during their missions. The fact that some of the combat cargo squadrons had lost planes over Burma recently illustrated the dangers they still faced.

When they arrived at the mess hall, they read the lunch menu posted at the door. It read, Homemade Potato Soup and Southern-Style Biscuits.

"Ah got ta see this," Bobby Joe said. "Specially the Southern-style biskits. That must mean they got boll weevils in 'em stead of the usual Burma bugs."

"I'm a little concerned," Sam responded. "Anytime Kerby uses words like *homemade* and *Southern style*, it can't be good."

They walked to the serving line and were cheerfully greeted by Kerby. "Hey, Sam, hey, Bobby Joe. Welcome to my soup kitchen," he said.

"Hi, Kerby," Sam responded. "Where did you get potatoes for potato soup?"

"Oh, I don't have any real potatoes. I just improvised with the powdered stuff," Kerby said as he ladled a portion into Sam's mess kit.

Sam looked at his serving and saw a thin watery gruel of powdered potatoes with greasy chunks of Spam floating in it.

"Have a Southern-style biscuit," Kerby said as he dropped a biscuit onto Sam's mess kit.

The clanking sound the biscuit made when it hit the metal mess kit told Sam his teeth would not be strong enough to bite into it. Looking at Bobby Joe, he noticed his friend had withdrawn his mess kit well out of Kerby's reach.

"Can y'all fry fish?" Bobby Joe asked Kerby.

"I can cook anything," Kerby answered, "but I don't have any fish."

"Meet me outside the mess hall at two o'clock," Bobby Joe said. "We're goin' fishin'."

"But I don't know how to fish," Kerby protested.

"Jus be there," Bobby Joe commanded. "Sam, git rid a that slop, and I'll see y'all back at the basha in an hour."

"What do you think he has in mind?" Kerby asked Sam.

"I don't know. Maybe he's going to stone the fish with these biscuits," Sam answered as he dumped his food into a garbage can. "Be outside at two o'clock, and you'll find out."

Sam walked back to his tent and eased his hunger with the remainder of some cookies Eleanor had sent a few days ago. He was surprised there were any cookies left, because anytime anyone received a care package from home, the guys in the basha usually made short work of it. After eating the cookies, he waited for Bobby Joe to return. True to his word, his friend showed up in an hour carrying a burlap sack and accompanied by three local Naga tribesmen carrying empty bamboo baskets.

"Hey, Bobby Joe, where's the fishing poles? I thought we were going fishing," Sam said.

"Ah, got everythin' we need in this sack," Bobby Joe said, "Let's go git Kerby."

They walked to the mess hall and found Kerby waiting for them. Bobby Joe led them to a wide pool in a nearby stream and then revealed the contents of the burlap sack. It contained four hand grenades.

"We're goin ta toss these grenades inta the water, and then these here Nagas is gonna collect the stunned fish when they float ta the surface," Bobby Joe said as he handed two grenades to Sam and kept two for himself.

"Hey, that sounds like fun," Kerby said excitedly. "Don't I get to throw a grenade?"

"Sorry, little feller," Bobby Joe responded. "Ah seen y'alls cookin'. Ah don't want ta find out what y'alls grenade throwin' is like. Okay, Sam, throw y'alls grenades over ta the right, and I'll throw mine ta the left. Spread 'em out ta cover a big area."

On Bobby Joe's command, both men pulled the safety pins on their grenades and threw them into the pool. A geyser of water erupted from the water as each grenade exploded and then everyone waited. Soon, fish of every size and description began to float to the surface of the pool. The Nagas immediately jumped into the pool and began filling their baskets with fish they knew were edible. Sam and Bobby Joe were watching the Nagas when they heard a shout from Kerby.

"Look at the size of this beauty," Kerby shouted as he pointed to a very large catfish floating near the edge of the pool where he was standing. "Hey, it's starting to float downstream. It's going to get away."

Sam saw the catfish was indeed very large and must have weighed twenty to thirty pounds. Sam could also see that the gills of the fish were still moving. Before he or Bobby Joe could respond, Kerby jumped into the stream and grabbed the large fish by the tail. Unfortunately, the catfish was just stunned and not dead. When Kerby grabbed its tail, the huge fish began to thrash wildly in the water. Whether he was just surprised or unwilling to let go, Kerby hung on while the big fish jerked him wildly about and dragged him into the middle of the stream. Sam and Bobby Joe began to laugh at the scene when Kerby suddenly disappeared under the water. A few seconds passed before Kerby finally came to the surface and began thrashing about.

"Kin that little feller swim?" Bobby Joe asked.

"Oh geez," Sam exclaimed, "I just remembered he can't swim."

"Ah, guess we better save 'em if we want ta git our fish fried," Bobby Joe said as Kerby went under again.

Sam leaped into the stream and began swimming toward the spot where they last saw Kerby. Bobby Joe was close behind him. As Sam neared the spot, Kerby came to the surface once again. His arms were flailing, and he was spouting water like a whale. Sam swam to his friend, but when he got near, Kerby grabbed on to him with a vice-like grip. Sam tried to break loose, but Kerby's wouldn't let go, and soon both men were sinking below the surface. Sam struggled to free himself, but Kerby's terror just tightened his grip.

Sam was reaching the point where he knew he couldn't hold his breath any longer when he suddenly felt Kerby release his grip. Sam quickly swam to the surface, gasping for breath. He spun around trying to locate Kerby when Bobby Joe erupted from the water a few feet away with Kerby's limp body in tow. Sam swam over and helped Bobby Joe get Kerby's body to shore. The Nagas helped the soldiers from the water, and one of them quickly turned Kerby over onto his stomach and stood on his back. The Naga gently bounced up and down on Kerby's back until the hapless cook ejected a mouthful of water and began gasping for breath. Everyone gathered around as Kerby regained his breath and his senses.

"I'll bet that damned fish got away, didn't he?" were the first words Kerby muttered.

All told, their endeavor resulted in six large baskets of fish and one half-drowned cook. The Nagas made quick work of cleaning the fish. They departed with three of the baskets leaving the other three for the drenched soldiers. That evening, the soldiers who ate in Kerby's mess hall were treated to a feast of fried fish and lumpy powdered potatoes. As the men were served, Kerby regaled them with the tale of his fishing adventure and about his heroic struggle with the big one that got away. According to Kerby's account, the fish was so big it would have fed them all with leftovers to spare. Sam and Bobby Joe sat at their table enjoying their fish and listening to Kerby brag. They just looked at each other and shook their heads.

NOVEMBER 29, 1944
MOSHANNON VALLEY, PENNSYLVANIA

Eleanor had just finished putting on Billy's snowsuit when May entered through the front door.

"Oh, I'm sorry, dear. I didn't know you were going out," May said.

"I'm just taking the boys up to the fire hall. The *Osceola Leader* has a photographer there today, and I want to have a picture taken of the boys together," Eleanor explained.

"That sounds wonderful. What are the boys wearing," May asked.

"I have Roger's christening outfit on him, and Billy is wearing his sailor suit," Eleanor responded.

"That's good. Billy looks so cute in his sailor suit, and Roger is such a beautiful baby," May said. "Why is the newspaper taking pictures?"

"They're going to have a contest, and the pictures of the cutest children are going to be shown in the paper under the heading of Our Future Generation," Eleanor said.

"Well, I'm sure these two will make it to the front page," May said. "Will you get a picture to keep for yourself?"

"Oh yes, I'll get several different sizes so I can give you one and send one to Sam," Eleanor said.

"Thank you for thinking of me, Eleanor. Your house seems cold, dear. Are you still having trouble firing your coal furnace?" May asked.

"Yes, this is my second winter trying to fire a furnace, and I just can't seem to get the hang of it," Eleanor said. "At night, the fire either goes out or it doesn't burn enough to warm the house. Sam never had problems firing the furnace."

"I'll have Paul come over and show you what to do," May said. "Have you heard from Sam lately?"

"Yes, I just received a letter this morning and it's so frustrating the way the censors block things out. Here, look for yourself," Eleanor said retrieving the letter from her apron.

May took the letter and began to read.

Pvt. Samuel Huber 33761617
5331st Air Supply Dropping Platoon
APO 487 %PM NY NY

Hello Eleanor,

I'm sorry I haven't written in a while, but they have been keeping us pretty busy delivering supplies to the troops in the ###### and in #####. As you have probably seen in the newspapers, the war in ##### is going well. We finally drove the Japs out of ######### and this has allowed our cargo flights to ##### to use a less dangerous route around the #### rather than over it. It's still a hazardous flight because of the bad weather around here. I'm sure you also heard ############# ## # ### ####################. That would not be good because we fly a lot of supplies there. I'm sure the censors will delete the names in this paragraph, but you will get the drift of what I'm saying.

I am doing ok. I am constantly tired from working all the time and the food we're getting is ##########################. It doesn't help that our friend Kerby is the cook. He tries hard, but he seems to have a knack for turning anything into slop. I've lost about 15 pounds over the past two months. I'd give anything for one of May's roast beef dinners.

I hope you and the boys are doing well. The pictures you sent of them really cheered me up. I have them pinned to the wall above my bed, and I go to sleep every night wishing I could be there with all of you. It was exactly a year ago today that I left you, and it seems like an eternity. At times I think this war is never going to end.

Well, it's almost time for lunch. I was thinking about skipping it, but maybe I'll go just to see what kind of mess Kerby has whipped up today. Write soon.

Love
Sam

"I know what you mean," May said, handing the letter back. "Don't the censors know we get newsreels and newspapers back here? We know how the war is going. By the way, did you hear the latest gossip?"

"I don't think so. What have you heard?" Eleanor asked.

"Well, Nan Herring was just over, and she told me she heard the government caught another group of German saboteurs, and they think one of their targets was the Horseshoe Curve in Altoona," May said.

"Oh my, that's so close to home," Eleanor said. "Do you think there are any enemy agents hiding around here?"

"You never know," May answered. "Those Germans are taught

to blend in and speak perfect English. Just be wary of anyone new in town. You better get the boys up to the fire hall. I'll see you later."

Eleanor bundled Roger up, took Billy by the hand, and started walking to the fire hall. Along the way, she couldn't help examining the face of every person she met.

December 23, 1944
Shingbwiyang, Burma

Kerby's fried fish dinner had been a big hit with the men, and his status as a cook vastly improved. His enhanced standing among the men inspired him to look for ways to continue his success, and he began trading moonshine with the local Naga tribesmen for fish and fruit from the jungle. He regularly served the fish in the chow hall, but he used the jungle fruit to make more moonshine. He also talked Sam into convincing his pilot friend, Sergeant Walt Grimes, to fly his small plane to remote native villages to trade moonshine for fresh eggs and chickens. The process was working well, and he was currently waiting for Sam and Walt to return from a flight to obtain eggs.

Walt had flown into many native villages in Burma, but today he and Sam were headed for a new village. A fellow pilot told Walt about the place and assured him the natives were friendly. The pilot also warned him that landing there would be very tricky. It was for that reason that Walt had chosen the L4 for this mission. The L4 was light and nimble and well suited for tough landings.

"We should be getting close to the village," Walt said to Sam.

"What should I be looking for," Sam replied.

"My friend said the village is perched right on the edge of a high cliff. So start looking at the tops of the cliffs," Walt said.

The area they were flying over consisted of jungle covered ridges that reached an altitude of around six thousand feet. Many of the ridges had sheer rocky cliffs, but so far none of the cliffs had a village at the top. Walt turned the controls of the plane over to Sam as they continued their search. It was another ten minutes before Sam thought he saw something.

"Over there on the left, Walt. That looks like a village on top of that cliff," Sam said as he turned the plane to the left.

"I've got the controls," Walt said as they approached the sheer two-thousand-foot cliff. "That's the village just like my friend described it."

Walt flew over the village so he could get an idea of what the landing would be like. The huts of the village were built on both sides of a main thoroughfare. The thoroughfare appeared to be about four hundred feet long and stretched from the very edge of the cliff to a solid wall of tall trees at the back of the village.

"That street doesn't look long enough or wide enough to land on," Sam said nervously.

"My friend said he's landed here many times," Walt said. "He did say it was pretty narrow and his wing tips barely cleared the huts."

"Surely you're not going to try to land down there, are you?" Sam asked.

"There won't be any room for error, but I've landed in worse places," Walt said. "Hang on, we're going in."

Sam was sitting in the front seat and had an unobstructed view of their approach to the village. Walt brought the little plane around and lined it up with the thoroughfare. He reduced power to the engine and began to descent toward the village. Sam could see the villagers watching as they approached. Walt started to slow the plane down and adjusted his glide path. Sam grew tense as the edge of the cliff drew nearer and nearer. He knew any sudden downdraft would drag the L4 into the face of the cliff. Walt continued to slow the plane's airspeed until it felt like it was about to drop out of the sky. Sam held his breath as the plane seemed to stagger toward the ground. Walt suddenly cut all power to the engine and plopped the airplane down just three feet from the edge of the cliff. He applied the brakes hard as he guided the plane down the narrow street and came to a stop just twenty feet from the trees.

"We're here, Sam. That landing was a piece of cake," Walt said proudly.

"If that was a piece of cake, I think I'll stick to pie," Sam replied with much relief.

"Let's see if we can trade for some eggs," Walt said as he grabbed a quart jar filled with moonshine.

Both men exited the plane and were met by the village chief and a group of warriors. None of the villagers spoke English, so Walt used gestures and hand signals to try to communicate. His efforts met with little success. Finally, Walt made drinking motions until one of the warriors got the idea and brought him a small wooden bowl of water. Dumping the water out, Walt poured some moonshine into the bowl, took a sip, rubbed his stomach, and handed the bowl to the chief. The man accepted the bowl, but a frown crossed his face as he sniffed it. Walt smiled and nodded his head to encourage the headman to take a drink. The chief remained unwilling to taste the contents of the bowl and instead handed it to one of his warriors. The warrior looked at the bowl and hesitated as a worried look crossed his face. The chief barked a command, and the warrior reluctantly took a small sip of the moonshine. His first reaction was to grimace and shiver as the strong alcohol slid down his throat, but then the grimace was replaced by a broad smile, and he took a much bigger drink before handing the bowl back. Noting the warrior's reaction, the chief also took a small sip. His initial reaction was the same as the warrior's, but then he too smiled and downed the remainder of the moonshine in the bowl.

Walt filled the headman's bowl again and tried to get the idea across that he wanted to trade the alcohol for eggs. Nothing seemed to work until Sam came up with an idea. He spotted a stone about the size of his fist on the ground and began strutting around making clucking sounds. He strutted over to the stone and crouched down over it clucking softly. The villagers looked at him as though he were crazy. Finally, he clucked loudly, pulling the stone out from beneath himself, and crowed like a rooster. The chief nodded his head in understanding and spoke to one of the women standing nearby. The woman hurried off and shortly returned with a basket of eggs. Walt took the eggs from the woman and handed the chief the quart of moonshine. A murmur of understanding rippled through the onlookers as the chief ordered the women to bring more eggs.

Walt was able to trade four quarts of moonshine for four baskets of eggs. The chief seemed genuinely pleased with the trade and gave two quarts of moonshine to his warriors and kept two quarts for himself.

"You're a genius, Sam," Walt said, "and you do a pretty good chicken imitation too."

"Thanks," Sam replied. "I knew being a country boy would come in handy someday."

Walt supervised the villagers as they loaded the eggs onto the L4. He and Sam then turned the plane around and pushed it backward until the tail was at the very edge of the jungle. It was then that Sam, looking down the village street, realized they didn't have enough distance to take off.

"It doesn't look like we have enough room to take off," Sam said apprehensively.

"Climb into the backseat and buckle up," Walt said. "This little bird can handle it."

Walt followed Sam into the L4 and strapped himself into the front seat. He started the engine and ran through the pretakeoff checklist.

"Are you ready, Sam?" he shouted over the noise of the engine.

"Are you sure you know what you're doing?" Sam asked in return.

"Just hold on," was Walt's answer.

Walt applied the brakes and applied full power to the engine.

The L4 strained and vibrated as the pilot held the brakes. Finally, Walt released the brakes, and the little plane leapt forward, gaining speed as they raced down the dirt street. Sam could see the village huts as they sped by just a few feet from their wing tips. Chickens and dogs scurried out of the way as the tail wheel rose from the ground. Sam looked over Walt's shoulder and saw the edge of the cliff quickly approaching. He expected anytime for Walt to pull back on the control stick and feel the plane rise safely into the air, but it didn't happen. He watched in horror as they reached the end of the village street and plunged over the edge of the cliff.

Sam felt his body strain against his harness as Walt lowered the nose of the L4 and plummeted toward the ground far below. It seemed like an eternity until the plane gained enough speed and began to fly. Walt slowly brought the nose of the airplane up until they were flying level about five hundred feet above the treetops.

"Are you doing okay back there?" Walt asked.

"Yeah," Sam answered weakly, "but I can tell you one thing. I'm going to enjoy every bite of these eggs."

32

JANUARY 6, 1945
SHINGBWIYANG, BURMA

S AM AND BOBBY Joe had just finished supervising the loading of their assigned C47 and were waiting for the rest of the crew to arrive. They were scheduled to fly three missions to deliver supplies to Chinese troops fighting along the Salween River in eastern Burma.

"I hate dropping supplies to the Chinese," Sam said.

"I know what y'all mean," Bobby Joe responded. "Ya never know when they're gonna start shootin' at ya."

Sam was about to say more but was interrupted. "Good morning, gentlemen. Are you ready for today's missions?" a familiar voice said from behind him.

He turned to see Lieutenant LT Thomas approaching; only he was no longer a lieutenant. He was now wearing shiny new captain's bars and a big smile on his face.

"Good morning, Lieu... er, Captain," Sam said. "When did you get promoted, sir?"

"The orders came through yesterday," LT said, "and you still don't need to call me sir."

"Well, congratulations, LT. It couldn't have happened to a nicer guy or a better pilot," Sam said.

"Amen ta that," Bobby Joe chimed in.

"Thanks, guys. Is the load all ready to go?" LT asked.

"We're all loaded, but the copilot and Wimpy haven't arrived yet," Sam answered.

"Okay, I'll start the preflight," LT said as he climbed aboard the C47.

The copilot arrived shortly afterward and introduced himself as Second Lieutenant Dwain Neusome from Ocala, Florida. The lieutenant was short in stature with bright red hair and an abundance of freckles on his face. He arrived from the United States two days ago, and this was to be his first mission. Sam and Bobby Joe welcomed the lieutenant warmly and told him where he could find Captain Thomas.

"Tarnation, that lieutenant cain't be more'n nineteen years old," Bobby Joe said as they watched the lieutenant enter the plane.

"They seem to get younger every day. I wonder what LT has in store for him?" Sam said with a knowing smile.

The words no sooner passed Sam's lips when they heard a shriek, and the young lieutenant came barreling out of the airplane shouting, *"Snake, Snake!"* He jumped to the tarmac and nearly knocked Bobby Joe over as he fled in panic. Shortly thereafter, LT appeared in the doorway holding a three-foot baby python. "I wonder how this got on his seat," he said with a grin.

The three men were having a good laugh over LT's practical joke when Wimpy arrived carrying a musette bag that was bulging at the seams. He immediately noticed the snake and said, "Whatcha going to do with the snake? Ya know they're good eatin'."

"I'm going to put it back in the jungle and find our copilot. You men wait here," LT said as he walked in the direction Lieutenant Neusome had run.

"I'm serious," Wimpy said. "Snakes are good eatin'."

"What y'all got in the bag, Wimpy?" Bobby Joe asked.

"Oh, that's my lunch," Wimpy said. "I have two tins of Spam, two packets of K-rations, a C-ration, and a bunch of water buffalo sandwiches Kerby made up for me."

"That ain't the meat he tried ta serve us last night, is it?" Bobby Joe asked.

"I suppose so," Wimpy answered. "He told me he traded with the local natives for a whole side of water buffalo."

"Dadgumit," Bobby Joe said. "I was hope'n he didn't have any more a that stuff. Ah never tried ta eat anythin' tougher 'n my whole life. I chewed on a piece fer half an hour and still couldn't swoller it."

"Aw, it ain't that tough," Wimpy countered as he removed a sandwich from his bag and took a bite.

"If'n that ain't tough, then my aunt's a brain surgeon," Bobby Joe said.

"Well, I like it," Wimpy said. "What does your aunt do anyway?"

"Les jus say she runs a business in the red-light district a Austin," Bobby Joe responded.

Their conversation was interrupted by the return of LT and his thoroughly shaken copilot. "Climb aboard, boys," LT said. "Let's get this show in the air. The weather reports are all looking favorable."

The weather was good, and they were well on their way to the drop zone when LT sent Lieutenant Neusome to get Sam. When Sam got to the cockpit, LT motioned for him to sit down in the copilot's seat. Sam hesitated at first but then settled into the copilot's position.

"Sergeant Grimes tells me you're doing quite well at flying the L planes," LT said. "I thought you might like to try your hand at a C47."

Sam looked stunned at first but then nodded his head in approval.

"Okay then," LT continued. "Put your feet on the rudder pedals and take hold of the control yoke."

Sam did as he was directed and watched as LT removed his hands and feet from the controls. "It's all yours, Sam. Just fly straight and level for a few minutes," LT said.

Sam felt the pressure of the control yoke against his hands as LT released his hold. His first reaction was to pull back against the pressure, which resulted in the nose of the airplane rising. Realizing his mistake, Sam eased forward on the yoke, allowing the nose of the plane to settle back to the horizon. LT watched Sam fly the plane for a few minutes before showing him how to use the elevator trim control to take the pressures out of the control yoke. Once he felt Sam could fly the plane straight and level, he demonstrated how to make right- and left-hand turns. Sam's first attempt at turning the C47 was a little sloppy, resulting in a loss of a hundred feet of altitude. LT showed him how to compensate for the altitude loss, and Sam was soon making acceptable left- and right-hand turns. Convinced Sam could handle the airplane, LT gave him a heading to the drop zone and then sat back and relaxed for half an hour while Sam flew the plane.

"Very good, Sam, you're doing very well," LT said as they neared the drop zone. "I have the controls now. Let Lieutenant Neusome have his seat and get ready for the drop."

It was a typical drop, and they had to make five passes to completely deliver their cargo. The first four passes over the drop zone went very well. Bobby Joe was in the kicker position while Sam and Wimpy moved supply containers into the open doorway. The target area was situated close to the front lines, but they were receiving a minimum of enemy fire. As was always the case when they were operating close to enemy lines, a timing error on their part could result in some supplies falling into Japanese hands. So far their timing had been perfect, and all of their drops were right on target. It was on this fifth pass that tragedy struck.

LT had the plane perfectly positioned when Bobby Joe kicked

the first bundle of supplies out. Sam and Wimpy immediately had the next bundle in position, and it was kicked out. The third and last bundle was quickly shoved into place. Bobby Joe gave it a mighty kick, and then it happened. A piercing shriek erupted from Wimpy's mouth. Sam turned, expecting to see Wimpy covered in blood from an enemy bullet. Instead, he saw his white-faced friend pointing toward the jungle below.

"What's wrong? Are you hit, Wimpy?" Sam asked.

"It's gone, it's gone," Wimpy cried as he continued to point outside.

"What's gone?" Sam asked as he looked to see where Wimpy was pointing. At first, he saw only the last parachute bundle floating in the air, and then he saw the source of Wimpy's distress. There, dangling below the bundle of supplies was Wimpy's musette bag. It had apparently become entangled in the ropes binding the supplies and was kicked out of the plane.

"My lunch, all that beautiful food is gone," Wimpy lamented.

Sam stood speechless as Bobby Joe joined them at the doorway and watched the Chinese soldiers below retrieve the bundle of supplies and Wimpy's bag.

"Well, Wimpy, look at it this way," Bobby Joe said. "Y'all wuz lucky. If the Japs got hold a them sandwiches, y'all could be charged with war crimes."

Sam and Bobby Joe laughed as Wimpy sat down and began gnawing morosely on a half-eaten sandwich he pulled from his pocket.

With the last of their cargo delivered, the crew settled down for the flight back to Shingbwiyang. LT took up a northwesterly heading back to base and was surprised to see a storm front looming in the windshield.

"Did you see any weather forecasts predicting anything like this, Dwain?" LT asked his copilot.

"Nothing I read indicated bad weather, Captain," Dwain responded.

"Well, it looks like you're going to get your first taste of flying in a tropical storm," LT said, not knowing this storm would turn out to be the worst weather front ever recorded in the history of India.

As the pilots prepared to enter the storm front, Sam came to the cockpit and looked out the windshield. What he saw made his heart freeze. He had seen storm clouds like this before when his plane flew through the equatorial front while flying from South America to Africa. He quickly returned to the cargo bay and told Bobby Joe and Wimpy what was about to happen. Helping the other men tie themselves securely to cargo tie-downs imbedded in the floor, Sam then secured himself in the same manner.

Expecting turbulence, LT slowed the airplane's airspeed as he entered the storm. At first, they encountered moderate turbulence, but then it began to intensify. Lightning flashed constantly all around them, and the strobe effect made the plane's propellers appear to be standing still. The pilots fought to maintain control of the C47 as it was jerked up and down like a puppet on a string. After a half hour of constant struggle against the storm, LT was able to get a radio fix on the Ft. Hertz station in Northern Burma. He was shocked to discover the bearings indicated that a terrific wind from the southwest was pushing them off course to the northwest over the Himalayan Mountains. LT pushed the throttles to full power in an attempt to climb above the twenty-thousand-foot peaks that surrounded them.

As they struggled to gain altitude, LT and Dwain began to hear numerous distress calls from other aircrafts that were caught in the storm. One pilot radioed he had encountered heavy icing, and they were bailing out. Another pilot's frantic calls for help went on for several minutes and then suddenly stopped. Everyone was warning against being in the air that day. LT managed to set a new course for Shingbwiyang before his plane was again slammed by extreme turbulence. He watched his gyrating instruments as the C47 was caught in an updraft that hurtled them upward at four thousand feet. Just as quickly, a downdraft plunged them downward to five thousand feet. A bright flash of lightning lit the scene, illuminating boulders and trees whizzing by the left. Realizing they were very close to the ground, LT struggled to gain altitude before the next downdraft could smash them into the ground.

Lightning continued to flash all around, and Dwain reported a thick layer of ice was forming on the engine cowl and leading edge of the right wing. LT began to feel sluggishness in the controls, and he could see they were beginning to lose altitude. He became aware of an unusual vibration in the airplane as another flash of lightning revealed the propellers were also heavily laden with ice. As he double-checked that the deicers were on, there was a brilliant flash of light and a thunderous bang hit the aircraft. The C47 shuddered momentarily, and an odor of ozone invaded the cockpit. Dwain looked outside the right window and reported a ten-inch hole in the wing near the fuel tank. LT could see fear on the young man's face and tenseness building up in his body. LT ordered him to release his grip on the controls and calmly handed him a stick of gum.

Luckily, the impact of the lightning bolt loosened some of the accumulated ice. Large chunks of ice began to fly from the wings and propellers. The sound the ice made as it impacted the fuselage of the airplane was terrifying to the men inside. The aircraft continued to shed its load of ice, and the loss of weight enabled LT to maintain control and gain some altitude. The hell that this storm had become lasted another fifteen minutes before the C47 finally broke out of the clouds into an area of thick overcast and dense rain.

The rain beat heavily on the windshield, but the air was relatively calm, enabling LT to get a radio bearing back to their base. The crew in the cargo bay untied themselves and talked excitedly about the storm. None of them had ever been through anything so violent, and they all agreed they didn't want to experience anything like it again. In the cockpit, LT settled into the routine of flying the plane while his young copilot shook uncontrollably in his seat. After a few moments, Dwain gained control of himself and asked if he could fly the plane. LT nodded approvingly and released the controls. He could still hear other pilots inside the storm frantically calling for help as they fought for their lives. Many of the callers eventually reported reaching safety, but some simply ended in silence. The voices of those lost airmen echoed in LT's ears, and he knew their voices would haunt him for the rest of his life.

The rain had finally stopped when they arrived at Shingbwiyang, but the view from the air revealed the extent of the damage the storm had inflicted on the base. As they circled the airfield, the crew could see toppled trees and damaged buildings. Litter was scattered everywhere, and a great deal of water was still standing on the runway. LT was hesitant to land on the water-covered runway, but they were almost out of fuel, and he had no choice. He lined the C47 up with the runway and lowered the landing gear.

LT's approach was near perfect and he touched down on the water covered runway. Everything appeared to be going well until he lightly applied the brakes to slow down. The brakes locked and the plane began to hydroplane and skid to the right. He applied right rudder and the aircraft began to skid in the opposite direction. As they sped down the runway, the brakes appeared to be ineffective. LT fought to control the aircraft as it slid from side to side. Each time the plane swung from one side to the other, the men in the back were thrown wildly against the sides of the cargo bay. The end of the runway was approaching quickly before LT managed to control the skidding motion. However, he was only able to slow the C47 down before it ran off the end of the runway and became mired in eighteen inches of mud. LT shut the engines down and rushed back to the cargo bay to see if the kickers were okay. He found a battered Sam and Bobby Joe bending over Wimpy.

"Are you guys all right?" LT asked.

"We're okay, but Wimpy was knocked unconscious," Sam said. "It looks like he's coming around now."

They watched as Wimpy's eyelids fluttered, and he struggled to regain consciousness. Finally, his eyes opened wide, and he looked at the concerned men bending over him. "Did we make it back in time for supper?" he asked.

JANUARY 7, 1945
SHINGBWIYANG, BURMA

All the talk around the lunch table was about the great storm of the previous day. Kerby was listening to the tales the flight crews were telling about their harrowing experiences. He sat in rapt attention as each man in turn told of the horrors the storm had inflicted upon them.

Finally, one of the men turned to Kerby and said, "As frightening as that storm was, cookie, nothing is scarier than the water buffalo you're serving."

"Aw, come on, guys," Kerby responded. "That's the only meat I could get."

"Yeah, maybe," another man said, "but you should have served it before you mummified it."

Kerby was about to respond when Bobby Joe entered the mess hall and approached with a glum expression on his face.

"Hey, Bobby Joe," Sam said. "You're looking kind of down. What's wrong?"

"I jus come from headquarters," Bobby Joe said. "Word has it there wuz eighteen planes lost in that storm yesterday."

Bobby Joe's announcement caused an immediate change in the men. All conversation stopped as a somber mood permeated the air. One by one, they silently rose and walked out of the mess hall until only Kerby remained. Looking around at the empty room, he turned his attention to the menu for supper.

Kerby had served the water buffalo fried, broiled, roasted, and boiled, and none of it had turned out palatable. Almost the entire side of buffalo still hung in the cooler, but he was reluctant to throw it away. As he walked into the kitchen, he spied the meat grinder. "What the hell," he said to himself. "I might as well try buffalo burgers."

Not many men showed up for supper that night, and they took one look at the buffalo burgers and turned away. Kerby was beginning to feel despondent when Wimpy walked in the door and spied the burgers.

"Oh man, my dreams have come true," Wimpy said excitedly. "Gimme a couple of them burgers."

Kerby placed two burgers onto Wimpy's mess kit and watched as the famished soldier grabbed some bread and sat down at a nearby table. Wimpy placed one of the burgers between two slices of bread and raised the sandwich to his mouth. Everyone in the mess hall watched with interest as Wimpy eagerly bit into his buffalo burger. The expression on his face turned from joy to consternation as he tugged and pulled without success to chew off a piece of the meat. Not wanting to give up, he tried again and again to bite through the sandwich. Finally, pulling out his jungle knife, he hacked off a piece of the burger and placed it in his mouth. The fascinated men watched as he chewed and chewed on the meat and finally managed to swallow it. Standing up with a triumphant expression on his face, Wimpy walked to a nearby garbage can and tossed the remaining burger away. He walked out of the door to a thunderous round of applause by the men inside.

After supper was over, Kerby finished cleaning up the kitchen and took the garbage cans outside. A stray dog that hung around the mess hall looking for handouts appeared. Kerby tossed him one of the buffalo burgers. The animal sniffed the meat, picked it up in its mouth, and tried to chew it. After several unsuccessful attempts to chew the burger, the dog dropped it on the ground, shook his head, and walked away.

Kerby went back into the empty mess hall, sat down at a table, and lit up a cigarette. He was contemplating what he could do with the rest of the water buffalo when a soldier he not seen before walked in and approached him.

"Hi, Mac," the soldier said. "I'm transporting a load of perishables up the Ledo Road, and I need some more ice. Ya got any?"

"Yeah, I've got plenty of ice," Kerby said, "The engineers installed us an ice maker last month. Come on, I'll show you."

Kerby led the soldier into the kitchen where he kept the ice in a cooler. "How much are you going to need?" he asked motioning to some five-gallon buckets nearby.

"I think four of those buckets will do," the soldier said. "By the way, my name's Christopher but everyone calls me Chris."

"Okay, Chris. I'm Kerby. I'll give you a hand with the ice," Kerby said as he proceeded to fill four of the buckets with ice.

Each man carried two of the buckets outside where the soldier's truck was parked. The truck was built on a six-ton Chevy chassis with a large cargo box attached to the back. Chris led Kerby to the rear of the truck and opened the double doors. Inside, cases of K-rations were stacked to the ceiling and a large insulated box resting on the floor. The box had the words To General Stern stenciled on the side. Chris pulled a plug on the insulated box, allowing water to pour out. He then retrieved a set of keys from his pocket and unlocked a large padlock securing the lid of the box. Kerby's heart nearly stopped when he saw what was inside. The box contained a full side of prime U.S. beef. Kerby helped fill the box with ice and stood back as Chris closed the lid and secured it with the padlock.

"Well, thank you, Kerby. I guess I'll be headin' on down the road to General Stern's camp," Chris said.

"It's getting pretty late, and it will be dark soon," Kerby said. "I have a spare cot in the kitchen. Why don't you spend the night?"

"I really need to get this stuff delivered before that meat spoils," Chris said.

"Hey, that ice will last until this time tomorrow, and I got a supply of good British liquor stashed in the kitchen," Kerby said with a wink of his eye.

"Well, I don't like driving that road at night, and I am kinda tired and thirsty," Chris responded.

"It's settled then," Kerby said. "Come on in and let's have us a drink or two."

Chris followed Kerby back into the kitchen and sat down as his new friend produced several bottles of scotch and a bottle of rum. The unsuspecting driver didn't know that Kerby had mixed some of his potent moonshine with the contents of each bottle. Chris turned out to be quite a drinker while Kerby only pretended to drink as he kept his friend's glass full. It took a bottle and a half of scotch and nearly the full bottle of rum before Chris finally succumbed and fell into a drunken stupor. Ensuring his victim was out cold, Kerby took the keys from his pocket and headed for the truck. He unlocked the insulated box but found the beef was too heavy for him to lift. Hastily relocking the box and covering the general's name, he headed for Sam's tent.

The sun had just set, and Sam was preparing to go to bed when Kerby entered the tent.

"Sam, I need some help at the mess hall," Kerby said.

"Can't it wait until morning?" Sam replied sleepily.

"No, I have to unload something perishable, and it's too heavy for me to lift by myself," Kerby said.

"Okay, okay," Sam said as he reluctantly pulled on his boots.

Sam followed Kerby to the truck parked by the mess hall. He watched as his friend unlocked an insulated box in the back of the truck. Kerby opened the box and pointed to the contents inside.

"I need help getting this into the mess hall," Kerby said pointing to the side of beef.

"Is that real beef?" Sam asked.

"As real as it gets, Sam," Kerby answered.

"Kerby, where did this meat come from?" Sam asked suspiciously. "Are you up to something?"

"No, Sam. Why do you think this truck is parked here? I ordered this meat months ago. See I even have the keys to the box," Kerby said, holding up the keys. "Now let's get this meat inside before it starts to spoil."

Sam reluctantly helped carry the side of beef inside where they placed it into the meat locker.

"Now can you help me put this side of buffalo in the truck?" Kerby asked.

"Why do you want to put that stuff in the truck?" Sam asked.

"The driver said he would get rid of it for me," Kerby answered.

Sam helped lug the side of buffalo to the truck. Kerby insisted it be put in the insulated box, so it wouldn't spoil and smell up the truck. When the box was securely locked, Sam wanted to go back to the kitchen for a cup of coffee. Not wanting to arouse any further suspicion on Sam's part, Kerby reluctantly agreed. They entered the kitchen and Kerby poured them both a cup of coffee. Sam took his cup and turned to leave the room. However, he stopped abruptly when he spied a body sprawled across a table in a dim corner of the kitchen.

"Who's that?" Sam asked.

"Oh, that's the truck driver. He got drunk and passed out," Kerby said innocently.

Sam immediately became suspicious and said, "This is all too convenient, Kerby. A truck carrying prime beef appears outside, and the driver somehow gets drunk and passes out in your kitchen. Tell me the truth now. That beef isn't meant for us, is it?"

"Well, it wasn't originally meant to be ours. I mean, it wasn't supposed to go here," Kerby said.

"Well then, who exactly is it supposed to go to?" Sam asked testily.

"It's supposed to go up the Ledo Road to General Stern," Kerby answered.

"Geez, Kerby you can't steal some general's meat," Sam exploded. "If you get caught, you'll be put so far in the brig they'll have to pipe sunshine to you."

"I won't get caught, Sam," Kerby said. "That driver's never going to admit he got drunk and lost the general's meat. Besides, we deserve something special for a change. When was the last time you had a good piece of meat?"

"I have to admit a nice piece of prime beef would taste pretty good right now," Sam said, "but the MPs are going to be looking for that meat at every stop the driver made, and if they find it here, you're going to wish you were the one hanging in that meat locker."

"I didn't think about that," Kerby said thoughtfully, "but I have the perfect solution. Go spread the word around camp for everyone to be at the back door of the kitchen with their mess kits in one hour."

"What do you intend to do?" Sam asked.

"They can't charge me without evidence," Kerby said. "I'm going to see to it that everyone gets a good meal tonight."

Sam stood there with his mouth agape. It was obvious he was not going to convince Kerby to give up the meat, so he went back to his tent and had little trouble enlisting his roommates in helping him spread the word. Soon, a long queue began to form behind the kitchen. At the appointed time, Kerby opened the kitchen door and began passing out large pieces of prime beef to the waiting men. In a little less than an hour's time, the side of beef was completely gone. Every man who showed up received a generous portion. Kerby had even ground some into hamburger for Wimpy. Small fires began to appear all over the base, and the smell of cooking meat permeated the air well into the night. Pilots flying into Shingbwiyang that night reported the twinkling camp fires made the base looked like a Christmas tree. For the hungry men on the ground, it was indeed Christmas.

The next morning, Chris awoke with a tremendous hangover. Kerby cheerfully plied him with coffee and quickly saw him safely on his way. Kerby noticed the grumbling in the chow line wasn't quite as bad, but he knew his respite wouldn't last long.

33

JUNE 1, 1945
SHINGBWIYANG, BURMA

SAM FINISHED PACKING his gear and looked around the tent he had called home since July of 1944. After nearly a year at Shingbwiyang, his unit was being transferred back to Dinjan Airbase in India. Shingbwiyang had become a major depot for trucks hauling supplies to China over the Ledo Road, and air activity from the base dropped off significantly in the past few months. Sam was looking forward to returning to less-primitive living conditions at Dinjan. There was little of life here that he would miss. He would miss Kerby, but he certainly wasn't going to miss his friend's miserable cooking. It still amazed him that Kerby avoided the stockade over the General Stern meat incident. Under pressure from the military police, the truck driver had broken down and admitted he got drunk in Kerby's kitchen. However, no evidence of the beef was ever found, and no one at Shingbwiyang admitted to having knowledge of its whereabouts.

Sam's musings were interrupted when an excited Bobby Joe entered the tent. "I jus come from headquarters and we been promoted ta corporals," he announced proudly.

"You're kidding," Sam replied.

"I seen it with my own eyes right there on the bulletin board," Bobby Joe said. "Y'all kin start sewin' on them corporal stripes anytime ya want."

"That's great news," Sam said. "Let's go to the mess hall and celebrate with some of Kerby's moonshine."

"Sounds good ta me, long as we don't have ta eat any a his cookin'," Bobby Joe said.

When they arrived at the mess hall, they found Kerby brooding over a cup of coffee.

"Hey, Kerby, what's wrong buddy?" Sam asked.

"Yeah, y'all look like yer dog jus had a dozen pups," Bobby Joe said.

"This is the worst day of my life," Kerby answered.

"What happened?" Sam asked.

"The MPs caught me at my still this morning," Kerby said. "They destroyed everything and hauled me before the base commander."

"Uh-oh, what did the colonel do?" Sam asked.

"He chewed me out good and then busted me down to buck private," Kerby said, pointing to the empty spaces on his sleeves.

"I'm sorry to hear that, Kerby, but you'll be okay. You're a survivor," Sam said, not mentioning his own promotion.

"Yeah, y'alls slicker than a card shark on a riverboat," Bobby Joe added.

"I guess you're right," Kerby said, "but I sure am going to miss that still, and you guys too. When are you shipping out?"

"Our plane leaves in about twenty minutes, but we'll be seeing you when we fly in here to pick up cargo," Sam said.

"Too bad you won't be here this evening," Kerby said with a knowing smile. "I heard that a bunch of supply trucks are stopping here for the night, and there's a meat truck among them."

JULY 2, 1945
SITTANG RIVER VALLEY, BURMA

Monsoon clouds enveloped the flight of three C47s soon after they departed from Dinjan. Although Sam never tired of the experience of flying, he didn't like flying in heavy weather conditions, because it deprived him of the pleasure of watching the earth slip by beneath him. From above, the earth's terrain and man-made objects always appeared pristine and untouched. It was like viewing things the way God had meant them to be, and the experience always touched Sam's soul. He dreamed of someday becoming a pilot and admired the flying skills of the pilots on this mission. He knew from past experience how difficult it was to find an isolated drop zone in monsoon weather.

Their mission today was to deliver supplies to General Slim's Fourteenth British army along the Sittang River in southern Burma. They had been dropping supplies to the Brits on a daily basis as the Fourteenth pushed steadily southward through Burma. General Slim's army now had seventeen thousand soldiers of the Japanese Twenty-eight Army trapped on the western side of the Sittang River. The Japanese were desperate to escape across the Sittang into the relative safety of the mountains in Thailand along the Burmese border. Fighting along the river had been fierce, and the British were anxious to keep their forces supplied. This was one battle General Slim did not want to lose. Along this same river in 1942, more than thirteen thousand British, Indian, and Gurkha troops were drowned or slain when the Japanese invaded Burma. General Slim's army was forced to retreat nine hundred miles through the mountains and jungles of Burma. With the Japanese hounding them every step of the way, twelve thousand men hobbled back to India. Their clothes were in rags, many were shoeless, and all were gaunt and weak from starvation. That defeat three years ago still haunted General Slim. He knew winning this battle would be retribution for the British and would effectively end the Japanese occupation of Burma.

Sam's plane was the first to arrive at the drop zone. The monsoon rains had stopped, and he could see the river below was swollen to near-flood stages. As they circled the target area, the other two C47s arrived, and preparations began for the supply drops. In addition to Sam, there were three other crewmen on his plane. Initially, Bobby Joe was to be part of the crew. However, he became ill with dysentery and was replaced by Private Harry "Harr" Burr from Chokio, Minnesota. Harr had just arrived in India, and this was his first mission. He was the quintessential Midwestern farm boy. Standing six feet two inches tall with blond hair and blue eyes, he was solid muscle, thanks to years of labor on his father's farm. On the way to the drop zone, Harr talked a lot and told Sam about his future plans. He wanted to return to Minnesota, marry his childhood sweetheart, buy a farm, and ride his Indian motorcycle. Sam liked the boy immediately and admired his simple outlook on life.

The pilot of the plane, Major Jim McDonald, was from San Antonio, Texas. Major McDonald was a small man with wizened brown eyes, a narrow aquiline nose, and light brown hair that was just beginning to gray at the temples. The major handled the C47 with the skill and confidence that came from many hours as a professional pilot back in Texas. Although this was Sam's first flight with Major McDonald, he felt confident because of the major's reputation for bringing his crews back safely.

Sam also had confidence in the copilot, Captain LT Thomas of Loveland, Colorado. Sam was good friends with LT and had flown with him many times in the past. One of the things that mystified Sam about LT was the secrecy surrounding his first name. The captain insisted everyone call him LT, and all the documents Sam had ever seen with LT's name on them only showed his initials. LT had a reputation as a practical joker and usually had a surprise up his sleeve for the crew. Today was no exception. When they encountered rough weather on the way to today's drop zone, LT tossed empty beer cans back into the cargo bay. Sam wasn't taken in by the stunt, but Harr was convinced the pilots were drunk and running over every pothole in the sky.

As the pilots prepared for the first pass over the target area, Sam showed Harr how to position supplies in front of the cargo door. He was amazed at the ease with which the farm boy was able to move the heavy cargo containers. Satisfied that Harr could handle the job, Sam took the kicker position. As he lay on the cargo bay floor, he could feel the steady vibration of the engines against his back. He had always been comforted by this feeling, and it gave him a sense of well-being. He began to think of the importance of this mission, not only to the troops fighting in the rain soaked jungle below, but to him personally. At the beginning of this mission, he had more than 1,140 hours of flying time to his credit. This would be his 287th mission, and under the current rules, it would qualify him for rotation back to the United States. Several times in the past, he was about to qualify, but each time, the rules were changed to require more missions and flying time. However, this time he was sure he would make it home. It had been a year and a half since he had seen Eleanor and Billy. He had never seen his eleven-month-old son, Roger.

"Do you think we'll make it through this mission okay, Sam?" Harr's question stirred Sam from his thoughts of going home.

Sam noted the concern in Harr's voice and recognized the first signs of fear on the young man's face. He had experienced fear many times in the past and knew he had to do something to help Harr through the moment.

"Hey, Harr, don't worry about it, you're with lucky Sam remember. I've flown over 280 missions, and I'm still here," Sam said.

"I know you've been lucky, Sam, but that doesn't mean I'll be lucky. I've heard stories about what can happen during these missions. Planes are shot down or disappear all the time," Harr said.

"At times like this, I like to think about home," Sam said. "Where are you from, Harr?"

"I'm from Minnesota," Harr answered, "and I'd give anything to be back on the farm with my girl and my motorcycle right now."

"What's her name?" Sam asked hoping to divert the young soldier's attention from their impending danger.

"Big Red," Harr responded.

"Well, I'll bet she's a real looker being tall and having red hair. How tall is she?" Sam inquired.

"Geez, Sam, Big Red is my motorcycle. My girl's name is Sally, Sally Berger, and she's a small blonde. God, how I miss her."

"Which do you miss more, your girl or your motorcycle?" Sam asked.

"Aw, Sam, of course I miss Sally more. We're going to get married when I get home. After our wedding, we're going to tie cans to Big Red and ride off into the sunset and have four kids. Two boys and two girls," Harr said.

Sam saw the tension easing on Harr's face and decided to continue talking about his life back in Minnesota. "Tell me about your life before the war, Harr, about your farm and Sally and Big Red," he said.

"It's my dad's farm, a small one near Chokio, Minnesota. It's only a hundred acres, but we can grow enough crops to feed the family for a year and have enough extra to sell at the farmer's market. I have three brothers and two sisters. I'm the oldest. There's no electricity to the farm, so Dad rigged up a lighting system using several car batteries. He even made a wind-powered generator to keep them charged. It works pretty well too. There's always a breeze blowing in Minnesota," Harr said enthusiastically. He was beginning to relax, and the tension slowly began to fade from his handsome face.

Sam could see his ploy was working and continued, "It sounds like your family doesn't have much to spare with eight mouths to feed. How were you able to buy a motorcycle?"

"Oh, I didn't buy it, Sam. I earned it. Big Red belonged to my neighbor, Mr. Berger, Sally's Dad. I agreed to help out on his farm for three summers in exchange for the motorcycle. It was hard work, and Mr. Berger was a tough taskmaster, but I eventually got Big Red. It wasn't all bad though. I got to see Sally a lot."

"That must have kept you hopping," Sam responded.

"Yeah, I was doing double duty on my dad's and Mr. Berger's farms. But every time I ride Big Red, I know it was worth it," Harr remembered the many pleasant times he spent riding his motorcycle through the Minnesota farm lands. He remembered the feeling of freedom he always got when he was on Big Red.

Sam wondered at the boy's determination in obtaining the motorcycle, and he could see how Harr had developed his powerful physique.

"Tell me more about Sally. How did you meet her?" Sam asked.

"Oh, I've always known Sally. She lives on the farm next to ours, and we grew up going to school and playing together. After I got Big Red, I would take her for rides through the fields and on the roads around home."

"So when did you realize you were in love with Sally?" Sam inquired.

"That wasn't until our junior year of high school. I took Sally to the junior prom, and afterward I kissed her. We both knew right then that we loved each other. It wasn't until the day before I left to enter the army that I realized how much we were in love," Harr said.

Harr stopped talking and got a faraway look on his face. He was remembering a special time...

It was the day before he left for the army, and he and Sally were riding Big Red on a beautiful midsummer day. The sun was shining, and puffy white clouds dotted the sky. The wind on their faces was warm as they rode along the country roads near their home. Sally rode behind him with her arms wrapped around his waist. She held on extra tight, and he felt the warmth of her cheek pressing against his back. He remembered the wetness that seeped through the back of his shirt and the realization she was crying.

He steered the motorcycle onto a dirt road and shut the engine off. When they dismounted from the cycle, he saw Sally's beautiful blue eyes were brimming with tears. Before he could speak, Sally flew into his arms and pressed her lips firmly against his. She kissed him like she had never kissed him before. Her lips sought every inch of his, and her tongue probed his mouth with desperation. When she finally pulled away, she asked if he would marry her. He remembered how difficult it was to tell her they couldn't be married until the war was over. He could still see the pain in her eyes as he explained he didn't want to take the chance of leaving a widow behind. In the end, they agreed to wait for each other.

They spent the remainder of the day riding Big Red, and it was dark when they finally arrived back at Sally's house. He knew the time had come to say goodbye. They stood on her front porch and clung desperately to each other. He didn't want to let her go, and finally had to force his arms to release her.

The memory of their last moments was still vivid in his mind. He tried to memorize every detail of her lovely face as tears streamed down her cheeks. He turned quickly away so she wouldn't see the tears welling up in his own eyes. As he walked to his bike, he felt Sally's eyes following him. He fought back the urge to turn around and rush into her waiting arms. He couldn't look back as he rode away on Big Red. It felt like he left part of his heart and soul back there with Sally, and he knew he would never feel whole again until he could return to her…

"Good Lord, Sam, look at all the dead bodies in the river down there," Harr said as his memories of home faded.

Sam rose from the cargo bay floor and peered out the open door. "There must be one hell of a battle going on down there," he said.

The sight of all the dead enemy soldiers in the river gave Sam an uneasy feeling. The Japanese were trapped and desperately in need of supplies, and experience had taught him the C47s were about to become serious targets. He felt even more uncomfortable when he saw the terrain below. Their drop zone was located at a point where the river flowed between hills that were three to four hundred feet high on both sides. The British were entrenched along the eastern shore while the Japanese were dug in on the western side. The winds were currently blowing from an easterly direction, so they would be making their drops from a very low altitude to keep the supplies from drifting into enemy hands. Japanese gunners positioned on the hills would be at the same level or above the C47's flight path, giving them a tremendous sighting and firing advantage. Sam remembered a similar situation the previous year when he was dropping supplies to British troops trapped at Kohima. That flight ended in the loss of many planes and a long ordeal for him in the Burmese jungle. He prayed for a different outcome this time.

On the ground, the Japanese commanders were well aware of the advantage the terrain gave them. When the American supply planes first appeared, they ordered all available automatic weapons be moved to the hilltops. Among those weapons was a twenty-millimeter cannon that had been scavenged from one of their wrecked Oscar fighter planes. The cannon was mounted on a small truck and loaded with quarter-pound high-explosive shells. The gun was meant for air to air combat, but it would serve their current purposes. The gunners were told to sight in their weapons on the passing planes but not to fire until ordered to do so. The Japanese had learned a long time ago to wait to fire upon the cargo planes until most of the supplies were dropped. Sometimes capricious winds would blow the supplies directly into their waiting hands. Once the supplies were on the ground, they would often launch attacks in an attempt to capture what they could.

Major McDonald raised his arm in the cockpit doorway as a signal they were approaching the drop zone. Sam returned to the kicker's position and watched the major's arm. When the pilot dropped his arm, Sam would kick the cargo out.

"Are you ready for the kick, Harr?" Sam asked his crewmate.

"Ready as I'll ever be," Harr responded.

Their first pass went off without a hitch, and all of the supplies landed in friendly hands. The next five passes were a repeat of the first, with only sporadic fire from the enemy. On the next pass, the last of the supplies would be dropped and their mission would be over. As he lay on the cargo bay floor, Sam thought about all the missions he had flown, and he began to wonder how many times he had been in the kicking position. Doing some quick calculations in his head, he concluded he must have been in this position about 1,300 times. The number stunned him, and when he realized he may be going home after this mission, he was struck with the thought that this may be his last kick.

Captain McDonald lined the plane up for their final pass. They were approaching the drop zone at two hundred feet and had slowed to 120 mph. Sam tensed his leg muscles in preparation for his last kick. Intent on getting his last mission in the logbooks, he was unaware that the enemy below was just as intent on literally making this his last kick.

* * * * *

On the ground below, Lt. Akio Hidaka barked last second orders to his gunners as the cargo planes approached. Corporal Yuki Tatsuta readied his twenty-millimeter cannon. On each side of him, other guns were readied and tracking the C47s as they neared. During their previous passes, the planes had accurately dropped their supplies onto the British side of the river. The starving Japanese had watched as British soldiers scrambled to retrieve the precious cargo of food, water, medical supplies, and ammunition.

The situation for Yuki's unit was desperate. They had eaten the last of their worm-infested rice four days ago. The monsoon rains kept everything wet, and their uniforms were rotting and moldy. Their bodies were raw from fungal infections. They were plagued by clouds of mosquitoes that pumped diseases into their weakened systems. Leeches grew fat sucking malnourished blood from their bodies. Yesterday, a spider crawled up Yuki's leg and left a walnut-size lump where it bit him. Today, swarms of red ants invaded his trench and left bites that burned like hot coals. Like the rest of his army, he had to endure the pain and discomfort because they had no medical supplies. Yuki's hunger intensified when he saw the British receiving supplies across the river. He knew if some of the supplies didn't drop on their side of the river soon, they would have to mount a suicidal attack across the rain-swollen river. It didn't occur to Yuki that the British had suffered the same miseries three years earlier when he and his comrades drove them out of Burma.

The first cargo plane was almost abreast of his position when Lieutenant Hidaka issued the order to fire. All thoughts and feelings of pain and discomfort disappeared as Yuki pressed the firing mechanism on the twenty-millimeter cannon. He and those around him filled the air with a wall of death and destruction. Yuki watched the tracer shells from his cannon arc toward the approaching airplane. He cheered with elation when one of the shells exploded near the plane's cockpit.

* * * * *

Sam saw Major McDonald raise his arm in the cockpit doorway and pressed his feet more firmly against the supply container. He waited to kick until the major signaled by dropping his arm. However, Major McDonald never gave the signal, and his arm disappeared amid a bright explosion that filled the cockpit doorway. Stunned by the explosion, Sam heard shrapnel ricochet through the plane. He saw multiple lines of holes appear in the wall of the cargo area and stitch their way back to where Harr was standing. He could hear the metallic ping of bullets as they pierced the fuselage. He saw a hole and a red splotch appear in the upper part of Harr's leg as the young man crumpled to the floor.

The plane tilted sharply to the left, and Sam could clearly see the jungle below through the open door. In an instant, he and the supply container began to slide toward the cargo door. He frantically grabbed for any handhold to stop his progress toward certain death, but it was to no avail. His foot was entangled in the webbing of the parachute harness and the container was pulling him out of the aircraft. As the lower part of his body slid through the doorway, panic seized him. His vision began to narrow as darkness invaded the periphery of his eyesight. He thought of Eleanor as his world began to fade.

34

JULY 2, 1945
SITTANG RIVER VALLEY, BURMA

S AM FELT THE relentless weight of the container as it pulled his body through the doorway. He grabbed wildly for anything that would stop his slide toward death, but there was nothing. He thought of Eleanor and his family and wondered what would become of them. He was halfway through the door when a strong hand grasped his wrist in a vise-like grip. At the same moment, the plane righted itself, and he felt a tug on his leg as the falling container yanked his boot from his foot. The grip on his wrist tightened as he was pulled back into the airplane.

Once Sam was safely in the plane, Harr released his grip and slumped to the floor. He was losing blood quickly, and the pain in his leg was intense. Sam saw that his young friend was in danger and quickly retrieved a nearby first-aid kit. He poured sulfa powder into Harr's wound and bound it tightly with a bandage. By the time Sam was done tending to the wound, Harr had lost consciousness. Sam thought of the strength Harr exhibited when he pulled him back from the brink of death, and he desperately wanted to do more to save his friend's life. His thoughts were interrupted by a shout from the cockpit.

"I need help up here. Can anyone hear me?" LT shouted.

"I'm on my way, LT," Sam yelled in response.

Sam moved Harr away from the open doorway before proceeding to the cockpit. As he ran to help LT, the C47 lurched several times, and he had to steady himself against the walls of the fuselage. When he finally entered the cockpit, the sight that greeted him was like a scene from hell. Shrapnel from the exploding shell had torn through the cockpit, wreaking havoc on the men inside. LT was bleeding profusely from a large gash on his forehead, and his left arm hung limply at his side. He struggled to maintain control of the aircraft. Major McDonald lay in a bloody heap in the pilot's seat. His right arm was missing, and half of his face was blown away.

"The major's dead, Sam, and I don't think I can fly the plane much longer," LT said.

"What are we going to do?" Sam asked.

"You're going to have to help me fly the plane," LT answered.

"I don't know, LT. All I've ever done in a C47 was fly it straight and level and make a few turns," Sam said.

"You can do it. I'll tell you what to do," LT said.

Sam stood there looking at the copilot in disbelief. If LT lost consciousness, he realized all of their lives would be in his hands. How could he navigate back to base? What if they flew into a monsoon storm? Could he make a crash landing? All of these questions raced through his head. The C47 lurched again, and LT struggled to regain control.

"I need help, Sam. Now get the major out of that seat and take his place," LT ordered.

Sam realized there was no other choice and sprang into action. He unbuckled the major's harness and gently removed his body from the pilot's seat. Luckily, Major McDonald was a small man, and Sam was able to drag his body to the cargo bay. He tied the body down with ropes and then checked on Harr. The young man was still alive, and the bleeding from his leg wound seemed to have stopped. Afraid his friend might get hurt if the plane encountered rough weather, Sam tied a rope around Harr's waist and secured it to the cargo bay wall. Satisfied that Harr was safe, Sam picked up the first-aid kit and returned to the cockpit.

Blood from LT's head wound had flowed into his left eye and severely blurred his vision. Sam cleaned as much blood from the man's eye as he could and bandaged the wound on his forehead. Satisfied he had done all he could for LT, Sam buckled himself into the pilot's seat. The shell that killed Major McDonald had shattered the pilot's side window, and the air blowing through the open window was somewhat of a distraction for Sam. However, he placed his feet on the rudder pedals and his hands on the control yoke and prepared himself to take control of the plane.

"Okay, LT. I'm ready. What do you want me to do?" Sam said.

"Maintain our current northwesterly heading and stay below the clouds," LT instructed. "The weather seems to be lifting, so I think we will be okay in that department. The engines seem to be operating okay, but the radios are not working."

"What's your plan?" Sam asked.

"Without the radios, we can't get a fix to navigate back to base," LT said. "We'll keep heading northwest until we cross a major river, and then we'll follow it north until we find an airstrip."

"Sounds good," Sam responded. "We control all the airfields north of here."

"Right, now you fly the plane for a while," LT said as he released the controls.

Sam felt the pressure of the controls in his hands as LT released them. He steadied the airplane and used the elevator trim to ease the pressures. The clouds began to break up and patches of sunlight appeared. He kept the plane on its northwesterly heading and began searching the ground below for a river or an airfield. Sam wasn't sure how much time had passed before he realized LT wasn't talking. He looked over and panicked when he saw the pilot appeared to be unconscious.

"LT, wake up, LT," Sam yelled.

At first, the pilot didn't respond and Sam kept shouting. Finally, Sam's shouts seemed to be getting through, and LT opened his eyes. He turned and looked at Sam as if bewildered.

"I must have blacked out. Is everything okay?" LT said wearily.

"It's okay. I'm still looking for a river," Sam said. "How are you feeling?"

"I feel weak and my head hurts," LT responded. "I don't seem to have any feeling in my left arm."

Sam felt he had to keep LT awake and decided to try to keep him talking. "Where are you from, LT?" he asked.

LT seemed bewildered by the question at first and finally answered. "I'm from Loveland, Colorado," he said.

"I've been there, Loveland's north of Denver," Sam said. "Do you live right in Loveland?"

LT's head seemed to be clearing. "No, I live with my parents on a cattle ranch just east of Loveland," he said.

"You must have a beautiful view of the Rocky Mountains," Sam continued.

"Yes, on a clear day, they fill the horizon as far as the eye can see from north to south," LT replied.

"What are you going to do after the war?" Sam asked.

"I think I'd like to stay in the air force and continue flying," LT said.

"Not me," Sam said. "I'm going back home to my family and my job on the Pennsylvania Railroad."

LT nodded but didn't respond. Sam could see his eyes were beginning to fade. "There's something I've wanted to ask you," Sam said.

"What's that?" LT said.

"Nobody seems to know what the initials *L* and *T* stand for in your name. Everybody just calls you LT. All the documents I've seen with your name on them just show first and middle initials," Sam said. "Do you have a first and middle name?"

LT seemed to chuckle before he answered. "Yes, I have a first and middle name, but it would cause confusion if I used them," he said.

"What kind of confusion?" Sam asked.

"Well, my father Theodore was an enlisted man in the First World War, and he always wanted to be an officer," LT explained, "so when I was born, he named me Lieutenant Theodore Thomas."

"So your first name is Lieutenant and your middle name is Theodore," Sam said.

"Yep, you can see how confusing it would be if I used my full title of Captain Lieutenant T. Thomas," LT replied.

"I see what you mean, LT," Sam said. "That could cause a lot of problems."

"Speaking of problems, I think we have a major one," LT said seriously.

"What's wrong?" Sam asked.

"We must have taken some bullets through our fuel tanks," LT said. "We're almost out of fuel."

"What are we going to do?" Sam asked.

"We're not going to have a choice," LT said. "When the fuel runs out, we're going down. You better hope we find an airfield before that happens."

As they flew on, Sam looked in earnest for an airfield. They were flying over open fields and rice paddies, but there was no sign of an airfield anywhere. The fuel gauges were indicating empty. He knew the engines couldn't run much longer when he saw clouds of dust on the horizon.

"Looks like some kind of vehicles ahead," Sam said.

"Let's have a look," LT responded as he eased the plane into a descent.

They were flying at about seven hundred feet when they passed over a column of vehicles on a road below. Sam immediately recognized the vehicles and the soldiers riding in them.

"They're Brits," Sam announced enthusiastically.

"Do you see any place to land?" LT asked as he circled the column of trucks.

"There are rice paddies on both sides of the road, but they look pretty rough," Sam said. "The road in front of the trucks looks straight for quite a ways though."

"Looks like the road will have to do," LT said as the right engine began to run rough. "We'll do a wheels-up landing on the road. You'll have to help me on the controls."

Sam placed his hands and feet on the controls as LT turned the C47 to parallel the road.

"I'm getting weak, Sam, you're going to have to take over," LT said.

"Tell me what to do," Sam pleaded.

"Start a shallow left turn until the plane is lined up with the road," LT instructed.

Sam followed LT's instructions and brought the C47 around until it was headed straight down the road.

"Okay, now push the mixture controls full forward. They're the handles with the red knobs on the throttle quadrant," LT explained as Sam found the controls and pushed them forward. "Now push the propeller controls, the gray knobs, forward," he said.

LT watched with satisfaction as Sam followed his instructions. "Now pull back on the black throttle knobs slowly until I tell you to stop," LT said.

When Sam had attained the proper throttle setting, LT told him to stop. The airplane began to descend in a gentle glide toward the road. Sam could feel LT making slight changes in the control yoke as they descended. Sam felt everything was going well until he felt the full pressure of the yoke in his hands. He looked over and saw LT slumped back in his seat unconscious. Panic immediately gripped Sam when he realized he was going to have to make the landing by himself.

He fought to maintain his airspeed as the road grew closer and closer. His panic deepened until he remembered what Sergeant Grimes taught him about landings. He began to slowly reduce power while keeping the nose of the plane level. He watched as the airspeed began to drop. He knew he didn't want the airspeed to get too low and tried to keep it around one hundred miles per hour. He made adjustments to keep the C47 aligned with the road and noticed dust from the approaching convoy ahead of him. When the plane was about five feet above the road, Sam pulled the throttles completely back and concentrated on the touchdown. Each time he felt the airplane begin to settle, he pulled back on the yoke to keep it flying until the last possible moment.

Finally, the C47 made contact with the ground. The propellers bit into the earth and bent as the plane skidded down the road. The noise was frightening as rocks and dirt scraped against the belly of the aircraft. Sam clung to the controls as the plane swung to the left into a rice paddy. The C47 came to an abrupt stop, slamming Sam's head into the window frame. Darkness enveloped Sam's consciousness.

Sam became aware of voices around him and felt his body being jostled about. He strained to open his eyes and finally saw the face of Sergeant Grimes hovering over him.

"Hey there, buddy. You're in good hands now. I'll be flying you to a hospital in an L5," Sergeant Grimes said. "They tell me you were in the pilot's seat when they pulled you out of that wreck. Good job, Sam. Any landing you can walk away from is a good landing."

July 5, 1945
Dinjan Airbase, India

Sam felt a gentle prodding on his shoulder and struggled to open his eyes. When his vision finally cleared, he didn't recognize where he was. "Where am I?" he mumbled.

"Y'alls in the hospital," a voice said from his right.

Sam turned his head and saw his friend Bobby Joe standing beside his bed. "How long have I been out?" he asked.

"Y'all got a bad concussion," Bobby Joe said. "Y'all been in an out a consciousness fer three days."

"What about the other guys in my plane?" Sam asked.

"LT and Private Burr is gonna be okay," Bobby Joe said, "but y'alls the lucky one."

"What do you mean?" Sam asked.

"The CO wuz here a bit ago, and he left a message fer ya," Bobby Joe said.

"What's the message?" Sam asked.

A tear formed in Bobby Joe's eye as he looked at Sam. "Y'alls goin' home, buddy."

EPILOGUE

THE WAR ENDED, and the American soldier returned home after winning the most destructive and costly conflict in the history of mankind. The Greatest Generation had survived the Great Depression and World War II. They picked up their lives where they left off and seldom talked about their wartime experiences. Through hard work and dedication, they continued to build the American way of life. Their greatest dream is that future generations will continue their legacy. Here is how some of them fared after the war:

Captain L. T. "LT" Thomas stayed in the army after the war and became part of the U.S. Air Force in 1947. He flew jets in the Korean conflict and became an ace with seven confirmed kills. He retired from the air force in 1973 with the rank of major general. His official title at the time of his retirement was Major General Lieutenant T. Thomas.

Corporal Bobby Joe Wilson returned to his home state of Texas and got into the oil business. He married and had a family of three children. He eventually became a millionaire and served three terms as a U.S. senator from Texas.

Sergeant Walt Grimes went home to Lock Haven, Pennsylvania, and resumed his job as a test pilot for the Piper Aircraft Corporation.

In 1947, he moved to Kansas, where he started a crop-dusting company. Two years later, he was killed when his plane ran into power lines while he was dusting a cornfield. He never married.

Corporal Virgil "Wimpy" Hutton stayed in India until December of 1945. He was on his way to board a troopship for home when the jeep he was riding in encountered an angry mob in the streets of Calcutta. The rioters were protesting British rule in India and had no sympathy for England's allies. Wimpy and the other men in the jeep perished at the hands of the inflamed crowd.

Buck Private Kerburt "Kerby" Kline barely managed to finish his military career without being court-martialed. He returned to his hometown in Pennsylvania, where he attempted several times to establish a restaurant. When no one ever returned for a second meal, he gave up in disgust and became a janitor in the local elementary school. Kerby was active with the local Little League baseball teams and had the distinction of gaining the reputation as the worst umpire in the history of the game.

Private First Class Harry "Harr" Burr recovered completely from his wounds and went home to Minnesota, where Sally was waiting. They were married in the spring of 1946 and took over the farm of Sally's father when he retired. With the help of their six children, Harr and Sally became successful farmers. Although Harr is now too old to ride, Big Red still occupies a prominent place in the family garage.

Corporal Samuel D. Huber departed from India by ship on the sixth of August 1945, the same day the atomic bomb was dropped on Hiroshima, Japan. Three days later, the men on board received the news of the bombing of Nagasaki. On August 14, four days after Roger's first birthday, Sam heard about the surrender of Japan. The remainder of his voyage to New York was uneventful, and he sighted the Statue of Liberty on the third of September 1945. Sam returned to his family and his job with the Pennsylvania Railroad. Six months after he returned home, Sam visited Dan Dury's parents in Maryland.

He presented them with pictures he had taken of Dan during their brief friendship. In the years that followed, Sam and Eleanor had two more sons and stayed in the Moshannon Valley for the rest of their lives. For his exemplary service to his country, Sam was awarded the Distinguished Flying Cross four times and the Air Medal five times.

Like so many men after the war, Sam's friends went their separate ways. With the exception of Kerby, he never saw any of them again.

CPSIA information can be obtained at www.ICGtesting.com
Printed in the USA
LVOW080102041212

309982LV00006B/263/P

9 781477 142943